LETTERS FROM EDEN

Thank you Dr. Douglam

— David McCasland

July 14, 2005

LETTERS FROM EDEN

POSTSCRIPT OF AN AMERICAN CENTURY

BY DANIEL McCASOWAY

cP
Aventine Press

Published by Aventine Press
1023 4th Ave #204
San Diego CA, 92101
www.aventinepress.com

ISBN: 1-59330-239-8

Library of Congress Control Number: 2004116967
Library of Congress Cataloging-in-Publication Data
LETTERS FROM EDEN

Printed in the United States of America

He was a man, take him for all in all,
I shall not look upon his like again.

HAMLET

CONTENTS

PART I
THROWING OFF DESPAIR

Chapter   Title

PART II
TEN MILES TO HOPETOWN

Everything changed after the fall except us.
We remained the same. And we never left Eden.

ANTON KORYENKO

For Susan, Jessica, and Emily.

Prologue

Human history had been an eternal struggle between hope and hopelessness. Somewhere in the twentieth century hope finally won. These are my father's victories.

PART I
THROWING OFF DESPAIR

Chapter 1

Up from Clay

He was the land got up. He was the hope of clay accumulated
for twelve billion years.
The soil didn't know it. But he did.

There is an incessant drumming in the furnace of infinity. It rumbles across the range of creation. It hums in the string of the heavens. It echoes through the myriad connections of the wider spectacle. It follows the pitch and moment of all of the motions of all of the particles in all of the compartments of space and time. It is the frenzied pulse of existence.

Yet unfastened between these popping conduits are tatters of nothingness. They are bleak provinces filled with unlit silence, without form or dimension, existing between the ticks of the clock. No word for their substance is in them. Were there, it might share properties with the word we call *Empty*. Still, in these voids there does stir some certain indelible thing. Call it *Possibility*. It is a tentacle of the possibility that we each have.

In timelessness possibility gambols unfettered. Odds are compressed. It is the crucible of the inevitable. It was in such an outlying reach of the unfathomable achievable, that an insensate awareness once did gestate. This conscious singularity knew neither beginning nor ending. It did not hold itself separate. In mystery and detachment it lingered for an indeterminate interval, reflective only of itself.

Then upon some ungaugeable, infinite instant, at an indiscernible threshold in the blurry backwaters of eternity, a faint tone arose to the sensibilities of the awareness. It was an irreducible hiss, like a noise we might recognize as the spilling of a waterfall, or sand buffeting a window glass. This crackle gradually disintegrated into the ovation of trees attending a morning breeze, finches singing, and the plop of a cool brook. Following quickly after, a dull glow pried in from the darkness. This ember romped, paused, and groped for a while - then all the colors came. *Adam just woke up as himself one day.*

The sheen of the world surprised him. He swiftly closed his eyes in fear. Yet the passion to know could not be contained. He looked out at the world again. There was no clarity, only penetrating brilliance. The impulse to recoil beset him. The sun scolded him. He did not blink.

Vacuums are said to be unstable. Thoughts can leak into them from the outside. Perhaps the universe is a thought that got loose in a vacuum. And so Adam awoke immersed in the residue of a collapsed nothingness. Molten forms steadily congealed out of the dizzying haze before him. Diffuse flickers became swaying leaves. Beyond was a striking sky of blue, crosshatched by jumbled clouds. Rays of sunlight warmed his face. It was the first day of history. *He would call this place Eden.*

He beheld the bustle of existence around him. There was some kind of magic here. This place did not exist until he woke up in it. He knew that an instant before he had been nothing, a residuum without cognition. For eternity he had been clay. *Now he was the king of Eden.*

Chapter 2

Empire of Hope

We come from clay and return to dust, or vice versa, either way, both being forms of the element earth. Through the ado between these two states courses also much moisture. Water gives earth mobility. We are earth and water in motion. Earth and water play throughout us and are present everywhere we venture. The traits of these modest ingredients also appear prominent among our natural faculties. They define our action and our aspect. They underlie and prop up our quintessence. Their properties explain our properties. We are collectively and individually as malleable and fragile as clay, as tenuous and insubstantial as dust, and as capricious and nimble as water.

Gathered in the vast, tossing gulf of time, the water of our race runs together and forms into a sea. It is an ocean fed from the land by mighty rivers. And each person, earth and water in motion, is a river. These are the rivers of people: they are expressions of the miraculous potential of Nature; they are powerful agents in shaping the world; an outward stillness in them buries unremitting momentum; they have a beginning and an ending; they have a direction.

To understand a river we must return to its origins. We must follow it back through the cities, past the factories, the bridges, and the farms. We must travel up the stream, against the torrent, tracing the tributaries that feed it. Then we must pursue the finer streams feeding these, in turn repeating this pattern until the branches finally meld into the texture of the earth itself. Yet what we call branches are really roots. The land containing these roots molds the grandeur of the river. My father came from good land.

To reach this land we must follow the river White beyond its wye with the Eel. We must trace it back to a valley where sycamores watch over sprawling lanes of wheat and maize. We must go to a place where a creek runs through a meadow of wild rose and purple amaranth. This journey is easy down among the groves of sweetgum and willow. But the strain builds as we move into the hedges and uneven fields higher up. Pausing for a while in a blue-green pasture, the path holds the stream in still pools and little pockets before hurling ever steeper up the rocky slope, never resting again until its ending beneath the hickories and the ancient oaks.

Nourishing this brook along the way are some springs. They seep through mossy fissures from the native layers of the earth. Eons have hewn the stone around the flow, forming terraced passes, ravines, and slender chasms. In places along these banks, jutty ledges yield a constant haze of easy mist and rain. Songbirds swoop and dip chasing midges in this spray. It is a hidden place where yearning creatures have always come to drink and sing, and to thrive. It is where the clan McCasoway built a house and a barn, raised their sons, and lived their lives.

In the County of Owen, from a farm atop these velvet cliffs, came five worthy brothers, all valiant, of good stead, each in their own season and time. What follows here is the story of a single child, the second son, Adam David. His light first shone upon the world in the twentieth year of the same numbered century. His meandering path carried him back across the veil on the 55th day of the 21st century. The range of affairs lying between these points in space and time, encompasses a gulf whose fathoms beck for sounding. The hope of this narrative is to outlay for posterity some cursory accounting of the most familiar anecdotes while they remain freshly booked upon the tablet of my memory.

My father's formative years coincided with a portion of the twentieth century traditionally known to historians as *the Great Depression.* This is an abstract term, concocted out of the cold, impersonal dogma of economists, social engineers, and politicians. It refers simply to the shape of a line on a chart. But to my father, as well as countless other children of this *Great Era,* the terms *the Great Poverty, the Great Illness,* or *the Great Toil,* would be considered more appropriate and more meaningful.

Despite the expression chosen however, it was still an era when most of the essentials we take for granted today did not exist. That is, it was a time before the life-saving miracles of antibiotics, magnetic resonance imaging, or transplant surgery. It was a time before the ubiquitous luxuries of supermarkets, ATMs, or interstate highways; and the technologies of DVDs, satellite television, laptop computers, and camera phones did not exist even in dreams.

A few well-off relatives owned automobiles but farming was still largely an enterprise requiring horses. Money was rare and the closest city was sixty miles away. Men were narrow of face, women gave birth without anesthesia, and sons were compelled to endeavor the arduous labors of the farm from dawn until dusk. The withering economic hardship and social isolation allowed little room for the felicities of childhood enjoyed by generations since. My father seldom spoke fondly of his younger days.

We however, only one generation removed, inherited entirely different circumstances. The sacrifices, discoveries, and victories of my father's generation afforded us with a luxury of hope never before known in America, or the world. For any who care to notice, this luxury continues to compound today. Yet there also seems to be an inexplicable dark thread of discontent and misanthropy entwined within the collective fabric of our times. It is like a self-inflicted disease, or a protracted suicidal binge that threatens to destroy all hope forever. Appreciation of this despicable trend exceeds the scope of this narrative, and I touch on it here only to better frame the fair outlook of my childhood, and to emphasize the towering image of my father in my eyes.

Life seemed more straightforward when I was a child. The collective uncertainty apparently so pervasive today did not exist. The fundamental tenets of civilization were absolute. It was a time when there was unquestioned hope - when hope was still ascending and novel. It was a time when things made sense, when truth was real, when there was a right and a wrong and knowing the difference between the two actually mattered.

It was a time when a dollar bought five gallons of gasoline. It was a time when each of the Seven Astronauts' names were household words. It was a time when automobiles were the best they would ever be. It was a time when the worlds of Darkness and of Light were separated by a Curtain of Iron stretching from Stettin in the Baltic, to Trieste in the Adriatic. It was a time when just being Americans made us all automatic winners.

The outlook of my father's youth was almost exactly the opposite. Everything was harsh. Little was certain, except toil, in that it was both grueling and constant. Sickness too was dependable, as were the twin specters Hunger and Poverty. Life from every angle was tough. This was the climate of my father's childhood season. Yet even as his youth was thus shaped by poverty and toil, so his early adulthood quickly after was marred by the spectacle of mass murder in the cruel arena of war. His comrades lives were extinguished before his unbelieving eyes. His wiry frame too endured the wrath of steel and fire. After surviving this madness, he returned home to the inequities and insults of endless injury, robbery, and destitution. But unlike other men whose demeanor might be permanently hardened by such events, he grew instead kinder, gentler, and more charitable.

Throughout his life he expressed these empathic qualities in many ways. They were little properties, humble, not pretentious or grandiose, often no more complicated than a heartfelt praise to a waitress, or a ride for a stranded motorist. His honest smile or pleasant greeting would disarm even the most cynical souls among both acquaintances and strangers alike.

By the constant pouring of this nectar into the wide vessel of life, it came to pass that his cup one day ran over. His humanity began to come back to him in the form of trust, respect, and investment by those who had been warmed by his universal largess and honesty. Perhaps they were attracted to him because everyone seems to hope that men like Adam D. McCasoway really exist in this callous world. Whatever the reason, once they met him, from that day forward they could never get enough of him. The year was 1949. It was the beginning of *the Empire*.

Chapter 3

Empire of Energy

en*er*gy n, pl. –gies. **1.** the capacity for vigorous activity; available power. **2.** a feeling of having an adequate or abundant amount of such power. **3.** Often **energies.** an exertion of such power; effort: *threw her energies into the job.* **4.** the habit of vigorous activity; vigor. **5.** the ability to act, lead others, or effect things forcefully. **6.** forcefulness of expression. **7.** *Physics.* the capacity to do work. *Symbol*: E **8.** a source of usable power, as fossil fuel or electricity.

Random House Webster's College Dictionary, 2000 Edition, p. 436

$$E = Mc^2$$

Albert Einstein, *Annalen der Physik*, September 27, 1905

"All of the above definitions apply, and more. Energy means many things. Energy means being warm when everything else is frozen, or being cool in killing heat. Energy means going where we want, near or far, when we want, for any reason we want. Energy means food, all we can eat, any time we want it. Energy means the illumination of darkness. Energy means being clean. Energy means medicine, healing, and health."

"Energy means abundance and its companions: tolerance, charity, and mercy. Energy enables our humanity. Energy means protection from the tyranny of evil men. Energy means children, family, and life. Energy means communication, learning, invention, amusement, and innumerable other things important to all of us. Energy is the fundamental fungible currency of civilization. Energy is salvation. Energy is hope."

"Energy comes in many forms. Some forms are theoretical. These are the energies of the future. Other forms are within our scope. These are the energies of the present. The energies of the present are simple and humble, they come from the ground."

"We cannot live without energy. So sometimes energy must be paid for with our lives. A coal miner dies every nine days in America. For each light that glows, for each song played on a radio, for each meal that is cooked, a coal miner must take a chance. The risk he takes is to show up for work. If he goes home alive at the end of his shift, then he wins, but for one day only. Tomorrow he must try again, and the day after that, and every day until he either quits, retires, or dies. Why does he do it? He does it for the hope."

-Adam D. McCasoway, February 5, 2000

To Adam McCasoway, the energies of the present came in two forms. One of these was petroleum. Oil is a pungent liquor of ethereal essences delved up from little compartments scattered within the imponderable crystalline depths. It is the integral working fluid of progress and the liquid electrum of modern civilization. It is a treasure that is pourable at room temperature. Petroleum is truly an elixir of success and a builder of empires.

Crude oil is an amalgam of natural spirits, in many ways comparable to fine cognac or bourbon. It comes in varying bouquets with regionally-derived names like *West Texas Sour, North Sea Brent,* or *Illinois Basin Sweet.* It is called crude oil because it is unrefined. In its natural state the gasoline, diesel fuel, kerosene, home heating oil, jet fuel, lubricating oils, and other ingredients are all mixed together. Refining separates these constituents, or alters them into the familiar products that are essential for the success of our society and our very lives.

Our lives are connected with petroleum in ways we may not appreciate. Technically, oil is the concentrated essence of life. Its origin is intimately connected with the abyssal reaches of the ancient seas and the teeming cycle of multicellular organisms constantly folding therein. Oil is strangely entwined in the mystery of Life's origin. It is a step in the succession of Life. An oil well peers back in time. It is a telescope aimed at the bridge between the mineral and the organic. Oil is life reduced to its precursor molecules. Oil is the colorful sheen floating on the pond of the universe. It hints of some large unseen thing lurking just under the surface. The vast reservoirs of oil trapped in the outer layers of our planet are the clumsy footprints of a universe that teems with life. Oil's existence points to intractable complexities and connections within the fabric of life that we have yet to fathom. When we fully understand oil and its origin, then we will fully understand the same about Life as well.

Chemically, petroleum is a concoction of carbon and hydrogen atoms. Oxygen from the atmosphere likes to combine with it. When this happens, copious quantities of electrons are emitted. That is, rivers of electrons are propelled from one place to another, like miniature fizzing pieces of the sun hurling through space. Curiously, two of the most mysterious phenomena in the universe seem to thrive exclusively along the banks of these rivers of electrons. Namely, the phenomenon of Life, and its ultimate companion, Consciousness. The roots of the Tree of Life cling enduringly to the fruitful banks along the proverbial Electron River. They have been planted there for as long as science can reckon. And as awareness seems to exist solely at the courtesy of life, every thought, idea, dream, and hope that ever occurred must have done so entrained within the magical pulse of the marching electron.

When petroleum and oxygen combine, we perceive the resulting deluge of electrons as heat and light. This is truly a blessing. Because in a cold, dark, and hostile universe, heat and light make life possible. Therefore, oil makes life possible. Its carbon and hydrogen atoms can be transformed into our carbon and hydrogen atoms. This transmutation is actuated by the interconnected alchemies of *Life*, and of the *Human Will*. It is a process essential to each of us individually and ultimately constitutes the foundation of that thing we perceive as civilization.

Adam McCasoway's second energy of the present was coal. Coal may seem less enchanting than oil. It appears after all, like little more than dirty rock. Its particles easily stick to us and make us dirty as well. Nevertheless, it too is the stuff of life concentrated. It too is a complex concoction of carbon and hydrogen atoms. And oxygen can combine with it as vigorously as it does with petroleum. Like oil, coal has an origin connected with the sea. But coal's origin is also tied to the land. The nurturing cradle of coal is a unique boundary zone between the sea and the terrain. In nature, boundary zones are places where opposing forces meet and co-exist in a pitching balance. Naturally, the forces involved can be compounded and concentrated in novel ways because of the closeness of the venue. The interface between opposing domains interacts to produce unique structures and phenomena. It could even be argued that all phenomena, at all scales, occur only at boundaries.

A boundary between two objects so great as a continent and an ocean is where a vast amount of power is focused and expended. Sometimes amid the hazard, a little piece of this power gets covered up and preserved. When this happens we call it coal. So coal is the product of transition and upheaval. Coal beds are the graffiti of the great ascents, plateaus, and declines in the biosphere of a young and fitful world. Coal is an artifact of the violent and fickle history of not only Earth, but of the cosmos itself. It betrays a heritage of carnage and universal natural indifference that inestimably predates and exceeds all of the blood-feuds between all of the tribes of humanity, for all time. It is sin more original than original sin. And like original sin, it also brings life to a world.

Like petroleum, coal also comes in many grades. They are as varied as the Ages and coastlines that generated them, or the uses for which they have been found to be best matched. In the east there is Pennsylvanian coal. In the west there is Cretaceous coal. There is steam coal and metallurgical coal. There is the bright, black coal they call anthracite; the dull, sooty bituminous coal; and a brownish coal called lignite. There is cannel coal and bone coal. There is Blue Creek coal, Blue Gem coal, Red Ash coal, Greensburg coal, and Black Mountain coal. In Kentucky there is *Number Nine Coal*. In the year 1946, Merle Travis wrote a song about loading a certain number of tons of it. Had Mr. Travis been a native of Indiana or Illinois, presumably he would have called it *Number Five Coal.* Nature has many recipes for coal. Some contain more leafy matter and ferns, or wood and tree parts, or abundant spores. There are smatterings of cinders, a few bugs, some mud, and assorted minerals from the sea and land. Mostly though, coal is a mélange of trampled mosses with either more or less of the rest. *Coal is a compressed forest.* Or more precisely, coal is a residue of native essences and durable resins left behind by a compressed forest. It is what results when a compressed forest is gently mellowed in the tepid outer tiers of Earth's oven. Most importantly though, coal is preserved *prosperity* that has patiently awaited our beck for two million centuries.

The Enigmas of Prosperity

Prosperity is a precious object. It will always be profoundly yearned for by those who are not prosperous. But curiously, in our modern world of bounty, it seems that some of the children of prosperity, in many cases those who have benefited the most from the freedom to achieve prosperity, are the ones who now most ardently seek its destruction. Organizations with noble-sounding names, whose memberships are peopled by the children of the prosperous, seem to unabashedly advocate the deconstruction of America and Her Constitution; and the eradication of every trace of human freedom and dignity She ever fostered.

By some aberrant and intrinsically contradictory metamorphosis of the spirit of liberty, they have transformed their own pursuit of happiness into a struggle to eliminate the right of everyone else to pursue happiness. That is, they claim that *the pursuit of happiness is harmful to the world.* In taking such a posture, they automatically deny the inherent need for the human spirit to be free. They propose the sacrifice of humanity in pursuit of a subjective notion of the world, *their notion.*

Technically, the world that they claim they are trying to save exists only in their minds. The ideal they seek is unattainable by the means they propose. Their ideal is an image propped up entirely by the abundance that human freedom has created. Their vision is nothing like the *real world.* The real world would eat them alive if the rest of us were to ever withdraw our protection.

They believe in the false notion that science can and ought to be used to limit human rights. That is, they think it is entirely proper to use scientific theories as justifications for decreeing the taking of rights from human beings. Unfortunately, none of their theories seem to allow for the expansion of human rights. Instead, they seem to require restriction of even the most basic rights. *This is a bad use of science.*

A good use of science has always involved finding ways to expand human rights, to expand human horizons, and to expand human choices. *This is a science of liberation.* The good use of science is the phenomenon that has given us our precious material essence, the complex technological organ that is an outgrowth of our will and the blossoming of our potential as rational beings. It is the thing that has propelled us from a species of soiled peasants teetering on extinction, to one of burgeoning cosmic notoriety, literally in the blink of an eye by all known standards of historical measure. This magnificent mechanical menagerie that we live inside of, like it or not, is what happens when free people are allowed to endeavor and invent, benefit from their efforts proportionally, and to have safety in the possession of their fruits. If this machine did not exist, we would not exist. Science and freedom made it possible. They made *us* possible. And here we are.

Yet there are now those who want to turn it around, to use science as an excuse to put up barriers. *This is a science of limitation.* Science cannot be used in this way. It is self-defeating and contradictory. It is unscientific. The use of science in this manner cannot endure simply because *those who would succeed the most at it would become extinct the quickest.*

Invention is the key. Science does not put up obstacles, it tears them down. Science that puts up barriers is not science. It is something else. Our science, our way of life, and our technology are rungs in a ladder to the stars. We are building it as we climb. All of the so-called, problems of the environment are rendered incidental when compared to what will be gained if we can remain a free people in the critical years ahead. That is, the day is truly approaching when what Adam McCasoway called *the energies of the future* will become the energies of the present. So called, industrial emissions will not be necessary. Not because of environmental compassion, but because the new technology will not generate emissions on the scale or with the inelegance of current systems. Such a future is coming. And it keeps getting here faster every day. When that time arrives, *the world will be a Better Place.* Then we will be able to *afford* to turn the whole planet into a garden if we want. There will be time enough to do it. To get there we must let the inventors keep tinkering. Don't kill the dreamers. They will give us the ability to heal the damage caused by previous technologies. They will bring back the extinct. It will happen.

That's how the payoff will work. That's what trumps the environmental alarmism of our time. All of this is going somewhere. It is a good place. It is an edge that keeps get sharper as it goes. *If you don't like it on the cutting edge, just stand still.* But please quit trying to block the way.

Other misuses common to the science of limitation include a tendency to inflate meaning or to take liberties with context, scale, and causality. The unavoidable scientific reality is that the precise understanding of the global and cosmic patterns of nature that some alarmists would suggest exists, actually does not yet exist. That is, although the current state of human knowledge of the universe is remarkable, it is still *very much in its infancy* and remains far too imperfect to be used as a justification for the stripping away of something so unanimously precious as human freedom and human life. Borrowing from T.S. Elliot's famous comment on Shakespeare:

At this stage in the understanding of Nature, the best contribution that most of us can hope for is to find a new way to be wrong about it.

The tyrants of the twentieth century had few reservations about invoking theories *(now proven to be incorrect theories,* by the way) as the just rationale for enslaving and slaughtering millions. That is why it is incumbent upon free people to measure very carefully any and all theories that are presented as a foundation for limiting human rights. And be seriously mindful of those who would be so bold as to promote a science of limitation rather than one of liberation.

It is likely that many of the popular theories that the environmentalists rely on to rationalize the destruction of freedom are imprecise at best and demonstrably false at worst. Most of their theories are relatively young, unverified, and in many cases unverifiable. Real scientific theories need time to age and endure new evidence, new technology, and new thinking. Einstein's relativity is over a century old and is still maturing. The paradigm that it augmented, Newton's dynamics, is approaching four centuries in age. These are solid theories because they have withstood new evidence, new technology, and new ways of thinking. They have successfully predicted physical phenomena to high degrees of precision. But they are not perfect. Eventually, they will be replaced by something more accurate. This could take another four centuries.

It is possible to construct a paradigm around untested theories, but not recommended. Like so many disproved theories of the past, such edifices may appear attractive on the outside, but upon close examination they are found to house only illusions. That is, at this stage of human knowledge, there is no person or group that is wise enough to demand that a scientific theory shall be a basis for rightfully determining the fate of the rest of us. The very fact that they even think this is appropriate indicates that they have overlooked some very important truths about the indelible human spirit. *People cannot decree the fate of others.* Every time it has ever been tried the justifications have always seemed rational to someone and the results have always been disastrous for everyone. The proponents of limitation also seem to ignore the reality of what the human race has become and what magnificent possibilities are at our frontier.

The means by which human fate is best determined has already been established. It is based on a simple idea with far-reaching consequences and responsibilities. Human beings suffered for thousands of years to achieve this breakthrough. A nation was finally created expressly so that this method could be put into practice. This idea is called *individual freedom.* After all, that is the purpose of liberty. That is the purpose of representative democracy. That is the purpose of a duly elected government that *derives its just power from the consent of the governed.*

Each of us gets to determine our own fate, right or wrong. In this society of *free people,* we are each protected from those who would control our lives. We are insulated, from those who would use the latest fad to justify telling us what foods we may eat, where we can live, how much property we can own, where we can travel or what means we use to get there. We are immune to the schemes of those who seek to impose limitations on the quality and quantity of our lives. The purpose of freedom is not to use its liberal latitudes to siphon away the happiness of others. *The purpose of freedom is not to restrict mankind's options, but to multiply them.*

Tempestuous Coal

The American coal business of the twentieth century was well known for its clashes and upheavals. The cultural perception of this conflict may be imperfect however. This may be partly because those who find their prosperity in the dissemination of information about current events to the masses are masters in the exploitation of conflict. No one should fault them for that. It is good business. It has been the source of enormous success for news organizations, their parent companies, their stockholders, and unfortunately, a few demagogues as well. The reason for this success is because when deprived of it, the human psyche tends to crave conflict. Fortunately, reading about conflict is about the closest thing to it most Americans ever experience. Those who have endured real life and death conflict typically want nothing to do with it ever again. They seem to prefer peace. Yet among the uninitiated, the natural craving for controversy appears so striking, that it could even be construed to be tantamount to one of the primary drives of the human animal. That is, if a newspaper could also be eaten, smoked, and squeezed to yield vodka, a man would never have to leave his house.

When news about the coal industry appeared in the media, or when average citizens contemplated the coal industry, the subject matter tended to have a great deal to do with things like the infamous *Herrin Massacre of 1922*, and not a great deal to do with the notion of *a continually improving standard of living for all people* (also known as *Progress*) that accompanies the use of coal. This is understandable. To the prosperous such things are at best boring, and at worst reviled. It is not cool. To the sophisticated, the cosmopolitan, and the urbane; to the rebellious, the irreverent, and the popular cynical, the evil Earth-destroying energy industry is an object worthy only of suspicion, scorn, contempt, and punishment. But despite all of the rhetoric reported in newspapers, magazines, and books of the time; despite the negative spin placed on depictions of the coal industry in movies and television programs; despite what people were, and were not told by the politicians and demagogues, most of the human race still seemed to remember the hateful and hungry times well enough to just naturally understand that *progress is good.*

So this was the method of the media, and thus much of the state of public thought on the subject for decades. Then one day, as if it were not enough to simply ignore the life-improving aspects of abundant and inexpensive energy, the method began to take a dark turn. That is, in the latter third of the twentieth century, it first became fashionable, then eventually seemingly *imperative* for the media to constantly remind the public that the production and use of energy will destroy the planet.

Nearly all of the world's problems were suddenly directly related to the use of energy. *Something had to be done.* It was more than the old-fashioned conflict portrayed in your grandfather's newspaper. This was conflict on a whole new level. This was conflict with *Progress*. We were no longer just passive bystanders reading about conflict between others. Now, each one of us (without our consent) had been made a party to the conflict. Under such conditions, neutrality became a very tricky proposition. Actually, according to the new plan, *we were the bad guys.* Their logic was irrefutable: each one of our pathetic, pointless, undeserving, unnecessary lives exerted an unsustainable and intolerable burden on Earth's increasingly finite resources. Suddenly the world was turned upside down and a brave new paradigm mutated: *progress is bad.* In the decades that followed, this initially quaint notion morphed into an enormous exercise in self-delusion and self-recrimination. We became a world of suicidal schizophrenics. We started confiscating tractors for making too much food, tearing down dams for impounding too much water, and banning mosquito pesticides for saving too many lives from Malaria.

We forced industries to raise the prices of the things we must have to live. We created new government agencies and layers of regulations with the expressed functions of restricting freedom, encumbering enterprise, punishing initiative, and redistributing wealth (particularly to law firms). We forced those who produce things to work increasingly harder for proportionally less and expanded the segment of society that creates nothing and demands everything. The producers must now work more hours. In families, both parents need jobs now to make ends meet. Why? To pay for a new class of burdens that accompany *Environmental Correctness.*

It is analogous to a man throwing boulders into the path of a delivery truck that is transporting groceries and medicine to his town. He does this because everyone knows that trucks are evil. They destroy the Earth with their emissions. The food that the truck carries is evil because of the farmers who produced it. They raped the soil and defiled the Earth with evil fertilizer and pesticides. They oppressed cows, pigs, and chickens. Some even owned the dreaded SUV. Medicine is evil because pharmaceutical companies conduct evil experiments with laboratory animals so that evil humans can be cured of diseases. The rock-throwing man believes it is all true because from the time he was a child he has been bombarded with the dogma of Environmental Correctness. It started when he opened that first issue of *Irrational Geographic Magazine* in the school library.

This kind of behavior is more than simply illogical, it is insanity. And to add insult to injury, not only have we been tricked into punishing ourselves for being successful, but we are paying other people outrageous sums of money to punish us as well. They are the professional punishers. There are individuals and organizations in this country that are shamelessly siphoning billions of dollars directly from the environmental movement (translation: *directly from us).* They are also the ones who squeal the loudest when free people resist their schemes. They are the ones who are the quickest to publicly demonize the free-spirited, the dreamers, the shapers, and the makers. Their power and prosperity depend on it. And we wonder why most mothers must work outside of the home now when it used to be only most fathers. We fret about our babies being raised by strangers in unhealthy daycare concentration camps where they are deprived of the kind nurturing that can only come from their mothers. Millions of our mothers are *nurturing the Earth* now instead of their babies. Or more precisely, half of their earnings are being confiscated from them to pay for the enrichment of those who are in collusion in what has become the *Great Environmental Swindle*.

The swindle is perpetrated by at least two distinct factions: a criminal element and a radical ideological element. The traditional criminals, the Boss Tweeds so to speak, of this confidence game are only interested in our wealth. They are the ones who used deception and hyperbole to actually get the regulations enacted in the last third of the twentieth century. Now they are billionaires. Their ideological radical accomplices played an important role in the legislative process as well. But their interest is more than monetary. It is something far more sinister. Those who comprise the ideological arm of the swindle ultimately have no less of an abomination planned for the unwashed masses than did the great socialist tyrants of the twentieth century. In their eyes, human beings seem to be a liability that must be controlled, hemmed-in and enslaved, or even *liquidated*. Individual Freedom is the enemy of the Earth. *It may even be worse than the internal combustion engine.* Growth is a scourge that must be crushed. And today the swindlers are still at it. A prime example is the Kyoto Protocol. It is a "global warming" treaty that has been signed by some of the more *progressive* (translation: *misanthropic)* nations of the world. The expressed purpose of Kyoto is to unabashedly and deliberately reverse progress (translation: *reduce the standard of living for all people).* Luckily, America has so far resisted this thinly veiled attempt to expand human suffering.

Aside from economic ruination, the only remarkable environmental impact that can be expected from adoption of the Kyoto treaty will be increased death rates among the elderly and the infirm during the summer and winter months because of the artificially inflated electricity prices required by the treaty to *reduce consumption.* Kyoto apologists might argue "...that the people who are dying of heat-stroke or freezing to death have only been unfairly enjoying *artificially propped-up life* beyond what the resources of the Earth are capable of sustaining." In other words, since there is a resource burden placed on the Earth for each person, if we *impose cuts in consumption*, then *naturally* a proportional number of us should be *expected to die*. It is the price that must be paid to save the Earth. It is the environmentally correct thing to do. It is a sacrifice they are willing to make. That is, they admit by default to having no reservations about enacting programs expressly intended to increase misery and death among their fellow human beings. And they offer calculated and dispassionate rationalizations of the necessity of it. All we have to do is sign on the dotted line.

Moscow, August 23, 1939, Soviet Foreign Commissar Vyacheslav Molotov signs the *German-Soviet Nonaggression Pact* as Joachim von Ribbentrop and Josef Stalin watch. A portrait of Lenin looms in the background. Within six years, 56,000,000 people would be killed. *(Photo courtesy U.S. National Archives.)*

We have been convinced that some kind of good can come out of such a plan. What it really means is that human poverty and suffering are worsened or prolonged. We have a self-hating, parasitic doppelganger feeding on our bodies and souls. It is trying to exterminate us. It claims that our simply being alive threatens the existence of a 4.6 billion year-old chunk of rock hurling at 66,000 miles per hour around a continually exploding hydrogen bomb that is a million miles in diameter. For some bizarre, deeply troubling reason, we have been willingly convinced that we are the Earth's enemy.

It is as if we are all diners in a really big restaurant. It's a place where we all must split the check. Half of us in this lunchroom usually try to order something simple and cheap to help keep the cost down, yet wholesome enough to make us happy. The other half seem to be doing everything they can to make this impossible. They force the restaurant to raise the prices through their constant complaining and unreasonable demands (not to mention the trucking company that delivers supplies has to charge the restaurant extra for the damage caused by the rock-throwers). And after a hard day of hurling boulders they are really hungry. But the higher prices are not an issue for them. They order anything they want, only the best. Why? Because they know someone else is paying the bill.

Everywhere we turn, in every reach of life, it's the environment this or the environment that - environment, environment, environment! *(Shouldn't it be people, people, people?)* There are environmental philosophies, environmental religions, environmental watchdogs, environmental trusts, environmental license plates, environmental activists, environmental citizen's groups, environmental lobbyists, environmental political parties, environmental careers, environmental educators, environmental protection agencies, environmental consultants, and even environmental terrorists. There are environmental laws, environmental lawyers, environmental crimes, environmental penalties, environmental settlements, environmental fees, and environmental fines. Environmental dogma lavishly flows from the mouths of politicians, television celebrities, news anchors, adult contemporary singers, rock stars, and movie actors. They line up in battalions and passionately sermonize the undisciplined multitudes with the party mantra *ad nauseum*.

And even if they were right, does it not seem odd that so many individuals whose personas are traditionally touted as free-thinking and rebellious should all be in such universal passionate agreement about *anything?* Is there no one who senses the menacing implications of a sociological phenomenon that infiltrates the collective consciousness so completely that even the James Deans of the world have become robots? Is there not some clearly existing dark connotation to such a comprehensive lockstep? And if *they* are the most cynical among us, then to what strength has this phenomenon affected the multitudes at large?

Where have all the real free-thinkers gone? Why are they no longer heard? Where are the guardians of truth? Where are the Churchills who warned us about the Curtain of Iron? Where are the Eisenhowers who pointed out the dangers of an unchecked military-industrial complex? Where are the heroes who once protected us from the looters and their phony claims of entitlement to our wealth, property, and freedom? Where is the common sense that gave us the ability to hear and appreciate their wisdom?

The people of this generation will be remembered as the victims of the greatest mass-brainwashing in history. It has become a paradigmic frenzy exceeding the imprints of Hitler, Stalin, and Mao combined. A new dark age looms on the horizon. The Crusades have returned. The rock singer and the movie actor are the pipers in this holy procession, followed by the television anchor as Supreme Inquisitor. Vast legions of boulder throwers make up the field. They march onward in the name of the *Holy Environment.*

Awareness and Existence

The environmentally-aware are against the *emissions* of technology. They seem more concerned with the *byproduct* than with the *product* of technology, even though it is the same technology that makes their lives possible. Actually, everything emits. Like all other systems in the universe, *Life* can be modeled as discrete ensembles of sequential states. These states cycle within defined limits, transforming energy and matter from their surroundings into new states. The things that get transformed are sometimes called resources. The things they get transformed into are called products and byproducts. For living systems, tiers of organization at all scales use and reuse the products and byproducts of adjoining scales and the planet is one big interconnected feeding frenzy.

To exist is to emit. Atoms emit. Snails emit. Snail darters emit. Humans emit. Our basic resources are air, water, and energy. Our product is our *awareness* of ourselves and of a complicated universe. Our byproduct, like that of most other life forms, is simple fertilizer. When environmentalists figure out how to have awareness without the fertilizer, what an extraordinary day that will be. Because that will be the day they finally shut their mouths.

Hating America 101 -
Environmental Science in Education and the Media

So complete has the indoctrination of environmentalism become that its confabulations have spilled out into our whole experience and fed upon themselves to the point that its absurdities have eclipsed all reason. The strength of imprintation has trumped disciplined, rational analysis. It is therefore, no longer a scientific question. It has by definition become a psychological question. In other words, it is a new religion. And like so many religions, it shrinks from analysis. Substantive argument quickly degrades to forensic posturing. Dissent is mocked. Heresy is not tolerated. Blasphemy is punished. Philanthropy abounds. Fortunes are made.

Highly qualified scientific experts such as famous American movie producers, actors, and singers of fleeting fame, trot across the globe cashing in on the popular cliché, enthusiastically professing to fawning audiences composed of equally qualified foreign citizens, how ashamed they are of their dim-witted countrymen back home in terrible old Earth-destroying, imperialist America.

If they are right about our national intelligence, might a review of modern American public school textbooks provide discouraging clues as to why? Perhaps. Because in virtually every subject, the traditional problems, examples, analogies, and methods that were employed to successfully teach useful knowledge to American students for decades, seem to have been infiltrated, adulterated, bowdlerized, painted over, and watered-down with useless environmentalist platitudes, truisms, and gibberish. Environmentalist dogma has often either superseded practical information or so obfuscated it that no one should be surprised that our students are performing poorly, or that our expectations have been eroded so deeply. The decline in American education is directly connected to the fact that environmentalism is the new religion of popular education and the convenient default subject matter for a massively inept educational system.

Declines cannot continue forever. They always hit bottom. The decline of American education is no different. There will come a point when the results of our experiment in environmentalism-centered education will be so plain that even its most inflexible apologists will have to confess failure. If not, then the deceit that has been put upon us will become unavoidably significant. The cows will come home. And when they do, the darkness will be right behind them. There will be suffering on a scale never before experienced in the history of our species. This will be the legacy of the radical environmental movement. The use of energy will not be the thing that destroys us. A lack of it will.

.

The radical environmentalists turn their misanthropic hand too easily. If their creed is purely benevolence and altruism, then let them work to enrich freedom, not dilute it. Let them be innovative, find options and develop them and bring them before humanity, not reduce options and hide the true purposes of a dark agenda. Let them *have a decent respect for the opinions of mankind.* Let them build up human life, not tear it down. Let them expand happiness and healing, not sadness and suffering. Let them survey new trails into the frontier, not put up barriers. Dear countrymen, the modern institutions of environmentalism *are not qualified* to determine the kind of world your children will live in, how they will live in it, or if they will even live at all. When the time comes, only your children will be qualified to do that. Until then, you are their only true protector.

Why have the well-fed strayed so far? Do they not eat? Do they not use electricity? Do they not generate waste, need medicine, and rely on delivery trucks? Do they intend to conveniently exempt themselves from the holocaust they are working to bring about? Actually, if what they propose were to ever come to fruition, there would first be unthinkable loss of life from disease, famine, and robbery as civilization disintegrated into anarchy. Then warlords and tyrants would emerge and enslave the survivors. The lesson is that if *any government* ever evolves the power to control human lives with such political machinations as a *Global Green Deal, acreage limitations,* or *steeply progressive income taxes,* then tyranny and enslavement will exist. Warlords are sharpening their swords right now.

The energy industry is not perfect. Anything so difficult could never be perfect. It is bloody, thankless, backbreaking work. Making energy is hard. Blaming is easy. That is what demagogues do best. They blame but never give credit. So it is not surprising that the complainers and the naysayers seem to conveniently disregard the spectacular achievements of the energy industry. For example, American oil and coal played a critical role in making the phenomenon of the twentieth century possible.

American oil and coal were the life blood of a vigorous industrial nation at a time when success was critically necessary.

Without abundant American energy, however imperfect, civilization of the twentieth century would have developed very differently. Life would not exist as we know it today. Human commerce would be coarser. We would be poorer. Suffering would be greater. Freedom would be rarer. Social injustice would be more common rather than less common. All because World War II and the conflicts that followed would have probably concluded less favorably for the free people of the world.

Without abundant energy, it is likely that no one would be disposed to join a radical environmental movement (it would more likely be a radical beans and rice movement). We probably would have less tolerance for the misanthropes pleading the necessity of our genocide as retribution for our crime of possessing abundant medicine, shelter, leisure, and transport (translation: medical research labs, apartment complexes, ski resorts, and sport utility vehicles). We would be too busy quarreling with our neighbors over a place in the soup line. Children and mothers would be crying. We would be too hungry to care about any protocol, Kyoto or otherwise, and too scared to speak against it. Or perhaps, we would be just another of the lost souls stacked like cordwood in one of the mass graves at the nearest state-run gulag.

In our struggles against Hitlerism and later Stalinism, coal forged the native elements iron, nickel, chromium, copper, and aluminum into trucks, locomotives, tanks, ships, planes, and guns. Oil made them mobile. Superior equipment in superior quantities gave America victory over tyranny and darkness. Coal and oil gave America victory over tyranny and darkness. By achieving victory, both militarily and economically, Americans of the twentieth century were finally able to bring to maturity the greatest civilization ever conceived in the history of the human race.

It was a civilization that held individual rights above those of the state. It was a civilization that expelled or outlasted totalitarianism and tyranny wherever they were encountered, even at home. It was a civilization that pierced the embryonic veil for the whole human race and took the first steps on another world. It was a civilization that reached out and tried to help others pull themselves up. It was a civilization that made possible all that we have today. And what we inherit in our time, like before, remains a treasure that the robbers, looters, thugs, and rogues want to plunder. It remains a civilization that the despots, the misanthropes, the jealous, and the backward want to destroy. Not surprisingly therefore, America is also still a principal source of optimism for the oppressed. To them, our dear America is now, and will always be the true *Empire of Hope*.

Chapter 4

Destroyers of Hope

America in the year 1919 was very different from the thing it has become in our time. The people of that era were not just mildly different from us, they were radically different. Their expectations were different. Their viewpoints were different. Their dreams were different. Although the underpinnings of the American psyche were no doubt well entrenched (e.g. individualism, independence, creativity, confidence), it is still likely that the cosmopolitan outlook of our time would have been completely unfathomable to most citizens of the period.

The physical landscape of 1919 was the same one we inhabit today. But the tangible infrastructure of civilization, the ponderous, interconnected technological and informational continuum encasing our world today, was scarcely in its embryonic stages. The safety net that comes with abundance was far weaker and contained enormous holes. This was because wealth was still small. The framework of our world was laid down, but the shelves were mostly empty space. Today, the combined accumulated produce of history has poured out and filled virtually every available receptacle in the manifold environment of humankind. The refrigerator is no longer bare. There exists today the highest standard of health, security, and affluence in the history of the our species. These conditions are enjoyed by unprecedented numbers of individuals as well as by the largest fraction of the population in history. Unless tampered with, this progression is destined to continue until everyone everywhere is healthy, wealthy, and wise.

Despite the warnings and gloomy predictions of the cynics, despite the confiscatory taxation and tyrannical regulations that our government continues to increasingly burden upon us, despite the endless parades and charades of the whiners, the complainers, the looters, the con-artists, the bloodsuckers, and the robbers, despite all these things and more, the additive fruit of toiling millions has finally brought the Free World to *inevitable, unavoidable prosperity.* This is where we were headed all along. *This has always been the promise of America* and the dream of the Founding Fathers. History has unfolded exactly like it was supposed to (déjá vu in reverse). But this near-Utopia we take for granted today was just another fanciful dream in the year 1919.

My father's formative years consisted of seemingly endless toil and despair. It was a time when labor was large and reward was small. It was a time when a man was expected to work himself to death without making a fuss about it. It was a time when both the entreaty and bestowment of pity were conspicuously scarce, and unequivocally considered improper of a man. But these were not phenomena exclusive to America. World War I and the immediate years subsequent thereto, tended to be even more compassionless in other parts of the world, and in fact remain that way even today in some backward areas.

In the year 1919 for example, much of Europe was still staggering from the insanity and devastation of the war. Of the sixty-five million men who served in the military for their respective nations between the years 1914 and 1918, at least thirty million were either killed or wounded (including 365,000 Americans), and another eight million became prisoners of war or were declared missing in action.

The country of France was coping with the psychological and economic consequences of having 1.4 million of her sons, brothers, and fathers killed, over 4.3 million maimed, and the creation of 650,000 new widows. Germany not only suffered similar injury but also, presumably, feigned a profound national shame, and so felt compelled to descend into the throes of an inelegant societal enema that ultimately deposited Hitler onto the world stage. Meanwhile, Russia writhed in an absurd, suicidal pogrom of unimaginable brutality and inhumanity.

Then to make matters even worse, right before the war ended, Mother Nature unexpectedly bestowed the human race with a particularly virulent epidemic of influenza. By the close of 1919, at least twenty million, and by some estimates, up to seventy million people had died from the disease (including at least 500,000 Americans). These staggering losses occurred when the world population was less than one-third of its current number. For the poor souls alive at the time, the inescapable hopelessness brought about by the war was suddenly compounded to indescribable severity by disease. Virtually everyone in the world lost an acquaintance or a family member to either war or disease, or both. Whole families were wiped out. People thought the world was coming to an end. It is easy to understand why. And of course for millions it actually did.

It is arguable that there is no contemporary frame of reference for Americans to realistically appreciate the above described events. An accurate modern comprehension of the impact to America's national spirit during the World War I era therefore, may not be possible. Nevertheless, there is one phenomenon that might be marginally instructive. That is, perhaps the most applicable recent example that may help modern Americans comprehend the scale of hopelessness prevailing between 1914 and 1919, would be the tragedy of September 11, 2001. Many Americans were deeply affected by what has come to be known as "9/11."

The impact of 9/11 on our national hope was profound. It was a unique kind of impact. It was not so much related directly to the deaths of friends or family like in the years 1914-1919. The impact caused by 9/11 was less direct. Therefore, 9/11 is not a perfect analogy, but is still useful because it lets us quantify hope in general, so that we may have a basis, however imperfect, for estimating the state of hope in the years 1914-1919.

An instructive method for translating the societal impact of World War I and the influenza epidemic into 21st Century terms is to examine the numbers. That is, the achievement of a relative loss of life today (adjusting for world population growth) that would be equivalent to the combined mortality caused by war and influenza in the years 1914–1919 would require at least one "9/11 event" to occur every 26 minutes and 40 seconds for five years. That is, it would require fifty-four "9/11" tragedies per day, every day, for 1,825 days, or approximately 100,000 "9/11" tragedies in all. Their souls would still be waiting in line to get into heaven.

To the casual observer, it would seem that the societal impact of an enormous global tragedy like that of 1914-1919 ought to continue to reverberate in the fabric of our civilization today, whether we are individually aware of it or not. It is likely that this is the case in many ways. However, in purely tangible terms it might be argued that just the opposite is true. This latter conclusion is predicated on two unscientific observational points:

1. Prior to 9/11, our expectations seemed to take certainty for granted. The magnificent advances in science and technology since World War I, have insulated us in a blanket of unprecedented security, affluence, and health. So much so that a single 9/11 event shocked many of us to the edge of our sanity.

2. Prior to 9/11, our perception of adversity had atrophied. That is, our national threshold for shock before 9/11 had been reduced to an almost child-like state. In the immediate aftermath of 9/11, many Americans were profoundly surprised by a very uncomfortable sensation they had never known before: fear.

But the fear experienced in September of 2001, as deeply troubling as it was, may have amounted to only 1/100,000th the level that must have existed in the years 1914-1919. Their fear came in smothering waves and surging rivers. It was a restless sea of fear, lapping and yelping at the hopeless shore of their souls for geologic time.

Veterans of the first world war had experiences that would forever shape their transactions with other human beings. Cruelty, harshness, and mercilessness became the norm. Widespread death and hopelessness were not unusual. In the numerical context, human life was devalued to its lowest level perhaps in recorded history. It seems that Hitler and Stalin both came out of the war years thinking so. The events of the period arguably shaped their collective mindset, establishing a template for atrocities they would later visit on humanity at an even grander scale. It was a tough time, perhaps not so far removed as we would think from the days when living human beings were fed to wild beasts purely for the perverted amusement of their mutual captors. Or when one person could own another, and pick their fate on a whim.

New Hope, Indiana, September 29, 1919

My father was born on this day and in this place. Considering the backdrop described above, it is little wonder that he seldom spoke fondly of his childhood days. There was a fundamental shortage of goodness everywhere. People were mean to each other. Races were mean to each other. Hope was a luxury beyond the reach of most of the citizens of the world, including millions of Americans, the nameless farmers of Indiana being no different in this regard.

Still hope is irrepressible. It will not be kept down. It springs up in places where we think none should be. Like life, it tends to assemble itself by trial and error from the available elements of its surroundings. It is self-generating. And it appears to follow life, particularly new life. Curiously, children do not seem to know they are not supposed to have it. So with each child born, a fresh chance for hope is put upon the land. The clocks are reset. Assumptions, prejudices, and dogmas are discarded and optimism is renewed.

Babies are miniature hope reactors. They generate hope and their families absorb it like a narcotic. The result is similar to a nuclear reaction. A trace of fuel produces a truly exponential output ($E = Mc^2$ again). The reaction is automatic. Simply provide a little sustenance, upkeep, and protection. It helps to jiggle it around a couple of times a day. The reward for this is an enormous output of hope that can be harnessed by the operators of the reactor, the nameless farmers of Indiana being no different in this regard.

Children seem to be able to wrest hope out of about anything, even dirt. Give a child a stick and he will use it to pry hope from a hole in the ground. Take the stick away and he will mold the dirt into a stick. His mind will become the lever. The creativity of a child is an X-ray of the immutable hope that smolders deep in the latticework of our genetic code. Obscured in layers of irreducible mystery, hope continually pulses, clicks, and roars in the boundless highland pastures of our nuclei. Twotrillion scintillating points weave into some emergent thing. Call it Hope. And this hope telescopes upward, spiraling outward, like the X-ray in reverse. It explodes from our cells, animating our bodies and illuminating the universe. Babies are our natural defense against a hostile universe. Children are the guns of hope. They are our letters from Eden.

Every child finds something in their surroundings upon which they can fix their hands and minds. The object grasped becomes their lever for prying hope from the world. This is our way. This is our instinct. It works for us. It saves us. It gives our lives meaning. The Universe has molded us to be this way for its own purposes. Perhaps we are the lever that the Universe uses to find its hope. Perhaps we are the thing that gives the Universe its meaning.

Chapter 5

Tiger Attack

During World War II, my father served his country honorably and faithfully in the United States Army. Adam David McCasoway entered active military service on September 7, 1944, twenty-two days before his 25th birthday. He received his training at Fort Jackson, South Carolina, and Camp Atterbury, Indiana. His military occupational designation was "Truck Driver Light 345." He was assigned to Company-L of the 423rd Regiment, of the 106th Infantry Division. The length of his service was eighteen months and twenty-two days, seven months and twenty days of which were spent in the European Theater of Operations. His rank was Private First Class. His decorations included the European/African/ Middle Eastern Theater Ribbon with one Bronze Campaign Star, Good Conduct Ribbon, American Theater Ribbon, and the Victory Ribbon. He was honorably discharged at Fort Custer, Michigan on March 28, 1946.

On March 25, 1945, my father embarked from New York City aboard the famed flagship of the Cunard line, *Queen Elizabeth*. She was a magnificent vessel, displacing approximately 84,000 tons, about twice that of the largest American and British battleships of the day. Built by John Brown & Co. Ltd., of Glasgow, the Queen Elizabeth was originally designed to provide luxurious accommodations for 2,283 paying passengers. During her final construction phase however, she was requisitioned by the British Ministry of War Transport and fitted out to carry 15,000 troops, with all facades of comfort discarded. In the course of her military service, the Queen Elizabeth is said to have traveled 500,000 miles and transported 750,000 American, British, Canadian, and Australian troops both to and from various war zones.

Crossing the Atlantic was a frightful ordeal for most of the men. Like my father, many had never even seen the ocean before. They had no idea what a sea voyage entailed. But they were very aware of the threat of German U-boats and surface raiders. They also knew that the Germans had a standing bounty on the Queen Elizabeth. At one time or another every sub captain in the Kriegsmarine must have dreamed of sinking her. It would have been a tremendous propaganda accomplishment for the Axis and a terrible loss for the Allies both psychologically and militarily. And in the frigid water of the North Atlantic, the cost in human terms would have been staggering.

The Queen Elizabeth seldom received naval escort. Were she sunk it could have taken hours, or even days for rescue ships to arrive, dooming any survivors unable to quickly get into a lifeboat. The Queen's primary defense against German submarines was her speed, said to have been in excess of twenty-nine knots. But such speed had a price. The hell-bent pace combined with the fitful Atlantic seas produced unremitting seasickness in thousands of the troops she carried. My father was among the unfortunate land lubbers afflicted by this wretched malady. He recalled spaces within the ship where vomit was pooled to a depth of two inches or more. It was as if ten-thousand stomachs had been turned inside out and grafted to the metallic interstices of the ship. They were both figuratively and literally, living inside their own guts. It was virtually impossible to move about without treading through this cheerless muck. And even in those places where it was in short supply, there still remained the stifling and unhealthful vapors, often in sufficient concentration to bring tears to the eyes. Many men remained topside during daylight hours to escape the pestilence. But the numbing temperatures and high winds forced them to return to their tainted, unhappy quarters at night.

Gourock, Scotland, was an important shipping center located on the Firth of Clyde, near Glasgow. It was in the dockyards there that ships like the Queen Mary and the Queen Elizabeth were constructed. On March 31, 1945, it was to Gourock that the Queen Elizabeth returned. Never were any passengers ever happier than the men who rejoined terra firma that day.

As the thousands of men filed off of the ship piecemeal, they were segregated into units and sent out to their varied assignments. Some departed in trucks, some in busses, and some by other means. My father left Gourock by train. Troop destinations were necessarily something of a sensitive topic, so the men seldom knew where they were going at any stage of their travels. Dad recounted that the information he received was only of the most vague type, such as: "You're going to ride the train." or "You'll know when you get there." Rumors were plentiful. Dad had found rumors to be generally unreliable, especially in situations related to transport. But based partly on the rumors and partly on what he observed, he was reasonably certain that their destination after leaving Gourock was most likely Portsmouth or Southampton. They were then ferried across the English Channel to the Baie de le Seine, landing at Le Havre. There the troops were again parsed to differing destinations and transport modes. He was assigned to a group that boarded a train and were then sped under blackout conditions across France and on toward the German frontier.

My father had been told that he was a replacement for one of the approximately nine-thousand soldiers of the 106th Division who were killed, wounded, or captured during the Battle of the Bulge only weeks before. He was also advised that he would not be placed immediately into combat at the front. Hitler was on the run. The Germans were expected to capitulate any day. His contribution to the war effort would involve truck driving, guarding German prisoners, or occupational duties. If given a choice, he had determined that the guarding of prisoners seemed to be the least desirable. There was something about the idea that he did not like. "Occupational duties" sounded a lot like police work, or at the very least trying to win the hearts and minds of the people. Again, this seemed like a vague assignment with implications that exceeded his tastes. Overall, he considered truck driving to be the best option to fit his skills and something actually productive. Bringing food, medicine, fuel, or ammunition to the front lines seemed like honorable duty.

Upon arrival at a train station near the German border, he and hundreds of other soldiers boarded canvas-covered transport trucks and were spirited off into the night. They continued to travel non-stop for another day and a half. The men were packed into the trucks to the point of standing room only. Traveling under such conditions was both miserable and exhausting. The vehicles seldom stopped. When nature called, the men would work their way to the back of the truck and relieve themselves over the tailgate. The concept of dignity became blurred under such circumstances. It was an awkward state of affairs for everyone. This included of course the passengers, any local citizens who happened to be out and about, and especially the drivers of the convoy vehicles.

For days, the drivers in troop convoys were an unenviable captive audience to the improvised mobile lavatories lumbering in front of them. Realizing this, Dad began to reconsider his options. Guarding prisoners didn't sound so bad after all. Occupational duties could even have previously unappreciated merits as well. It was a tough call. Nevertheless, one thing remained unequivocal: being the truck's driver had to be better than being the truck's cargo.

By the second morning, on or about April 3, 1945, the convoy had reached the foothills of what Dad believed may have been the Harz Mountains. The pace slowed with the increasing grade. The cool spring climate transformed to one of deep winter. Within two hours they crossed the snow line as the modern highway they had been following gradually narrowed into a slender trail that switched back and forth through a dense forest of rime encumbered firs. The advance slowed to a near crawl in the building snow, now at least a foot deep. To many of the men this was worrisome. They had been riding for thirty-six hours and it seemed like they were not getting closer to anywhere. And wherever they were now, it was a hell of a long way from everywhere. It was sensed by everyone: *they were lost.* A winding, one-lane road walled on either side by thick, snow-blanketed, mountainous woods makes a nice picture for a postcard. But for an unescorted convoy in a war zone, it is among the worst of places to be. There was an inherent menacing aspect to such a setting. For my father and the others, there was a sudden and new perceived vulnerability.

They could only hope that the leaders of this procession knew what they were doing. The tension could be seen in their faces. Their conversations were subdued. No one seemed eager to be the first person to interject defeatist rhetoric. Perhaps they were waiting for some seasoned veteran among them to blurt out that everything was okay and that the cavalry was just over the next hill. No one said a word.

Outside, the temperature was painfully cold in its own right. But the bitter wind coursing for hour after dreary hour through the mostly unprotected, metal frame of a moving truck, dangerously compounded the chilling effect. First their limbs went numb. Then their minds began to wane. The chill reached into the marrow of their bones. Starving men in the throes of their deprivation are said to fantasize about lavish dinners and rich desserts. Their visions become so persuasive that some claim they have smelled chicken frying and biscuits baking. The men in these trucks were probably quite hungry, considering all they had been through to reach this juncture. Yet now their hallucinations would have more likely been of flickering fireplaces or glowing potbelly stoves; and their conjured aromas more the rustic fragrances of hickory smoke, smoldering coal, or that tinge of scorched of cotton that comes when we stand too near the embers.

The convoy's sluggish progress continued toward the first glint of morning. The men were little more than zombies as dawn teased their weary eyes. Weakened from the recent sea journey and the urgent pace of the current excursion, Dad and most of the others had not received appreciable rest or held down a decent meal for days. Like the snow-encrusted wheels beneath them, morale was beginning to slip.

Surprisingly however, with the mounting light outside, a curious optimistic consensus began to emerge in their conversations. They surmised collectively that their situation was surely about to get better. This logic seemed largely predicated on the notion that since they were so miserable, things couldn't possibly get any worse. They all agreed. In their hearts they probably knew it was self-deception. But the morning sun had brought a ray of hope. However tenuous, they intended to cling to it. Then during a brief lull in the conversation, for reasons he could never explain, Dad started whistling *God Bless America*. Everyone in the truck immediately joined in and began to sing the song. The drivers just looked at one another in puzzlement. They must have thought the poor fellows were loopy, that the cold had finally gotten to them.

Just then a powerful explosion jolted the truck. Their vehicle lunged, spun to the left and abruptly stopped. In a sorrowful chain reaction, the trucks following them also veered abruptly to avoid their successive collisions. The report of automatic weapons could be heard outside. The convoy had driven into a German ambush.

The attack began when two Tiger tanks unexpectedly came rushing out of the woods and stopped in the middle of the roadway. One tank blocked the front of the convoy and the second tank stopped about ten or twelve vehicles back from the front and about three or four vehicles ahead of my father's truck. German troops in the woods and surrounding these tanks in the meantime unleashed a devastating weight coordinated rifle and machine gun fire into the convoy. Bullets were striking the truck and whistling through the air all around. The drivers of Dad's truck were killed instantly. The canvas cover of their truck was then shredded with multiple hits.

Men started falling as the bullets ripped into their bodies. Dad felt a body tumble against him and a sharp burning sensation in his neck, as the living started bailing out of the back. One man remained on the truck shooting at the Germans with his rifle. The closest tank brought its 88 millimeter main gun to bear and fired. The truck exploded, presumably killing this soldier. Dad believed that the bravery of this man distracted the enemy long enough for the others to escape.

My father ran with scores of other men down the road, away from the German tanks and in the opposite direction his column had been heading. They ran past many stalled convoy vehicles extending around the tree-lined curve. The scores of fleeing men quickly became hundreds. Then about 150 yards ahead, near the rear of the convoy, a third tank entered the road and began firing. It became obvious that the convoy was hopelessly trapped and being cut to pieces. The situation then collapsed into chaos as the men panicked and began running in all directions. Dad could feel blood running down the back of his neck and soaking his shirt but he did not have time to investigate. He was actually afraid to feel of the injured area. Something in him did not want to know.

The artillery explosions and rifle fire eventually compelled Dad and many others to seek safety away from the road. Dad veered out into the woods heading northwest. The others scattered into the forest at random. Like my father, in their haste to exit the trucks, most of them left their rifles, packs, and helmets. Dad had only the clothes he wore, which luckily included a winter overcoat. Once out in the forest, many of the soldiers quickly re-grouped into small, haphazardly organized squads. Near dusk on the first night, Dad was with a group of about six soldiers, who against my father's advice, decided to start a campfire to try to get warm. There were no officers among this group of men. Dad and another soldier whose name was Baird, reminded them that they were in enemy-held territory and that lighting a fire at night would surely attract attention when stealth was much more desirable. They built the fire anyway.

In fearful frustration, Dad and Baird then separated themselves from this group by a distance of about 50 yards where they discovered a mass of tree roots hanging over a creek bank. They concealed themselves behind this natural barrier. There they found some welcome protection from the wind and were able to collect their thoughts for the first time in hours. The sharp burning in Dad's neck had by now transformed into an excruciating throb superimposed on a bothersome itch. Hesitantly, he explored of the area with the tips of his fingers. He could feel dried blood. But he could find no major entrance wound. However, there were three small cuts greatly swollen and tender to the touch. When striking something hard, bullets sometimes shatter with their fragments fanning out at a much reduced energy. Dad thought this is what must have happened - a bullet shattered against the metal frame of the canvas top and some of the fragments hit him.

When he touched these lumps the pain was quite intense. He thought he could feel the metal protruding from one of them. Obviously it was embedded only superficially. So he decided to squeeze the wound on the odd chance that it might come out. The pain was more robust than he had hoped but he finally managed to extract the fragment. He subsequently removed the fragments from the other two wounds and collected them in his pocket.

Signals, commands, that is, information is propagated through our bodies in two basic ways. One occurs when neurons release neurotransmitter molecules across enclosed synapses, analogous perhaps to Morse code pulses traveling through wires. These signals follow discrete pathways between specific origins and destinations, just like phone calls. Another method of information exchange occurs when the endocrine system releases specialized molecules directly into the bloodstream. This approach might be comparable to a radio broadcast. The signals go everywhere in the body but affect only those cells that have their radio dial on the proper channel, i.e., that possess specific protein receptor molecules in their plasma membranes. When the signal molecule is received, a series of chemical changes cascade through the target cell. When these chemical changes occur in the millions of cells comprising certain tissue or organ systems within our bodies, we perceive them outwardly as physiological changes.

In humans, the adrenal glands are encased within masses of fatty tissue attached to the top of both kidneys. The adrenal gland consists of two major concentric regions, with each producing a specific range of molecules important in regulating many complex functions of the body. The approximate outer third of the adrenal gland constitutes a region called the cortex. Embryonically, the cells of the cortex trace their origin to the mesoderm, the same primitive gastrula cells from which the muscles and bones ultimately differentiate. The cortex produces classes of molecules called glucocorticoids and mineralocorticoids which among other things, help regulate developmental growth of the body.

Beneath the cortex region lies the core of the adrenal gland, the medulla. Embryonically, the cells of the medulla derive from the ectoderm region of the primitive gastrula, the same cells from which the brain and central nervous system differentiate. The medulla is composed of bundles neuron-like chromaffin cells which produce large quantities of the neurotransmitter molecules adrenaline and noradrenaline. The medulla releases these molecules in response to elevations in physical or mental stress. These chemical sentinels quickly reach receptors all over the body, triggering physiological changes in very rapid response to elevations in stress. These effects include among other things, an increase in the rate and force of the heartbeat; a reduction in blood flow to the skin and digestive tract with a corresponding increase of flow to the skeletal muscles, heart, liver, and brain; increase in metabolic rate; expansion of the respiratory passageways; dilation of the pupils; and a reduction in the clotting time of the blood. Fear is particularly effective at stimulating the release of adrenaline.

Adrenaline is the panic-button rocket fuel of both predator and prey. It chops time into little pieces and then magnifies each for the mind's eye. It transforms normally sedentary muscles into extraordinary instruments of propulsion and combat. It helps us to out-think and out-maneuver danger. But adrenaline without motion can overcharge the mind and poison the spirit. Within the suddenly hushed confinement of their makeshift foxhole, adrenaline's alchemy transmuted the seconds into hours. Time was dilated almost relativistically - like the analogy of the astronaut who leaves Earth and travels at near the speed of light for a day, and upon returning discovers that one-hundred years have elapsed. On the night of April 3, 1945, the span of a few hours everywhere else in the world was stretched into a lifetime for the men in these woods.

In the apparent sensory deprivation of the moment, their eyes became locked on the hypnotic flicker of the campfire in the distance, the fire that they fled some indeterminate period of time ago. Sounds near and far were wildly amplified. They heard the cavitation of air in the branches of their lungs. Between the beats of their hearts, they could almost make out the roar of corpuscles ratcheting through their capillaries. Yet with the passage of time, the sphere of their awareness began to expand beyond the noise of its own machinery. They slowly started to dissect the din of the battlefield around them. It was not just static. The sounds contained information. By cogitation of its nuances, the night's acoustics began to congeal into a phenomenon with curious sonar-like qualities. This provided them with occasional, tantalizingly clear mental glimpses of the surrounding landscape. The reports of rifles composed the most prominent ambient noise riding on the shoulder of the wind. The shots seemed to come from every direction. A few were nearby, perhaps a hundred yards off. Some were so far away that the direction was ambiguous. They were mostly singular reports, or in compact bursts of two to eight rounds. Also amid the mix were the frightful discharges of automatic weapons. Finally, in the distance was artillery fire broadcasting in sporadic cadences reminiscent of a midsummer thunderstorm, gently shuddering the frozen kingdom beneath them.

Then around midnight the wind began to die down letting a previously unheard noise slowly materialize from the darkness. It sounded like the howls of coyotes, except far more eerie and troublesome. Dad tried to figure it out. Maybe it was the wind in the tops of the trees, or artillery shells streaking overhead in the thin alpine atmosphere, or the squeaking of tank tracks. Dad thought his mind was playing tricks on him. Then it became shockingly clear that he was hearing the pitiful cries of scores of wounded men slowly freezing to death. Men but not men, that is, mostly boys, many not older than nineteen years, but still dying.

Everyone has heard stories about how wounded soldiers in their declining minutes, sometimes call out for their mothers. Patriots, citizens, cynics, please know: it is true. This is not a sign of individual cowardice. It is a sign of human fragility. And it is a sign of our innate folly - that we would allow worldly grievances to compel us to ever cause harm any mother's child.

Of all of my father's tribulations in his lifetime, before, during, and after the war, he professed that enduring the dismal beckoning of those boys was the greatest horror ever known to him. Their pleading tugged at his soul and mocked his hope. Any man, even a misanthrope, would surely have been compelled to go to them. It is a race instinct propped up by our convergent heritage in the mystery of the primordial past. It exceeds politics or personalities. Some unfathomable button within us is pushed by the pleading of a suffering fellow. And the suffering of a child is carried to us by ten-thousand angels more. But there were so many boys. They were everywhere. Without resources, without order, nothing could be done for them. This night anarchy and suffering would prevail.

My father said that as he listened to their cries fade with the evening hours, the mirror of the human soul revealed itself to him. He realized that what we call our Self, our personality, our identity, the inner corporate thing that converses with itself when we think, this emergent property is nothing more than a summation of the layers of all of our thoughts and experiences accumulated through time. Each day of our lives adds a living layer to this calculus - like the rings of a tree. And the reflection of these experiences in the mirror of the soul is what we define as our self-awareness. These layers converse with one another and fix themselves in, and give dimension to the universe of our consciousness. Each layer supports and empowers the successive layers above it and is a gateway to the layers below. And when the loss of blood, or the loss of hope, or great injury punctures the soul, the layers are lifted back one by one as the life drains from them, like the layers of an onion being peeled away, or turning the pages of a book, thus going backward in time. And somewhere in the frigid darkness, when time grows short for the poor wounded soul, all that remain are the layers of a little boy; a little boy who knows only that he is caught in the throes of a nightmare he does not understand; a little boy calling for his mommy to come and make everything better. A scared inner child orphaned in the snow. Somewhere in the horror of that glacial night, my poor father called for his mommy too. He cried quietly with those dying boys. This lament of the dying continued into the frozen depths of pre-dawn, slowly noticeably receding because of the obvious. In the mercy of the numb indifference that comes with absolute exhaustion, it was to this decrescendo of death that my father and Baird finally fell asleep. Then there was silence.

About an hour before daybreak they were suddenly awakened by the sound of gunfire nearby. A squad of about ten German soldiers had surprised the Americans at the campfire, subsequently shooting them without warning or provocation. Some were asleep when they were killed. Some were awake. All were shot in the head with pistols after being riddled with machine gun and rifle bullets. Every soldier at the campfire was brutally murdered. Dad and Baird watched the executions in horror but could not respond because they had no weapons. To attempt surrender would have clearly been suicide. So they remained silent and motionless as the Germans searched the bodies of the dead for loot. They took some coats, cigarettes, a few other items and then leisurely meandered back into the malevolent darkness.

Dad and Baird roamed through the forest for five days without seeing another living human being. They used snow as their source of water but had no food whatsoever during this period. Using pine needles and branches for materials, Dad was able to build several small shelters that he called "squirrel nests." They were by no means perfect, but they did offer considerable protection from the wind and cold. They also had excellent concealment properties which after the executions, was a paramount concern. The two men slept in these shelters during the day and traveled at night, heading northwest whenever possible, with artillery and small arms fire around them continuously. Because of their separation from their unit, their lack of information, and the limited visibility associated with the terrain, they were unable to determine who was shooting at who.

Essentially, anything seen or heard got shot at by someone. Under such conditions it was not only pointless and suicidal to participate in the action, but counterproductive. That is, it was impossible to distinguish between one's own forces and those of the enemy. They were caught in a peculiar phenomenological trap that effectively neutralized their combat potential. Under the circumstances, the only practical recourse was to remain concealed and try to survive until some measure of order was established within the theater.

It is truly noble to be brave. The two terms are often used interchangeably. Success in warfare cannot be achieved without bravery. But maintaining one's wits is also within a soldier's purview. Brave men are frequently asked to commit suicide in war, unfortunately too often routinely. But there ought to be some goal worth achieving in order to give balance and purpose to such extreme sacrifice.

Occasionally, victory is not so much destroying the enemy as it is denying him the achievement of your own destruction. If the enemy cannot kill you, he is robbed of complete victory. In the chaos that Dad. found himself, committing suicide would have been easy, but pointless. His suicide would not have shortened the war. So his focus became to simply survive long enough to rejoin his regiment. If he could achieve this, maybe he would get a chance to make a meaningful contribution to the war effort instead of a meaningless one. He was determined to live. He would make this his battle – survival.

On the fifth day, Baird and Dad observed a farmstead in a cleared valley below them. It was the first sign of civilization they had seen since the ambush. They quickly spotted a flock of six to eight tame geese in the barnyard behind this house. They subsequently hatched a plan to sneak down to the farmhouse during the night and obtain one or more of these geese. While they waited for darkness to fall, they saw a man come out of the house and remove several objects from a hole in the ground near the edge of the woods.

When darkness finally came, Dad and Baird slowly approached the barnyard, crawling on their bellies most of the way. Unfortunately, the geese detected them and began to protest loudly, forcing abandonment of the plan. Consequently, with utmost anticipation and hope, they went to the place where the farmer had been digging and discovered a cache of objects that had the heft and feel of potatoes. But in the darkness, it was impossible to tell for sure. It seemed clear enough though that the objects were probably edible. So they stuffed their coat pockets with as many of the rude vegetables as they could, then pawing two or three in each hand they excitedly dashed back to the safety of their shelter.

Upon reaching their squirrel nest, Dad was somewhat dismayed to discover that the pilfered vegetables were not potatoes after all. They were rutabagas (see Chapter 12). Before he even got settled in, next to him in the darkness, he could already hear Baird gnawing off frozen chunks of the vegetables and hurling them down his gullet with mindless urgency, seemingly oblivious to Dad's dilemma. A flake of peel or a droplet of saliva from the vaporous plume of Baird's feeding frenzy would occasionally pepper Dad on his face. He sounded like a herd of pigs. He paused only once to assert that he had never before eaten rutabagas, but that he found them to be quite palatable. My father of course eventually ate the rutabagas too. It was the only sustenance that he received during the twelve days he was lost. After surviving solely on the dreadful vegetable during that hellish period, he vowed to never eat rutabaga again, even on a lark. As far as anyone knows, he remained true to this promise for the fifty-six years he lived after his ordeal in the war.

On or about the seventh day, they were hiding in a patch of woods on a hill overlooking a road intersection at the edge of a small village. They noted some military vehicles parked at this intersection. There were soldiers milling around as though trying to stay warm. They appeared to be Germans. After several hours of intense consternation, Baird decided to surrender. Before he departed he assured Dad that he would not tell the Germans about him. They shook hands and said their goodbyes. Baird then climbed out of the squirrel nest and went down the hill in a circuitous path so as to better protect Dad's hiding place. A few minutes later, Dad watched the Germans take Baird prisoner. He never saw or heard from him ever again. My father always believed that Baird was executed that day.

On the ninth day, Dad was forced to seek refuge in a hedgerow when he discovered he was trapped in the middle of a Nazi armored infantry battalion, possibly the same unit that originally ambushed his convoy. German troops and tanks were passing on a road next to him only inches away. They appeared to be in retreat. He could see their mud-covered boots and hear their conversations as they marched past. Even though he was surrounded, he felt secure. They were moving too fast to pay attention to him. But there was a catch. As the tanks came down the road they periodically swerved into the hedgerow, presumably to pass around the troops or vehicles. The tank's immense weight would smash and rip the hedgerow to pieces each time this happened. Accompanying these collisions were the frightful sounds of breaking timbers and the trembling of the ground beneath him. He could not predict where and when the tanks were going to hit. All he knew was that the collisions were getting closer. Dad feared that at any minute he would be ran over and mangled under the treads of a tank. It was at this point that he determined his only choice was to surrender.

Just as he was preparing to climb out of the hedgerow, a stray cat, presumably flushed from its own hiding place by the tanks, unexpectedly jumped onto his leg. He thought that it was a Nazi reaching into the hedge and grabbing his leg. In the suddenness of the act he instinctively uttered a startled "Ahhhh," of an appreciable volume and kicked out with the affected leg. When he saw that it was only a cat, he realized that his yell may have been loud enough to attract the attention of the Germans. But apparently they did not hear him. He decided to not surrender.

Since leaving New York, Dad's weight had gone from 160 to 120 pounds, a loss of forty pounds in twenty-two days. He was dehydrated, malnourished, frost bitten, and could not get warm. By the tenth day he had reached his physical limit. He knew if he did not find help soon the consequences would be grim. He had been continually hobbling northwest for the last seven nights. As daybreak approached on the eleventh day he hastily constructed a squirrel nest and collapsed into it, subsequently falling asleep quickly.

He was awakened in the mid-morning by the noises of truck engines and men talking. They appeared to be speaking German. He carefully peered out of his shelter and observed a team of Germans apparently assembling a V2 rocket near him. The site was in a large oblong clearing in the woods, approximately 175 feet by 250 feet in its dimensions. A one-lane dirt road lead away from the clearing to the east. His shelter was about two-hundred feet south of the edge of this clearing, and slightly above it, located on the side of a gentle slope. The trees were quite tall and closely spaced on the slope, providing him with excellent concealment.

Technical personnel appeared to be preparing the rocket for launch. There were several trucks parked around the clearing. Some had cables or hoses connected to the rocket. Dad tried to think of ways to sabotage these hoses but quickly gave up the idea because he was simply too weak to move. And in fact he did not know if it was even real. He was so ill and feverous that he could of imagined the entire thing. No matter, he finally fell asleep watching them. He remained in the squirrel nest the entire eleventh day and night, too exhausted to do much else. When he awoke on the twelfth morning the rocket was gone. It had apparently been launched or moved during the night but he was sleeping so deeply that the sound did not awaken him. Or, as he freely admitted years later, it may have never existed at all, being an hallucination brought about by his fever.

He remained in the nest hoping to accumulate enough strength to resume his journey. He drifted in and out of consciousness through the morning. Then toward the middle of the day he was awakened by what sounded like approaching vehicles. Much to his disbelief, he saw a pair US Army 6x6 trucks approaching on the dirt road. They entered the clearing and stopped. He thought he was hallucinating again. He saw about ten soldiers get out of these trucks. They appeared to be inspecting the launch site. My father immediately tried to climb out of his squirrel nest but found that he was too weak to break free. In his clouded mental state all he could think of was to get their attention before they left.

The soldiers heard the commotion and immediately moved toward him with their rifles locked and loaded. They ordered him to put his hands over his head. But all he could do was get on his hands and knees. He was too weak to go forward, backward, or stand up. And his voice was too low to be heard. He could not even raise his head. All he could do was look at the ground as whisper over and over: "Don't shoot...I'm an American."

When the soldiers recognized that he was in distress, they carried him out of the woods and placed him into the cab of one of the trucks. He recognized the Screaming Eagle emblems on their uniforms, indicating that they were members of the 101st Airborne Division. They asked him if he was okay. He tried to speak but his voice was too weak. One of the men, a sergeant by the name of Rowe, gave him a drink of water from a canteen. Dad was then able to tell them that he was fine, but that he was a little hungry. The paratroopers lavished him with cans of fruit cocktail, potted meat, saltine crackers, candy, and all the fresh water he could hold. To the day he died, he professed that no food he ever ate tasted better or was more welcome.

The soldiers had many questions: Where were the rest of his platoon members? Why was he out here in the middle of nowhere? What unit was he with? and so on. Dad answered each of their queries. He recounted the events of the ambush and the executions at the campfire. He told them about the dying boys calling for their mothers. He confessed to them that he had cried for his momma too. After hearing this, the soldiers told Dad not to worry anymore. He was going to be okay now. The war was all but over. The Germans were folding on every front. Thousands were surrendering daily.

The 101st took good care of my father. In the midst of their kindnesses he suddenly became overwhelmed with emotion. He tried with all his strength to contain his feelings. He found himself laughing and crying at the same time. Someone in the truck covered him with a blanket. The next thing he remembered was waking up at a hospital in Paris.

While in the hospital, Dad was interrogated by an Army Intelligence officer. This officer told my father that he would be contacted again concerning the events of the ambush, but for now he should try to forget about it and return to duty as soon as possible. After regaining most of his strength, Dad was reunited with the 106th and assigned the duty of driving his company captain's jeep.

On several occasions during this period, Dad was sent out at night on reconnaissance missions with a squad of ten to twelve other soldiers. He was told that these maneuvers were part of a program described as *tactical training before the enemy.* His initial impression was that they were joking. But he soon discovered they were dreadfully serious. Presumably the program was dreamed up by a committee of bureaucratic geniuses in response to the shellacking that the 106th Division took during the Battle of the Bulge, when in a three day period 564 men were killed, 1,246 were wounded, and 7,000 were declared missing or captured.

The Army had been sharply criticized by many for placing an inadequately prepared division directly on the front lines. The criticism may have been undeserved however. True, the 106th was green, and they were spread a little thinly. But the fact remains that the Germans launched a blistering surprise offensive along the portion of the front where under all conventional assumptions of war such an attack was least likely to occur. This is precisely why the 106th was positioned there.

The Germans were a resourceful and dangerous enemy. Their forces comprised the equivalent of 29 divisions and approximately 600,000 troops. The timing of their attack showed great cunning. It came early on a Sunday morning nine days before Christmas when Allied air forces were conveniently grounded because of bad weather. Under the circumstances it is likely that any military force located in the path of such a juggernaut in such a place and time, regardless of training, would have suffered equally horrendous losses. In fact, the 106th is credited for actually thwarting the German offensive by refusing to relinquish the village of St. Vith. Their steadfastness distracted the Germans and caused them to expend precious time. This delay was a major contributing factor in the failure of the German battle plan.

For my father's reconnaissance squads, the standing order under the *tactical training before the enemy* scenario was to aggressively probe the lines but to not directly engage the enemy. One night Dad was among a group of ten soldiers patrolling a wooded area when they encountered an emplacement of Germans. Upon detecting the approach of my father's squad, the Germans fired a flare into the air, illuminating the area. The Germans then threw grenades and opened fire with automatic weapons. One of the grenades exploded approximately ten feet from Dad, knocking him to the ground and stunning him briefly. Although the blast was devastating, he credited it with saving his life. Because while he was on the ground the Germans saturated the area with a hail of bullets. Had he been standing it is likely that he would have been killed. He returned fire and then retreated with the rest of his squad.

Back at camp, medical personnel determined that the grenade explosion had given Dad a perforated eardrum and a concussion. By the following morning his knees and ankles had swollen to the point that he could not walk. Dad was consequently transported back to Paris, to the same hospital as before, where he stayed for at least two weeks.

After recovering for a second time, he returned to his unit and resumed his duty as a jeep driver. During this period he was also involved in occupational duties in eastern France. While working in this area his unit encountered large numbers of German soldiers who were attempting to surrender to the American Army before members of the local underground could capture them. Germans were reportedly being executed by the French in retribution for atrocities.

Dad recalled an episode when a high-ranking German officer who spoke fluent English, attempted to surrender to my father's commanding officer. The American captain, well aware of the gravity of the situation with regard to the executions, nevertheless refused to take him prisoner. The German then *demanded* that he be taken prisoner immediately, in accordance with the Geneva Convention. The American captain had been hearing this same demand for days. The Germans suddenly seemed to be very familiar with the Geneva Convention now that it was convenient. So much for German honor. They were shamelessly appealing to the clemency of civilized men to avoid the same kind of justice they had been handing out for five years.

Presumably, the arrogance of this particular German strained all that was left of the American officer's patience. He promptly produced a .45 caliber semiautomatic pistol and fired several shots at the ground near the German's feet, then pointed the weapon at his face and told him that he would blow off his g...d.... head if he uttered another word. The German was then reminded that as a defeated enemy combatant, he was in no position to demand anything. Furthermore, not only would he not be taken prisoner by the Army of the United States, he would be summarily executed if he did not remove himself from this operational sector.

Before the German was sent on his way however, my father confiscated his caliber 7.65 millimeter Mauser pistol, his ammo belt, and dagger. Dad kept the pistol for the rest of his life. The fate of the German officer is unknown. He was last seen walking off into the forest expressing what were believed to be extremely coarse profanities in the German language.

In the weeks after the formal surrender of Germany, Dad was assigned to a demolition team that destroyed captured weapons and ordnance. There were enormous stockpiles of cannons, machine guns, grenades, mortar shells, rifle cartridges, and so forth at locations throughout Germany. These instruments of war were either burned with fuel oil and thermite grenades, or blown to bits with high explosives. Many of the rifles they destroyed were in pristine condition. Dad and his associates were permitted to keep a few of these rifles.

One of the more exotic German weapon types that Dad helped destroy were several hundred Sd.Kfz.303b/Gerät-672 *Leichter Ladungsträger,* or *Goliath* remote-controlled mines. The *Goliath* was a small tracked vehicle that looked like a miniature tank without a turret. They came in a variety of configurations, both electric and gasoline powered. They were operated remotely by an electronic control box that was connected by a wire that spooled from the rear of the vehicle. The Goliath carried 100 kilograms of high explosives. The weapon did not see a lot of use in combat however. Members of my father's ordnance disposal squad played with some these mines before detonating them.

After completing his weapons disposal duties Dad was returned to England and interrogated by a panel of officers. He was told that he was to be part of a special study concerning the events of the Panzer ambush in early April. Other soldiers who survived the attack would also participate. Baird was not among them.

He was asked to recount his daily activities in great detail between the time of the ambush and the time he was rescued. The Army was interested in learning how he and the other men had survived not only the attack but also the deadly environmental conditions. Dad had always figured that his survival was attributable mostly to luck and did not understand why the Army was making such a big fuss about it. He was then informed that the convoy in which he had been riding was composed of over forty vehicles and at least 350 men. He was one of only twelve soldiers to survive. In a fit of barbarism, the Germans had systematically killed every American in the convoy. Dad was one of a handful who had managed to elude their executioners. Each man's story was different, but they all shared some important elements. Among these were:

1. Each survivor was an experienced hunter.
2. Each survivor actively sought and located food.
3. No survivor built a fire.
4. No survivor surrendered to the Germans.

The Army was profoundly interested in this information. They were also greatly captivated by Dad's description of his squirrel nests. Their interest was in fact sufficient for them to send him to meet a group of about one-hundred British and American commandos at a forest training area in Scotland where he demonstrated squirrel nest construction. He instructed them on all the variations of the nest that he had built. The commandos were very thankful for his input.

Dad recalled that his voyage back to America was considerably more pleasurable than the original trip to Scotland, even though the ship was still generously appointed with pestilent attributes. The difference was that he was going home. That knowledge alone seemed to make everything more tolerable. Upon entering New York Harbor and observing the Statue of Liberty, many of the soldiers shed tears of joy, including my father. From New York, he was sent to an army hospital in Michigan for about two weeks before being permanently discharged.

Dad later officially inquired as to why he had not received a Purple Heart for being wounded in action. He was told that he did not qualify because he was wounded while engaged in tactical training before the enemy. He accepted this explanation and never pursued it further. He was buried having never received his medal for being wounded in combat. He was mildly disappointed at this turn of events, but never expressed anger. The way he looked at it, the great size of the bureaucracy required to win a war against an enemy like the Germans, sometimes rolled over the individual. It was an unfortunate reality. Everybody made certain little sacrifices as a result.

Most men never complained. Dad was one of these. Some of the men who made the ultimate sacrifice were friends of my father. And then there was the fellow who stayed on the truck shooting back at the Germans during the ambush. My father believed men like that deserved the medals. Besides, the way he looked at it, if he needed an occasional reminder of the battle he could always strip his sleeve and show his scars.

Chapter 6

The Reign of Lawlessness

Men with guns came to take my father away.

September 1939, Nazi troops parade through Warsaw. *(Photo courtesy U.S. National Archives.)*

My father's experiences with crooks and gangsters were too numerous to comprehensively recount within the scope of this document. He battled the dark forces of collusion, intimidation, and extortion in virtually every commercial enterprise that he pursued. These agents took many forms, from the common to the arcane, from the laughable to the vulgar. For example, there were deceitful court house clerks who "lost" his oil leases after he dropped them off to be recorded. The leases would end up in the hands of crooked officials or their friends. There were contractors who charged for new equipment that either never existed or that was stolen from the project site as soon as it was delivered. Usually however, they simply switched used equipment in its place when no one was looking, and took the new equipment to their warehouse. Any equipment put into an oil well is particularly suspect in this regard.

There were less than truthful landowners who claimed that their property had never been drilled when in fact it had so many dry holes that it looked like a 640 acre piece of Swiss cheese. There were dishonest weigh station operators. A truck could be within the legal weight limit but they would tweak the scales to make it read overweight. This was a very simple scam. The solution was also simple: a couple of sawbucks passed under the counter for each load. Failure to comply resulted in punitive action taking the form of a fine in the amount of ten cents for each pound overweight, plus a safety inspection. A ton overweight equaled two-hundred dollars (or about two-thousand modern dollars). You slipped the tens through the window and moved on.

There were county road commissioners who required regular payments. Their methods were very straightforward as well. They would wait until my father had invested all of his solvent resources into a project and it was time start hauling out truckloads of coal or oil. On the day, or sometimes even the very hour the trucks began to run, five-ton load limit signs would miraculously appear along the county roads surrounding the project area. A monthly payment of between five-hundred and five-thousand dollars, depending upon the audacity of the commissioner, would make the signs disappear. A missed payment caused them to reappear and the involvement of the local sheriff. All payments were in cash, usually hundreds or fifties, but not in envelopes like in the movies – U.S. currency, folded once, hand to palm, while sitting in a car.

Since my father was an independent businessman, he was fair game for every corrupt official in virtually every county he operated. In a few of these counties, corruption was more than just a simple venerable tradition, it was considered a constitutional right. Most commissioners are honest, they do an essential and unenviable service for their communities. However, the harsh reality is that during much of my father's career, a certain fraction of them were bloodsucking criminals. Staying in business meant paying them. It was cheaper to pay than to fight.

Sometimes the local contractors that my father hired were crooked. Owners of trucking companies often had at least one family member on the county road commission. It was planned that way. They could shake down anyone who needed to haul things in trucks. The contractor kept the corrupt official apprised of the status of the project and the quantity of coal or oil being produced. The flow of information was so complete that the commissioners sometimes knew more about my father's business than even he did. This level of collusion allowed them to maximize their cut. That is, the amount of extortion was then tailored to match the output of the project.

Some would demand a flat rate per ton of coal or per barrel of oil, amounting to a few hundred dollars per week or month. This was taxing but sustainable. There were others who would incrementally raise their rate until they were taking most of the profit. Some got out of control and demanded all of the profit. This was done presumably to run my father out of business so they could seize the project for themselves. This happened more than once. However, even though they could knock him down and pick him clean, each time he hit the ground running. He was irrepressible. They could steal his resources but could not steal his resourcefulness. In sight of the shore, he endured wave after wave of these senseless obstacles. When others would surely have given up, he tried harder. He knew that if he just kept kicking, he would eventually reach the *Promised Land.*

The SMWA

Dishonest commissioners and contractors were troublesome. However, the real pros at corruption were the criminals who ran the crooked unions. They made the local government officials look like amateurs. But before unfolding the following account of events, so that there can be no misunderstanding, let it be known that Adam McCasoway had nothing against the lawful unions. He considered whatever they did as being between them and the Creator. Their business had nothing to do with him, unless it made the price of diesel fuel or explosives increase. He also felt that any person should have the right to join, or *not to join* a union. He did not think that it was moral to force a person to join a union if they did not want to, as so often is the case for school teachers for example.

Members of crooked unions are masters at taking statements out of context. They will take the statements in this narrative out of context, bend them, spin them, and regurgitate them before any who will listen. They necessitate this disclaimer. They will try to provoke condemnation of this narrative from other unions by claiming that what is said here is a criticism of them all, thereby acquiring endorsement of their criminality. So let it be known that this chronicle applies to *one union only*. It was the union that *killed many men* and some women and children too. It was the union that *tried to kill Adam McCasoway*. This account therefore, does not apply to the unions that did not try to kill Adam McCasoway. Only one union did that. And because of this, it was my father's wish that this story be told.

Unlike corrupt local officials who usually got what they wanted with a few well-placed signs on bridges, union thugs relied on violence and intimidation as the means to achieve their goals. That is, if their demands were not met, the penalty was not merely monetary, it was arson, sabotage, mayhem, and death; usually being delivered via projectiles of caliber-30 or greater, high explosives, flammable liquids, or some combination of the three.

Sometimes a wife would receive a phone call from an unidentified man who would tell her which stores she had shopped at that day, or the color of the dress that her daughter was wearing at school right that moment. *"We are watching you. We know that you are alone."* they would say. "Tell your husband to close his mine or you're going to regret it." In today's vernacular, I believe this sort of thing is called *terrorism*.

At the time, the above described activity was completely normal. There was little recourse. It was just the way things were done in SMWA country. It was a game of power. The unions had to sustain their tough image. To do this, a certain level of *terror* was continuously promulgated. That is, a few bulldozers and trucks would be incinerated periodically, some office trailers would be overturned, and there would be a few broken bones and soft-tissue injures bestowed upon you and/or your employees. It is unclear what percentage of union members actually engaged in the commission of these dishonorable deeds, admittedly and hopefully only a minority. What is extremely well known however, is that of those union members who did participate in the atrocities, most seemed to outwardly derive a form of sadistic gratification in demeaning and whipping the poor, loathsome, leprous scabs.

When my father filed charges under the rule of law, the perpetrators were exonerated every time. The union was apparently very influential at all levels of the local legal system. Jury members have laughed at my father, taunted him, and called him names in open court. The prosecutors, judges, and police were either sympathetic to the union, or afraid to stand up against them. This behavior betrayed a dark undercurrent of disrespect for the law that would eventually become unsustainable.

On average, for one month out of every twenty-four, the coal fields became battle fields. In the states of Indiana and Illinois during this period, it was not uncommon for one or two men to be killed each cycle. In Kentucky, Pennsylvania, or West Virginia the number of deaths might be three times that. These deaths did not result from falling rocks or power equipment accidents however, but from the bullets of high-powered rifles. Snipers liked to hide in rock cliffs overlooking haulage routes. From there they could kill truck drivers and others with relative impunity. This brutality was understood to just be part of the industry, a very distasteful and insane part, but still a part nonetheless.

The cycle of violence surged in ferocity. Some years it would be fairly benign. But frequently it would be vicious, perfectly in character with the tactics of socialist organizations all over the world since at least October of 1917. If a small operator wanted to stay in business, he had to have the stomach for either armed combat or humiliating acquiescence.

It usually began in one of two ways. On a day around the beginning of hunting season, the national contract of the Socialist Mine Warfare Alliance (SMWA) would expire and thousands of union miners would go on strike. Or, on a day around the beginning of hunting season, some disgruntled union member would cause a ruckus at a coal mine far, far away, resulting in a *wildcat* strike. Sometimes the wildcat strike would spread into a nationwide strike. Either way, about seven hours later, approximately two-hundred pickup trucks filled with armed men would suddenly appear on the haul road at our mine. Dad always operated small mines, so there were usually no more than ten or twenty employees present when the union armada arrived. A few dozen SMWA members would get out of the lead vehicles. They would casually walk up to my father and encircle him.

"What are you going to do McCasoway?"

"We're going to honor the strike. We will shut down."

"We figured you would. There's no need to tell you what will happen if you start up again."

Then they would leave. But not without driving through the mine, brandishing their weapons, and shouting "SCABS" and other disrespectful epithets at us. *"This is our coal!"* and *"You're stealing the food out of my kid's mouth."* seemed to be the commonest slogans. Some threw out empty beer cans as they passed. I was present on at least two occasions when the armadas came. I could not believe my eyes. I had never seen adults behave in such a manner, except perhaps in a cheap, formulaic, made-for-TV movie. *"How could anyone think like that?"* I thought.

We were too occupied with trying to rip through hard limestone while standing in mud up to our necks, to drive around the countryside inciting anarchy. We were too busy dealing with recurrent equipment breakdowns, cut-outs in the coal, water problems, and a list of other operational difficulties, not to mention constant physical exhaustion. And now a bunch of arrogant, pampered thugs are threatening to kill us for doing this? They want to fight for the right to be covered in mud and blood for twelve hours a day? There was something wrong with this concept.

It was perhaps the single greatest brutally shocking epiphany that I ever had. That is, to suddenly find out that everything I believed in, every tenet of the American Ideal, was apparently meaningless. I now realize that this is untrue of course. The American Ideal is not meaningless. Yet it is certain that there are those who for their own selfish motives, render it meaningless to themselves and those around them by disregarding the principles of democracy, civilization, and the law.

The attitudes expressed by the union members seemed very strange to me. My father taught me to love our country. He taught me to shake a man's hand firmly when it is offered. He taught me that wealth is created by both toil and invention. He taught me not to be a complainer. He taught me to recognize and accept responsibility for my own errors. He taught me that the true test of a man's worth is how he alone faces life's obstacles; that a man's character is reflected both in his victories and his defeats; that there is no obstacle too great if we are willing to do the work. The union members' dads seemed to have forgotten to tell their sons these things.

That is, their disrespect for democratic principles seemed to convey a fundamental disrespect for America. They refused our hands when we offered them. They seemed to believe that wealth is not created, but instead extorted. They complained constantly. They blamed someone else for every imperfection in their lives. They did not face obstacles individually but as a swaggering, clumsy mob. They were in effect admitting that life's impediments were too great for each of them individually. They were too weak as individual men to make it honestly in this world. So they gave up their individuality in order to get a cut of the loot. They sold their souls to the devil. The problem was however, not everybody shared their mindset. They can sell out all they want, but there will always be people who refuse. The union had no power over the entrepreneurs like my father. They had no control over the independents. They had no control over the landowners.

Since this is a free country, the coal actually belongs to the party holding title to it, typically the landowner. The landowner has the right to sell or lease the property to the person who offers him the best deal, or any deal at all. Dad mined small tracts of coal that the large union-controlled companies could not afford to mine. The owners of these tracts were very happy to lease to him. They had thousands of dollars worth of coal on their land that the large companies did not want. Dad wanted it.

The large companies had been taken over by the union. The mobsters running the union knew that was where the big money was. The inherent inefficiency and added cost brought about by having a mafia-like organization running a coal mine, made it economically challenging to operate. These same pressures made it fiscal suicide for them to mine the small tracts. That left a niche for independents like my father. This infuriated the union. Dad had a "live and let live" outlook, he felt that there was more than enough opportunity to go around for everybody. The union did not see it that way. When free men were able to mine coal and sell it on a free market, the union monopoly was eliminated.

The large union mines had evolved into cumbersome dinosaurs. Their profitability was continually eroded by the inflexibility and inefficiency resulting from the union's influence in the day-to-day operation of the mine. In most union operations at that time, unproductive, incompetent, or disruptive employees often could not be disciplined. Employees were generally locked into designated tasks and could not be asked to help out with other tasks, even when they had nothing to do, without risking a walkout. Wages had to be paid for millions of man-hours in which no work was done. Attempts to increase efficiency, reduce waste, or any move whatsoever to make ordinary adjustments in the operations could result in a strike. Rather than risk such a reaction, the mine owners often had to severely alter, or altogether give up their plans for operational improvements. In other words, the union ultimately ran the mines instead of the rightful owners. At first glance this may not seem extraordinary. For who better to run a privately-owned company than a group of caring, philanthropic, honest, altruistic union bosses? It only seems like the natural thing to do. Why can't our nation have such good folks running all businesses – people who won't let petty, selfish things like profitability or productivity interfere with operations?

The problem with a union having so much control was that there was a fundamental conflict of interest. The union was an entity with its own mindset. It had its own agenda that operated independently of the interests of the mine. The profitability of the mine was not an item on their agenda.

The collective attitude perpetuated by virtually the entire membership seemed to be that *they were getting screwed so badly by the company* that anything they could do to harm it was justified. Thievery, sabotage, and deliberate waste of resources were rampant. And for union members of the period it was a matter of common conversation to brag about it to anyone who would listen. There are millions of anecdotal tales of how union members continually discovered and re-discovered innovative ways to get back at the evil company. I have personally heard hundreds of these stories gleefully recounted by union members.

Small entrepreneurs like my father were too flexible and adaptive for the union to pin down or hem in. Moreover, the employees at small mines like Dad's seemed to be a different breed than the typical SMWA members. Most had been union miners in the past and had experienced directly the criminality and arrogance prevailing among the typical union membership.

"They were there at the 1964 convention and saw the District-19 boys in action. Most of them hate what the Union has become. They are independent types - rebels. They do not want to belong to an organ. They do not want to goose-step with the oppressed, victimized masses. They do not want money extracted from their paychecks to fund the outrageous lifestyles of corrupt, self-inflated, megalomaniacal leaders."

They liked having autonomy and they liked working for an autonomous company. They knew my father as a man and not as *The Company.* They knew that when he prospered, they prospered. They knew that they were not just employees, they were partners. They knew the most fundamental tenet of the American Dream is the notion that any man is free to start a business. Each of them wanted to someday. Many have. To them, viewing American enterprise in terms so simple as *worker versus company* was not only antithetical to the very core of the American Ideal, it was tantamount tyranny.

"In the apparent professed mindset of the SMWA, a man automatically becomes evil the moment he hires someone. He becomes the enemy. He becomes an oppressor. He becomes a counter-revolutionary."

My father was not evil. He knew it. His men knew it. Neither were they evil because of a dream to be self sufficient, to have an enterprise of their own someday.

"No one wants Draconian bosses. No one wants deplorable working conditions. And the Union was useful in helping to bring needed change in those areas. I respect them for that. But they went too far. They considered themselves above the law. They became more Draconian than Draco. They took themselves too seriously and chose to go from a defensive posture to one of offense. And once offensive maneuvers have precedent in such an organization and the apparatus for prosecuting them is in place, it is only a matter of time before the power is abused. Someone of poor judgment will get control of the apparatus. When that happens, destruction is inevitable."

(Photo courtesy of Library of Congress.)

"Independent thought becomes illegal. If a nation were ran according to that mindset, there would be no company. No man with a dream could ever realize it. Unions would control the means of production instead of free men. A man would be dissuaded from creating something wonderful to call his own. Why should he even try when someone always comes and takes it away, or destroys it? What kind of world is that? Obviously, in every nation where this has been tried, it has resulted in great human suffering and diminishment of hope. The people there ride bicycles a lot. They also seldom get to express their opinion about too much unless it mimics the party line, you know - tyranny."

"Our people left tyranny on another continent three-hundred years ago. Then it followed us here. So we formalized the concept two-hundred years ago. We decided among ourselves to outlaw tyranny. But tyrants are born every day. They never rest. So we had another great test a little over one-hundred years ago. Now tyranny springs up once more. So we must again mobilize ourselves to defeat it. And as long as we remain vigilant in this regard:"

" ...government of the people, by the people, for the people shall not perish from the earth."

Over a span of nearly thirty years, the SMWA made numerous attempts to *organize* my father's coal mines. His employees overwhelmingly voted against unionization every time.

My father paid landowners as much or more per ton than they would get from a union mining operation. Seemingly unknown to the union at that time, a landowner is free to choose the mining company he or she wants. They have the full legal right to make a deal with whoever has the will, the skill, and the wherewithal to perform the job, i.e., the firstest with the mostest.

Dad tried to convey this idea in discussions with the SMWA members many times, but he always found that open debate and reasoning were not a part of their agenda. Debate was not an option. Either allow yourself to be organized or prepare to be exterminated. Resistance is futile. The way they looked at it, they had already been incredibly gracious by not killing us. I mean after all, who in the Living Hell did Dad think he was? What made him think he could come into an area and engage in the honest pursuit of Free Enterprise? Between 1960 and 1980, the Free Enterprise system was a fanciful illusion as far as coal mining was concerned, thanks to crooked local officials and thug-controlled, terrorist organizations like the SMWA.

The SMWA method was to visit each small mining operation and intimidate them into compliance with the national strike. Failure to comply meant instantaneous retaliation. To avoid outright warfare, Dad usually complied for as long as he reasonably could. My father's creditors however, didn't care about his union problems. They still wanted to be paid for the diesel fuel, spare parts, lubricants, and explosives required to run the mine. The utility companies still wanted the coal, delivered in the quantity and on the schedule stipulated in the sales contract. And since the union mines were all idle during the strike, the demand became even more critical.

The utilities had no sense of humor in this regard, however. Dad expected some degree of understanding from the utility companies based on their mutual vulnerability to the union. It did not seem to work like that. He therefore was caught between three hostile elements. The union would physically destroy him if he did haul coal. The utilities would economically destroy him if he did not haul coal. However, the creditors ultimately were the most persuasive of all the forces. They explained how his bones would be first scraped and then boiled to remove every trace of meat if he did not pay them. He hauled the coal.

He would delay for as long as possible. Then he would put the trucks on the road at the peril of all. It was either resume operations, or face total financial ruin and loss of his sales contract. The imposing pressures and forces were relentless and withering--all just to get a few tons of preserved plant material out of the ground. It was insanity. My father often commented on these seeming contradictions of American Freedom:

"Thomas Jefferson and the framers designed and laid the foundation of a magnificent work of architecture. It is the greatest structure every conceived in the history of the human race. It is a mansion of unparalleled beauty and elegance. It aspires to the most express and admirable notion of the angels. It reaches to the sky. It is a stairway to the Higher Thing. The light of Heaven glimmers on the windows of its many rooms."

"But its hallowed halls, offices, and conference rooms can be filled with criminals who promote their own dark ends. This is what is happening in our country. Never blame the architecture. It is solid. It has withstood

worse. Put the blame where it belongs: on the criminals themselves and
those whose neglect has empowered them. Put the blame where it belongs
and good men will walk here again: men who do not rule with law, but
men who are ruled by law. Put men like that in these rooms and we will
all walk among the stars."

Dad's prediction was eventually realized. The election of a few good men and a combination of other factors finally came together to render the SMWA irrelevant. Perhaps the most significant factors in their demise were their intrinsic corruption and audacity. The SMWA as well as other unions at the time, were thug organizations and they unabashedly advertised it. Their leaders routinely murdered their way into power. And once there, they methodically eliminated anyone who could threaten them. Typically the opponent would simply disappear. Sometimes their bodies would be found in a river, sometimes in the trunk of a luxury sedan. Sometimes they would never be found. This sort of thing went on mostly behind the scenes for decades. But eventually it became fashionable to perform rival eliminations in excessively brutal and flamboyant ways.

Many theories can be put forth to explain this behavior. It could have been intended to flaunt the degree of their immunity from the law. Maybe the intent was to intimidate the company owners. Perhaps it was a window into the true core of the human soul. However manifold the complexities, it is very likely that the main purpose of this brutality was to impress the rank and file. Crystallized in the bottom of this crucible was the irreducible fact that the dues-paying members wanted a strong leader who could get them the biggest cut of the loot. They wanted a leader who would hold the company by the throat. They wanted a leader who would not let some trivial inconvenience like *the law* be an obstacle. They wanted a man with good solid murder experience. It was war after all. And it was in a time and environment marked by such phenomena as the assassination of John F. Kennedy. Violence was power. "If we can kill presidents, we can kill you." Being part of the mob gave a man power. Not unlike Germany in the thirties perhaps, joining a corrupt socialist thug organization was considered a completely normal career option in America thirty years later.

This ruthless behavior trickled both ways: it went up in the sense that the members elected leaders with a mandate of violence. Then in turn, the leaders' novel injustices naturally trickled downward, expressed in the form of individual cruelties and atrocities at the local level. America tolerated this insanity for too long. Then in 1969, a few days after Christmas, Brownshirts from the infamous District-19, brutally murdered Jock Yablonski, his wife Margaret, and their daughter Charlotte, as they slept in their home. The executions were carried out on the direct order of union president Tony Boyle, and the assassins were paid with union money. It took four years to convict Boyle. He died in prison in 1985.

For some reason the Yablonski murders seemed to strike a chord with the public. The ghastly nature and timing of the executions may have been the straw that broke the camel's back. It is arguable that the Yablonski murders caused irreparable damage to the public's perception not only of the corrupt unions, but of all labor organizations everywhere. It was the kind of bad publicity none of them needed. It was the kind of cultural erosion that they could not afford. And it was just the beginning of their troubles.

VHS, SMCRA, MSHA, and 401(k)

There were many factors that expedited the elimination of the SMWA's stranglehold on the coal industry. Among these was the invention and widespread availability of the hand held portable video camcorder. This tool enabled victims to record crimes as they were being visited upon them. The thugs quickly learned that they could no longer perform their acts in the anonymity or with the impunity that they had before. Now their faces and their license plate numbers could show up as footage on the six-o'clock news, or in court rooms. In venues of real jurisprudence, there were legal consequences to such acts. SMWA members, like anybody else, do not like legal consequences. The crimes quickly began to diminish.

Another major factor affecting the practical value of labor organizations in general was the introduction of simple and affordable private retirement accounts for all Americans. This was made possible by the Revenue Act of 1978. This legislation included a provision that became Internal Revenue Code, Section-401(k), under which a portion of an employee's income would not be taxed if placed into a deferred compensation account. This suddenly gave small companies a way to provide retirement plans for their employees that were comparable with union pensions. Since the core (legitimate) membership incentive of a union was its pension, interest in unions began to decline.

The reduction of union violence may have been aided by the passage of two Federal Laws in 1977: one, entitled the Surface Mining Conservation and Reclamation Act, also known as SMCRA (called "Smack-Ra"), was intended to address the perceived environmental problems of unreclaimed mine lands. The other was the Federal Mine Health & Safety Act, which created the Federal Mine Safety and Health Administration, also known as MSHA.

The new safety standards and enforcement mechanisms brought about by MSHA helped reduce annual U.S. coal mine fatalities from 272 in 1977 to 86 by the year 2000. This was accomplished by putting hundreds of mine safety inspectors in the mines. SMCRA and MSHA were intended to help mining companies be more environmentally responsible and to make coal mines safer for people. Both of these programs were very successful in their goals. But they also had the unanticipated effect of helping to attenuate coal field violence.

Suddenly the coal fields contained hundreds of mostly young, highly-educated, idealistic state and federal officers. These people had eyes. They had cameras. The majority were not colored with the mob mentality. Their sense of fair play was still intact. And they were walking, talking, highly credible witnesses. If anyone attempted to perpetrate a terrorist act in a coal mine, these people were in positions either to see it first-hand, or to learn about it quickly. This permanently eliminated the isolated theaters in which the thugs had traditionally operated unmolested.

With the new legislation, all activities at a coal mine now required authorization by the applicable state regulatory authority and the U.S. Department of Interior. Mayhem is not an authorized activity. Any violation became a federal matter. Each little one-horse coal mine was now able to strut and fret its hour upon the stage of a national theater. In principle this turn of events was tantamount to President Hoover's enlistment of treasury secretary Andrew Mellon to solve the Prohibition era organized crime crisis in Chicago. And it came just in time.

A Bad Night at the River Camp

The 201st winter after Thomas Jefferson and fifty-five other men signed the Declaration of Independence was one of the worst of the 20th Century. The winter of 1977-78 brought record low temperatures and snowfall in the Midwest. The Upper Saline River froze shore to shore in places with ice up to four feet thick. People were able to drive automobiles from bank to bank, without a bridge. That same winter also brought the worst coal field violence ever endured by my father. On one particular night that dark season, hundreds of miners came out of a union meeting in Tikrit, Kentucky, with the expressed goal of burning my father's house to the ground, along with any people who happened to be inside.

Fortunately for our family, their battle plan called for them to first attack a nearby coal loading facility at Har Megiddo. It was a coal barge loading dock on the Upper Saline River. Local people referred to it as the River Camp. The attack provided a local TV news station with an opportunity to broadcast live streaming video. And the operation took time. The delay gave my father an opportunity to evacuate my mother and sister to a safe location.

Finally, when it became clear that things were getting out of control, the governor personally ordered a large contingency of state troopers to intercept the miners and put down the riot. By the time it was over, at least two-hundred SMWA members had been taken into custody.

December 1977, Somewhere in Kentucky

My father learned of the impending attack at approximately 5:00 p.m. I was a sophomore in college at the time. It was on a Saturday. I was playing cards in my dorm room with some friends. I was holding heart flush, ten-high. There was about three dollars in the pot. At approximately 5:15 p.m. the phone rang.

"Hello."

"Danny, is that you?"

"Dad!"

"How's your classes going son."

"Not bad. I think everything is working out."

"I want you to know I'm very proud of you. We all are."

"Thanks. I hope I don't let you down."

"I know you won't son. Hey Danny, I need for you to do something for me."

"Just name it."

"I need you to come home son."

"Right now?

"Yes."

"What's going on?"

"Some SMWA members are causing trouble. I need for you to watch the house tonight while I stay at the mine."

There was an urgency in his voice that I had never heard before, nor would ever hear again. No further elaboration was needed. I knew Dad would not have called unless it was serious. I had to go.

"I'll be on the road in a few minutes."

"Come on home son."

I put the receiver on the hook, grabbed my coat, said goodbye to my friends, and exited the dorm. Within five minutes I was in my 1970 Mustang and headed north. The trip from Oran to Har Megiddo usually took two hours. This night it would require only fifty-six minutes. The car was seldom under 130 miles per hour virtually the entire way.

As I entered the city it became obvious that something was gravely awry. Hundreds of men were gathered in the middle of U.S. Highway 321. There were scores of state police cars lining the streets. To get home I had to pass through this mob. A policeman flagged me down.

"What's going on officer? I need to get through."

"The road is closed, nobody can get through."

"But it's an emergency, I really have to get home!"

"I'm sorry sir, the road is closed."

I turned my car around and took another route through the countryside on a highway called Bronzedale Road which bypassed the city and came out on U.S. 321 about three miles north of Har Megiddo. It was on this road that I came to a place where scores of men were standing outside their vehicles and blocking traffic. There were no police cars here. These men flagged me down. I had to either stop or run over them. I stopped. About thirty of them surrounded my car. It was a very disturbing sensation. One of them came to my window. He was a tall, thin fellow with nearly shoulder-length blond hair. He was wearing a heavy denim coat. I rolled down the glass: He leaned over and spoke:

"Hey buddy, how's it going?"

"Not bad, what 'bout yourself?"

"I'm making it. Nice car."

"Thanks. What's going on here anyway? Is the bridge out?"

"We're just waiting for the ball game to start. Say there buddy, you wouldn't by any chance know where the residence of Adam McCasoway is located would you?"

"I'm not from around here. The police told me to come this way because the main highway is blocked. There's a bad wreck or something. Cops are everywhere."

"Never heard of him huh?"

"Sorry, I can't help you!"

"Alright then - you can pass on through. Move back boys, let him past."

The crowd parted and let me by. I was scared prior to this encounter. But afterwards I was nearly hyperventilating. If they had figured out who I was, it is difficult to say what might have happened. Also, I determined that if they continued to stop and interrogate each driver who came through their roadblock, eventually they would find someone who would tell them what they wanted to know.

Our house was located adjacent to State Route 107, about eleven miles northeast of Har Megiddo. It seemed like a hundred. As I approached I did not know what I would find. When I got there the house was completely dark. The only illumination was from the dusk-to-dawn light near the garage. No one seemed to be home. I unlocked the door and went inside. I had been there about two or three minutes when the phone rang.

"Hello."

"Son, are you okay?"

"Yes, where is everybody?"

"Your mother and sister are at the State Police Post in Hegira. They will be safe there."

"Where are you?"

"I'm at the mine. Is everything okay at the house?"

"Yes. You're not out there alone are you?"

"No, Big Jim is here, and Glen. There's a couple of other boys too. Lloyd brought mortars. Mr. Bosco has the fifty-cal set up under a dozer on the south haul road. Don and Buster are up there with him. We're ready. I pity any man who tries to get into this mine tonight. Did you come through Har Megiddo?"

"Yes sir."

"How was it?"

"The main highway was closed. The state police had hundreds of men detained. I couldn't tell what was happening though, it was chaos. I had to drive around on Bronzedale Road. But when I got out there, a bunch of SMWA guys were stopping cars and asking people for directions to our house. It's only a matter of time before they show up here."

"Did they stop you?"

"Yes."

"Did you see the River Camp?"

"No, I couldn't get that far, the road was blocked. What do you want me to do?"

"Okay, stay there. Don't worry. Remain calm. Go and get the automatics out of the vault. Find a box or a sack to put some ammo and extra clips in. Get yourself some blankets and a couple of heavy coats. Try to pick something with a hood on it. I'll be there in a few minutes. I'll explain everything. Don't forget your forty-five pistol."

As Dad drove up in his 1976 Blazer, I rushed out to meet him.

"Danny, hundreds of SMWA members are supposed to be heading here tonight. They plan on attacking the mine and burning our house too. They've already destroyed the River Camp and beat up a bunch of men there. I'm going back to the mine. Do you remember where the defense point is on the hill?"

"Yes sir."

"I want you to take the guns up there and wait. Don't shoot until you see somebody light a fire or break into the house. Shoot the flame before it gets out of their hands. Aim at people only after they shoot at you. But don't let them kill you. Pick your shots well. Take them out cleanly and quickly. If you run out of ammo, head southeast across the back forty and into the river bottoms. They will never find you there. Save some pistol rounds just in case. Lay low until daylight and then link up with Foster and his men at the scale house. Don't come to the mine and stay out of the open. Do you understand?"

"Yes sir."

"I'm sorry it's come to this Danny, but they've gone too far this time. We have to make a stand tonight."

"I won't let anyone hurt our house Dad."

"I know you won't son. Good luck and keep your head down."

Dad gave me a box of fried chicken and a six-pack of sodas and then drove away. He had the Mauser that he captured in World War II. He waved goodbye holding the pistol in his hand.

In anticipation of this eventuality, Dad and I had constructed a very robust defense position on a hill about 120 yards from our house. From this location the entire valley could be commanded. The previously mentioned dusk-to-dawn light was situated directly between the fox hole and the parking area. The light was pointed toward the house, illuminating the entire yard and parking lot. The hope was that rifle fire could be directed from behind this light and those receiving it would have greater difficultly trying to pinpoint the defender's location because the light would be in their eyes.

I had with me in the foxhole a matching pair of caliber 7.62 millimeter M-14 combat rifles, each with ten, twenty-round clips. One M-14 was configured with armor-piercing ammunition, the other with antipersonnel rounds. Also in my possession were a pair of caliber 5.56 millimeter, fully automatic M-16 machine rifles with about a dozen extra thirty-round clips each. I also had a Marlin .30/30 lever action rifle, and a Model 1911-A1, .45 caliber ACP combat pistol. I had about a thousand rounds of ammunition configured so that it could be delivered quickly and effectively. As I completed arranging the weapons and ammo magazines around the perimeter of the foxhole, I noticed that I could hear my heart pounding inside my chest. It was beating very rapidly.

That's when I saw the pickups pull into the driveway. There were four of them - three Chevies and a Ford. They eased up the drive and made the loop around the parking area behind the garage, maintaining a very rigorous single file pattern. They stopped with their headlights facing the house. They just sat there for over a minute. Then the driver's side door opened on the lead truck. An empty beer can fell out and slowly rolled down the driveway, making a *clinkety--clink--clink--clinkety* sound for several seconds until it came to rest at the edge of the lawn. The dome light revealed the frames of three men in the truck. But no one got out. They were looking at my car.

In my haste to reach the foxhole I had neglected to remove a gun scabbard and several empty ammo boxes from the trunk lid of the Mustang. These objects stood out quite prominently on the flat metal surface. A small amount of steam or smoke gently coursed from the grille of the car, betraying the engine's accumulated strain in my mad hurdling dash to get home. The visitors seemed to be sizing up the situation very carefully. The driver finally got out of the lead truck and stood there staring at the car for a moment. I immediately recognized him as the person who had spoken to me at the roadblock on Bronzedale Road. I carefully drew a bead on him with the M-14. He looked toward the people in the other vehicles. He said something but I could not make it out. He walked around to the back of my car. He picked up one of the ammo boxes.

7.62 MM
FULL METAL JACKET

would have been the lettering that he saw. He then moved to the front of my car and placed his hand on the hood near the radiator. He pulled his hand back quickly. He looked toward the others. Then, he screamed out into the arbitrary darkness these words:

"NOT FROM AROUND HERE YOU SAY? YOU LYING BASTARD!"

My rage boiled over. I was tempted to respond, both verbally and ballistically. The rifle was fused to my hands. I forced my breathing into steadiness. I tightened my finger against the trigger. This rifle was loaded with 180 grain, jacketed soft point bullets - extremely formidable projectiles when traveling half a mile per second, or any speed. I have seen these bullets flip a full grown deer around end-to-end before. If they strike a deer at an oblique angle, they will take off an entire leg. There is no way to conduct a *clean kill* with a bullet like this. It is by definition an extremely messy affair because of the enormous energy delivered. My father routinely hit fence posts at distances exceeding eight-hundred yards using these rifles. I liked to shoot soda cans at more modest distances of around 150 yards. All the rifle knew was that this man's chest was twenty times larger than a soda can. He was in my sights for over four minutes. The slightest pressure increase on my fingertip and his ribcage would have exploded. His heart and lungs would have been turned into pudding by the explosive shock. His death would have been brutal and instantaneous. As I contemplated this, my focus waned momentarily.

Then I saw a fire. It was the flame of a match. My finger tightened against the trigger to the brink of no return. The diameter of little more than a single hair lay between chaos and hope. The cold December breeze stressed the fire. He was lighting a cigarette. The match went out. I let off the trigger a little. He ignited a second match, cupping it in his hands. He gazed around the perimeter of darkness as he brought the flame to his cigarette. He seemed to do this as though to illuminate his face. He looked in my direction. He knew I was out there somewhere. They all did. They must have thought that the gun case and the ammo boxes on the car were put there as a deliberate warning. It was purely accidental. But the effect was the same. Someone in the lead truck finally yelled:

"COME ON THEN!"

My finger tightened again. I would kill him with the M-14 and then immediately kill the occupants of the last truck in the line. That would trap the other vehicles long enough for me to fire four to ten rounds into each truck in turn. Exiting a truck cab with a rifle in one's hand cannot be done quickly. Maybe under fire a person might react a little faster, but the advantage was clearly mine. They were sitting ducks. I would have killed every one of them in a matter of seconds. All of this was on my mind. Praise God in Heaven, he got back into the truck and they drove away.

Sunday Morning, 3:00 a.m.

The actions of the state police took the momentum out of the SMWA for the rest of the night. The union organizers were evidently detained at Har Megiddo sufficiently to thwart the entire plan. Any stragglers who managed to slip away gathered in sporadic pockets around the countryside waiting for guidance that never came, or proceeded on their own initiative, like the group that stopped me on Bronzedale Road. Since their command and control had been neutralized, they were unable to prosecute a coordinated counterattack. In frustration, most of them returned to Tikrit and burned the headquarters of King-Herod Trucking Company.

Dad returned from the mine at around 3:00 a.m. He informed me that the main threat was over. We had apparently dodged another bullet. But roving squads were still causing trouble. So we decided to remain in the foxhole until daybreak. The rest of the night proved completely uneventful. Then, around 8:15 a.m., just as we were preparing to go to the house, we observed a compact procession of vehicles coming up Highway 107, consisting of about twenty pickups and three station wagons. This armada filed slowly past the house. Each vehicle was packed with armed men. Their intense collective attention appeared to be focused on our home and the immediate environs. They drove on past and went out of sight around a curve about a quarter mile from our driveway.

"Watch them for me."

"Don't go down there!"

"They aren't going to hurt anyone. There's not enough of them."

"Don't do it!"

"Watch them for me."

Dad climbed out of the foxhole and headed for the house. All he had with him was his semiautomatic .32 Mauser pistol. He made it to the far side of the garage just as the SMWA vehicles started coming in the driveway. Dad entered the garage unseen through the backdoor. The trucks stopped. Approximately seventy-five men got out of these vehicles, most carrying what appeared to be hunting rifles and/or shotguns. I drew a bead on the man who acted like he was in charge. My finger was tight on the trigger. They formed into a loose congregation, drifting generally toward the house. It looked like a CPO jacket convention.

That is when Dad hit the button on the electric garage door opener. The loud clanking of the old door startled the mob, causing them to stop. I could easily hear the noise from my location. As the door slowly raised, it dramatically presented my father standing there, relaxed, arms crossed, poised, casual, calm, unsullied, deftly holding the Mauser in his right hand. None of them uttered a word. Dad smiled and said:

"Can I help you fellows?"

The man that I had in my sights responded:

"Yes you can! Stay the hell out of the way, we're going to burn this house to the ground."

A tall man standing behind him then displayed what appeared to be an improvised Molotov cocktail. I recognized him as the same man who had confronted me at the roadblock on Bronzedale Road and who had gotten out of the lead truck in our parking lot hours earlier. He held the makeshift incendiary device high up for all to see. It was a half-gallon orange juice jar filled with kerosene. The crowd cheered. Still holding the jar above his head, he spoke:

"And that damn Mustang gets it first!"

The crowd cheered again. I carefully compressed the trigger. The bullet struck the jar about two inches from the top. An atomized cloud of the straw-colored distillate was propelled sharply outward, engulfing dozens of men, causing them and all the rest to duck to the pavement with great zeal. Some gagged from the effects of the kerosene. Luckily, the fuel did not ignite. My father was the only person who remained standing. Some principled soul in the crowd felt compelled to utter the words:

"Lord help us!"

"Gentlemen, nobody is going to burn anything here today. And I'd appreciate it if you'd not move any of your guns around. I want you to leave them alone right now. Is that understood?"

No one responded. There was only wheezing. Some men clearly ignored him and began fumbling for their firearms. Dad motioned his pistol in the air. So I used a fully automatic M-16 to discharge 30 rounds of ammunition in approximately one second. I aimed for the midsection of a large cedar tree at the edge of the parking lot. Branches and wood fragments were scattered for a considerable radius, much of it falling on and around the huddled mob.

"You should not touch those guns. I told you not to mess with the guns. Can you people hear okay?"

"Yes sir Mr. McCasoway. We hear you fine."

"If anybody touches a weapon again, you guys are going to look like about ten tons of raw hamburger. They'll have to scrape you up with shovels. Your poor old mommas won't even recognize you. Do you understand?"

"Yes sir."

"Now if you fellows have a problem with how I run a coal mine, then take it up with me, man-to-man. This house hasn't hurt you. My wife and children live in this house. They've never hurt you. What were you going to do—burn two kids and a woman to death over some lousy, stinking coal? Don't you guys have families somewhere? What in the world were you thinking? Don't you realize that's murder? Are you people *murderers?*"

"No sir, we are not murderers."

"Well, you sure seem to be going to an awful lot of trouble to act like murderers. You people need to calm down. I thought this was America. I thought we were all on the same side. There's no good reason for us to be killing each other here today. This is crazy."

"You're right Mr. McCasoway, we shouldn't have come here. May we get up now?"

"I strongly recommend against it! Danny is pretty upset with you fellows. He gets excited easy. The boy ain't right. I'd stay still for a few more minutes if I were you."

"What do you want us to do then?"

"What do I want you to do? Well let's see...I want you to leave my family alone. I want you to quit calling my wife on the phone and scaring her and telling her you're watching her when she goes to the store or takes my daughter to school. I want you to go back to work and end this strike. I want you to stop burning things. I want you to promise me that you will never again do what you have tried to do here today."

"Mr. McCasoway, if you will give us safe passage from this place, we will never harass you, or your family ever again, this I promise, sir."

"Will you give me your word?"

"Yes sir, you have my word."

There was a pause as my father contemplated what had been said.

"I believe you. I don't know why, but I do. I think you are sincere. But how do I know that some of your associates won't sneak back in on their own later? Forgive me, but I don't have much reason to trust you fellows."

"No sir. That won't happen. I speak for every man here. DO I SPEAK FOR ALL OF YOU?" he called to the mob.

There was a massive cheer from the inch-like masses.

"Mr. McCasoway, you have the word of every man here."

"Then if I allow you to leave, as gentlemen, we all agree that this matter is closed?"

"It all ends here sir."

Dad looked over them. After a short pause he spoke:

"Alright then. Stand up. Go at your leisure. No one will harm you here today. Please drive responsibly."

Dad waved for me to cease fire. I lifted my finger from the trigger but kept the mob in my sights. The SMWA members began to get up off of the pavement.

"May we take our guns?"

There was another pause as Dad considered the question. In the meantime, men continued getting up, some helping others. Many were brushing wood chips off of their clothing. A few of them looked in my direction intermittently. All stood still waiting for Dad's answer. No one dared touch any of the weapons on the ground.

"I don't want your guns. You take them...take them all...pick them up. And get those beer cans too while you're at it."

The men retrieved their weapons from the pavement. They also policed the area for the empty beer cans that they had thrown down. As they returned to their vehicles, some of the men coursed past my father, like a reception-line, and put out their hands. He transferred the pistol to his left hand and firmly clasped the hands of all who offered. Some men apologized. Others thanked him. Some did both. Dad spoke briefly with each of them as they came by. At least one man asked if there were any positions open at my father's coal mine. Although I could not hear the bulk of these conversations, based on the gestures that I observed, it is likely that most went something like this:

"Where're you from son?"

"Wheatcroft."

"You're not too far from home then."

"No sir. Mr. McCasoway, I really don't know how to tell you how sorry I am. This is the first time I ever did anything like this. I don't know what I was thinking. I learned a valuable lesson today. Please forgive me."

"Don't worry about it son. *Just go home and hug your momma.*"

"Yes sir."

The armada then quietly left without further incident. It was one of my father's greatest victories. He never had union problems again.

Model 1914, cal. 7.65 MM semiautomatic pistol,
confiscated from a Nazi officer in 1945 by Adam D. McCasoway.
Inscription reads: *MAUSER-WERKE A.G. OBERNDORF A.N.*

PART II
TEN MILES TO HOPETOWN

Chapter 7

Why Squirrels are Nervous

As a child my father for the most part remained undistracted by the chronic adversity of the times. This may have been partly because of his precocious aptitude for science. At a very early age, without any formal guidance, he instinctively implemented his own rigorous examination of the world around him. He found the mystery of nature irresistible. He gathered rock, plant, insect, and animal specimens and cataloged them according to their similarities. His collection contained at least one sample of every insect and small animal species in the local environment. He carefully dissected and studied each specimen. He traced functional connections between organ systems across species boundaries. This gave him a unique insight into the underlying symmetry of all life on earth. He maintained highly detailed drawings and notes.

When he was eight years old he showed this compilation to his uncle Woodrow McCasoway at a family reunion. Recognizing the potential in my father, Woodrow, who was a retired school teacher from Boston, sent my father some old college textbooks, including an original 1859 edition of *On the Origin of Species* by Charles Darwin. The book was almost worn out but sufficiently intact for Dad to glean from it the fundamentals of Darwin's reasoning and conclusions. Also among the books given to him by his uncle Woodrow was a three volume set by Sir Charles Lyell entitled *Principles of Geology*.

My father's natural scientific talents proved to be very useful around the farm. For every chick that hatched, every puppy whelped, and each calf that was born, he was present from start to finish. He observed in intricate detail each stage of the birth cycle in every life form in the area. He compared the similarities between the various species, formulated hypotheses, and tested them for validity in the field, eventually honing his observational and deductive skills until he was able to make predictive conclusions that could be used to save the life of virtually any farm animal in distress.

The local veterinarian quickly recognized my father as *a Natural*. He subsequently requested Dad's assistance in scores of medical and birthing emergencies for horses, cows, pigs, and sheep. By the time Dad was eleven years old, he was the go-to guy for half the county's farmers. Dad's highly detailed recollections of these adventures kept me enthralled for hours on the many long trips we took together.

Another of the rare childhood pleasantries my father sometimes reflected on was the art of hunting, squirrels in particular. Natural science and squirrel hunting were Dad's only real avocations and he pursued them with equal fanatical devotion for his entire life.

Depression Era children sought diversion in fundamental ways. They used methods probably entirely incomprehensible to their modern counterparts. The boy who would one day be my father found his purest escape within the undulating and undying woodlands of Indiana. There was a practical aspect to his hunting as well. Because of their poverty, his family became dependent on the extra food that hunting provided. So my father hunted for squirrels as much as the farming obligations allowed. Throughout his childhood, under the guidance of his grandfather, Virgil McCasoway, my father continued to refine his hunting skills. Meanwhile, the constant farm work bestowed him with a very robust frame. By his twelfth birthday he was an expert marksman, hunter, and trapper. By his sixteenth year he was strong as a mule.

The management of the landscape was straightforward in those days. Valleys were reserved for cultivation. The middle ground contained the pastures, barns and the houses. And the uplands were engulfed in creaking swaths of hickory, oak, and walnut.

These are the species whose seeds the squirrels rely on for the bulk of their sustenance. Since the output of these trees is seasonal, squirrels

have evolved the ability to maximize their resources. That is, they alter
the environment in such a way to make the supply of nuts endure for more
than one season: the squirrels gather and transport the nutritious tidbits
with mad efficiency. They hoard them in any cavity that can be found in
the forest, mostly in the hollows of trees. When all of the available tree
space is full, they then bury the nuts in the earth wherever they are found.
In the autumn, the woods explode with the frantic motions of squirrels
engaged in this endeavor. They urgently secure every nut in the forest. No
fruit escapes their attention. The buried ones not later recovered for food,
become the next generation of trees. This cycle has presumably gone on
for as long as there have been trees and squirrels.

Squirrel hunting worked so well at diminishing my father's stress that
it became his preferred mode of natural absolution. And he retained this
passion throughout his life. For as long as I can remember, he carried a
rifle or a shotgun in his vehicle expressly to be used for squirrel hunting.
At the slightest provocation he would lay waste to the jaunty creatures by
the bushel. He brought a sack of squirrels home nearly every night. Even
during the routines of his daily business travels he kept a constant eye out
for their habitats. Likewise, he had no qualms about seeking anecdotal
intelligence from local informants regarding these isolated niches.

For example, there were many times when, while passing through a
small rural town, Dad would suddenly stop the vehicle and ask the first
person he saw about the hunting potential of a particular patch of trees we
had just driven past. The informant, usually a cantankerous, misanthropic
geezer, would frequently obnoxiously attest that said woods had been in
his words, *hunted-out,* or *used-up,* and that no squirrels were in there. The
old guy would generally say something to the effect of:

> *"Forget it you young punk...there ain't been no damn squirrels in them
> woods ever since my wife got her tit hung in the apple-picker back during
> the flood of '37. And why in the hell are you askin' me anyway, do I look
> like Davy Crockett?"*

Dad always loved such assessments because it was a sterling opportunity
for him to demonstrate to another collection of misinformed locals how
real hunting was supposed to be conducted. Usually within seconds after
he entered even the smallest grove of trees, a frightful barrage of gunfire
would ensue. A few minutes later he would emerge with the unequivocal
evidence that the local hunting experts were grossly mistaken - a sack

brimming with freshly dispatched squirrels, some so fresh in fact that a leg or two would still be twitching.

By pursuing the art with the same competence and zest for virtually his entire life, it is now widely rumored that between 1924 and 1996, my father killed in excess of 250,000 squirrels. And every single one was eaten, if not by him then by some hungry person. It is unclear whether or not records are kept about such things. Regardless, it is likely that my father would rank among the best of all the squirrel hunters who ever lived.

Preparing Squirrels

Although there are many representatives of the squirrel family populating the rural Indiana landscape, only two are considered worthy for the rustic dinner table, both from a sporting and a regulatory perspective. The diminutive Eastern Gray Squirrel *(Sciurus carolinensis)* tends to inhabit the thicker forests, while the larger Eastern Fox Squirrel *(Sciurus niger)*, often occupies the open wooded areas that border fields, meadows, and pastures. The Gray Squirrel is preferred overall by hunters because it is easier to skin and is generally more palatable. The Fox Squirrel on the other hand, sometimes has nearly twice the mass of the Gray, although it is considerably more difficult to skin, and dining on its meat is said to be comparable to gnawing the rivets out of a saddle.

As difficult as squirrel hunting is, it still represents only half of the process. The true challenge is to convert said arboreal quadruped into a palatable food product. To achieve this the hunter must efficiently separate the edible sections from those elements generally considered unfit for the human palate. That is, both the outermost layer and the core of the animal must be selectively differentiated, while leaving the intermediate layer intact and uncontaminated. Disconnection of the outer layer is performed via a special, and often very rigorous procedure called *skinning*. Removal of the core of the animal is universally termed *gutting*.

These distinct individual processes are together generally referred to in the back country vernacular as the *cleaning* of a squirrel. All squirrels must be cleaned prior to consumption. This type of cleaning however, does not involve the application of detergents or soap products. Nevertheless, failure to adequately clean a squirrel before consuming it can cause serious quality issues to arise. Like anything else, there is also a learning curve involved with the cleaning of squirrels. It is an art not easily mastered.

My first attempts at cleaning squirrels were very awkward to say the least. The skinning of a dead squirrel is perhaps the Universe's most extreme natural punishment for hunters. Pound for pound, the squirrel is arguably the most difficult of all game animals to skin. The hairy hide of a sweet, delicate, Bambi-like little squirrel conceals a dark and horrible secret: it is genuinely tougher than a mother-in-law's heart. Grown men have gnawed their own knuckles off trying to clean squirrels. For the uninitiated, it can require hours of intense labor to separate the tenacious hide from the iron-like sinews of even a single squirrel. And when the task is completed, because of the inherent inefficiency of the process, the meat becomes liberally appointed with loose hairs, dirt, gravel, flea legs, and macerated blowfly carcasses, making the whole affair more than just a little unpleasant and significantly distasteful. But Dad was a true artist at cleaning a squirrel. He had the process reduced to a calculated procedure of four basic movements, together taking somewhat less than a minute to complete. In addition, when he finished the task not even a single loose hair would be stuck to the meat. It was more than simply clean, it was sterile, just like the meat one would expect to find being served in the thousands of modern Chinese all-you-can-eat super-buffet restaurants throughout the United States.

My father had over the years refined squirrel cleaning into an efficient series of steps that basically went something like this: (1), he would pick the animal up with his left hand, bend its tail back with his thumb, and make a slit in the skin just above its asshole; then (2), while holding its back legs with his right hand, pull the tail toward the front of its body thereby drawing the reversed hide down over its hindquarters, exposing the raw meat. Next he would (3), flip the animal over, pull the skin down over the legs, then grab the exposed meat of the back and with one enormous tug, like a weight-lifter tearing a phone book in two, pull the rest of the skin toward the head. This would leave the entire squirrel skinned with the inverted hide now draping over its head and feet. He then (4), chopped-off each foot at the last joint and lopped-off the head. Compounding the inherent efficiency of the procedure, the entrails would remain affixed to the skin and be removed in this same final motion.

When skinning an old squirrel (which are very tough) he would often multiply the force by standing on the partially-separated skin of the squirrel while pulling up on hindquarters of the animal using both of his arms. This sometimes became troublesome and a little awkward, especially if the squirrel ripped into pieces. But for ordinary squirrels the skinning process was a very trim operation. Anyone who has ever observed a farmer shucking corn - that's what it was like. Dad shucked squirrels as if they were ears of corn. He could skin and gut fourteen squirrels in nine-minutes.

Passing on the Art

Dad started taking me hunting with him when I was about three. My first job was to carry the dead squirrels after he shot them. Sometimes he would kill so many that I couldn't carry them all. I recall many occasions when Dad would shoot a squirrel and it would fall within inches of me, often still alive. I was required therefore, at a very impressionable age, to learn how to effectively dispatch a wounded squirrel with a stick. This has ultimately contributed to my overall confidence in life because I now know that if I'm ever attacked by a wounded squirrel, I will be able to defend myself fairly handily, if there's a half way decent stick anywhere within reach.

As the years went by and I became more confident, I began to serve the role of hunting caddy for Dad. During this period I would carry a golf bag containing several different kinds of firearms instead of golf clubs. Some of the weapons were intended for long range shots, some for short range, and some for other specialized applications. For extremely long shots (over 500 yards) Dad would request his Model-700 Remington magnum sniper rifle in caliber 7 millimeter. For short range shots he would use a Model-63 Winchester .22 caliber rifle.

For extremely close-in encounters, or for squirrels displaying hostile intentions; that is, what today might be called *hand to hand* engagements, he would deploy his standard issue Model 1914 Mauser semiautomatic pistol. This weapon was very effective at dissuading even the most aggressive squirrels. For engagements involving multiple squirrels, or those attempting to flee, he frequently relied on his battle-hardened Browning Auto-5 semiautomatic shotgun. When thick brush or dense understory was a problem, he would deploy his reliable 7.62 millimeter, M-14 rifle.

There were a variety of other weapons in the golf bag, each designated for a specific range of hunting scenarios. Occasionally, we encountered other hunters in the woods. Perhaps because of our appearance of great professionalism, they often allowed us to *hunt-on-through.*

When Dad would find a tree densely populated with squirrels, which was not uncommon, he had a technique of being able to reload his Browning Auto-5 while still firing it. This is an art form that should not be tried by novices. He had the ability to fire the weapon with his right hand while simultaneously feeding fresh ammunition into the magazine with his left hand. Whenever he performed this gunnery feat, squirrels would fall like rain. I once retrieved thirty-seven squirrels that Dad killed in this manner. His shotgun held only three cartridges but he could fire it with the precision and speed as though it held thirty-seven cartridges.

Even after he had ceased firing and the bodies were still raining down through the canopy, he continued to reload and keep his sights high as a part of his follow-through procedure (all true marksmen have a follow-through procedure). After the bits of leaves, clouds of smoke, waves of hair, plumes of splattered retinas, segments of intestine, chunks of liver, blood droplets, and other organic debris slowly receded, he would finally stand-down and carefully examine each carcass to ascertain the effectiveness of his marksmanship.

A part of this protocol also usually involved me mopping up any last pockets of resistance by ranging about the general theater and whopping the stragglers with a stick. Sometimes I even smacked the dead ones a couple of extra times just to make sure that they were not faking it, because as far as I was concerned during that period of my life, there was nothing more dangerous than a wounded squirrel. I have grabbed them by the tail before thinking they were dead only to have the onerous rascals flip around and bite the living hell out of me. Although I never actually received my rocket science degree from an accredited institution of higher learning, I have learned how to bring to bear sufficient mental resources to properly deal with situations involving razor-sharp rodent teeth.

Not only was Dad a superior hunter of squirrels, he was also one of history's greatest connoisseurs of squirrel-based cuisine. Over time he had managed to master many of the most effective preparation methodologies. For example, he routinely fried it, baked it, broiled it, grilled it, steamed or boiled it, roasted it, toasted it, and even stewed it.

In terms of recipe dishes based on squirrel meat, there was really no limit to Dad's creativity. Some of his specialties included: squirrel sausage, squirrel jerky, squirrel loaf, squirrel-kabob, sweet & sour squirrel, squirrel Rangoon, Peking squirrel, squirrel Newburgh, Manhattan squirrel,

squirrel Alfredo, Salisbury squirrel, squirrel dip, and of course, Dad's all-time favorite, squirrel gravy.

When witnesses observed him tearing into a heaping plate of squirrel and slurping-down a huge serving of biscuits and squirrel gravy, they would quickly analytically dissect the phenomenon until only two irreducible ontological possibilities remained: 1, he was a starving man freshly escaped from a vegetarian commune, or 2, he had an extraordinary fondness for squirrel.

A Native American Perspective

My mother, Ruby Hawkfeather, wasn't just a simple run-of-the-mill squirrelophobe. She absolutely, categorically, and unequivocally hated the very fundamental concept of a squirrel, or anything remotely related thereto. She also cultivated an extraordinary, almost pathological hatred for rodents in general. She even hated squirrel gravy. Needless to say, Dad's passion for squirrel hunting was over the years the cause of more than just a little bit of disharmony in our household.

My father's reputation as a master squirrel hunter was well known among my mother's family. One day when Dad came home with a bushel basket heaped full of freshly harvested squirrels, my grandmother, Ellen Leaping Fawn, started referring to him as *Dead Squirrel*. It was a big joke at the time, but the name stuck. After that, any time we would go to reunions on my mother's side of the family, people with names like *Roy Floating Beaver* and *Sally Muddy Buffalo* would make fun of my father and call him *Dead Squirrel* and obnoxiously laugh about it. The children would form a daisy chain around him and sing the name out loud:

"Uncle Dead Squirrel...Uncle Dead Squirrel...nanna–nanna, na na."

He just smiled. Dad's charisma and germane skills actually made him extremely popular at these reunions. Many of my uncles and cousins consulted with him on the intricacies of squirrel hunting. Dad conducted safety demonstrations, weapons drills, and gave one-on-one marksmanship tips. He planned and carried out a complex series of skinning seminars with breakout sessions on field hygiene and cooking techniques. He gave scholarly lectures on supersonic ballistics and squirrel biology. Scores of my mother's relatives would attend these presentations, many taking notes. Afterwards, lively discussions would often erupt. The participants would ask sophisticated questions and freely offer their opinions. A genuine rapport would develop between Dad and his audience. He received standing ovations at the conclusions of many of these programs. Dad became so popular that eventually even members of the public at large started attending. His acceptance by my mother's family was complete. Still, this did nothing to assuage her intolerance of squirrels. In the years ahead, as my father continued to bring home legions of dead rodents on a perpetual basis, a powder keg slowly simmered.

The struggle of pent up strife came to a head one morning in October of 1964, when Dad suddenly brought home his obligatory compliment of dead squirrels that he had ambushed somewhere only moments before. He dropped six of the wiry rodents, some with a foot or two still twitching, onto the kitchen counter and told Mom something to the effect of:

"Hey woman...cook these sumbitches. I'll be back around noon to eat them."

Evidently Dad must have had something else on his mind that day because he left just as suddenly without skinning them. I recall watching Mom stuff the squirrels into our brand new heavy-duty pressure cooker, the microwave oven of the era, pour in a gallon or so of water and then go through the ten-minute lock-down safety procedure required by law to fasten the forty-some-odd pound lid to the main boiler assembly. She then turned the gas burner on the stove to the highest setting. She had a diabolical look on her face and was mumbling something like:

"Oh yeah, I'll cook them, yes sir-ee Bob!"

As previously referenced, I wasn't exactly the sharpest tomahawk in the teepee, but I did know enough to realize that whatever she was up to seemed improper at best, perhaps criminal at worst. But I was just a kid. Maybe grownups somehow knew that it's okay to cook squirrels with their hair and guts under certain conditions. So I didn't think much else about it. But I do clearly recall noticing how violently the pressure cooker's steam flapper was reciprocating, how the indicator needle on the analog pressure gauge was well past the DANGER ZONE, and how jets of superheated steam were shooting from every joint on the boiler. The thing that stands out in my memory more than any other however, is the dynamically pungent aroma that filled the kitchen. I can only describe it as being like a cross between roasted hickory nuts, wet dog hair, and a municipal landfill sometime around mid-August. Dad arrived right on time, with his mouth severely yearning for a big plate of steaming-hot fried squirrel. As he neared the house in his 1963 Ford F-100 pickup that morning he must have been thinking something like:

"Man...I just can't wait to sink my teeth into those damned squirrels!"

He walked through the doorway and sniffed the air. He seemed to get an odd look on his face, not unlike how a buffalo might appear as it admires its reflection in the grille of an oncoming charter bus. Mom was sitting in the living room reading the latest edition of *New Yorker.*
"Are my squirrels ready yet, sweetheart?"
"They're in the pressure cooker, dear."
"Pressure cooker? That's a great idea! I bet they're really tender."

Dad innocently sauntered over to the stove and deployed the attached catalytic heat shield, pulled down on the hydraulically-assisted safety levers on either side of the lid assembly, removed the two titanium shear-pins, and then reached across the primary bulkhead collar to trip the high-output pressure release valve. This was standard safety procedure for opening the boiler, right out of the operating manual. It was necessary because even under normal conditions, pressure cookers back in those days operated at extreme pressures and temperatures. Unfortunately, what Dad didn't know was that in this particular instance, normal conditions did not even come close to applying.

The engineers who designed the pressure cooker undoubtedly considered many safety-related scenarios during the development process. However, nobody probably ever built a pressure cooker that was intended to handle the hellish contents brought forth on that day. When he finally tripped the release valve, the escaping gasses rushed out with such force that it sounded like a jet engine at full throttle. There was so much trapped pressure that the boiler flew across the stove and lodged itself between the toaster and the refrigerator. It vibrated itself free from this position after a couple of seconds and roared across the counter, destroying mom's new antique spice rack. From there it spun into the sink where it rotated at about 1,500 rpm for approximately twenty more seconds. The foul and pestilent congregation of vapors became so thick that all light was cut off, plunging the entire kitchen in total darkness.

The horrible images I saw that day will be with me for the rest of my life. All I could make out in that terrible blackness of chaos were some occasional distorted glimpses of my poor father desperately trying to get the pressure-release valve closed. After we aired-out the house for about half an hour, and Dad rubbed first-aid cream on his burns, and dug cinnamon bark from the wounds on his face, he finally got around to unbolting the approximately four-dozen carbon steel retainers that held the main bulkhead of the pressure cooker to its heavy-duty boiler assembly. When he finally broke the last o-ring seal, rotated the bulkhead three-quarters of a turn counterclockwise, and lifted it over to the side, he was suddenly noticeably shocked at the profound sight before him.

In the pot were the remains of six bloated and putrefied squirrels steeped in an unsavory gruel of hair, viscera, and other unidentified hideous matter, all of such an agonizing disposition that any normal man would have abruptly set free the entire contents of his alimentary canal on the spot without advanced-notice-in-writing. He looked at the squirrels, then he looked at Mom, he looked at the squirrels, and then at Mom. Without saying another word he went straight to the cupboard and took out one of Mom's best *Sunday-go-to-meeting* Chinaware plates she collected from boxes of laundry powder back in the fifties. He grabbed a fork, jabbed one of the fermented rodents in its hyper-extended rib-cage and unceremoniously sloughed it onto the premium dinner plate, taking care not to let the intestines drag across the stove and dangle onto the floor.

He then sat down at the table where I was attempting to enjoy the remains of a delicious peanut butter sandwich and a glass of artificially-flavored green Kool-Aid. I remember observing the dead mammal lying there on the plate. It seemed to be more than just staring at me, it was looking into my soul. From across the wide, wide metaphysical abyss it was pleading for me to somehow end its agony. I was powerless to do so of course. But I was overwhelmed by a profound sense of pity. The outward appearance of the squirrel reminded me of one of the mutated calf fetuses they kept preserved in jars of formaldehyde in the basement at our school.

The sudden pressure release had caused its eyes to swell up and pop out. They looked like a pair festering cantaloupes lodged in the nostrils of a dead walrus. Its tongue was grossly enlarged and hanging out of its mouth. On its face was the look of absolute, 100% pure misery. Its grayish-blue intestines were draped off the edge of the plate and welled up in a pile on the table.

Dad looked at me and winked. He then peeled back the hide of the animal and gouged out a hunk of the bloated, putrid, greenish-yellow meat. He dashed some salt onto this hell-sprung morsel and chucked it deep into the cavernous recesses of his massive iron jaws. As he chewed, I could see in his eyes the full magnitude of the human torment he was enduring. He swallowed the first bite really, really hard, like it had claws and was trying to climb back out of his esophagus. When he finally got it down, he shook his head, beaming with approval:

"Not bad!"

The whole time he was exerting what can only be described as pure Herculean strength to keep the bite from expelling itself back onto the plate. Then the secondary odor plume must have reached me and I finally lost what remaining traces of my appetite that still inexplicably lingered after the pressure release valve incident. With each offensive event that unfolded, I learned more about some of the most important subtleties of my father's character. Chief among my epiphanies that day was a new and unqualified appreciation for the formidable strength of his willpower. Dad ate a few more bites and put the rest of the bloated carcass back into the pot.

"Honey, it was pretty damn good, but next time let's cook those intestines separately! What do you think?"

She did not respond. Not a sigh, a grunt, or even a nod. There was only silence. Finally, he removed the 20-gallon boiler from the sink and hobbled outside with it. He quickly surveyed the yard in search of a suitable place to deposit its contents. He finally decided on a convenient spot at the edge of our back yard beside an old hackberry tree *(Celtis occidentalis)*. The neighborhood dogs immediately came over to investigate this pathetic pile of unsavory mayhem, but it soon became clear that they wanted nothing to do with it. The dogs actually seemed to be overwhelmed with a streak of genuine sympathy for the poor squirrels.

The squirrels ultimately became the focal point of countless impromptu canine gatherings for the remainder of that winter. The following spring the squirrels were still there until Dad and I finally buried them in the garden.

Dad never brought unskinned squirrels into the house again. And he became considerably more attentive afterwards when Mom cooked squirrels for him. My aunt Little-Dove realized possession of the pressure cooker within a week of the alleged incident. The hackberry tree died in April of 1965. We never knew if it was the squirrels, or the dogs that actually did it in.

Chapter 8

The Good Neighbor Policy

A phone rang in Moscow.

It is difficult to appreciate the full scope of my father 's experiences with irate waitresses. The traditional folklore of our family contains countless examples of this complex sociological phenomenon. The first major episode that I witnessed occurred in the summer of 1963 at a coal mine in Kentucky, near the small rural community of Wounded Mule. Dad was mining a block of No. 9 coal at this location using a fleet of obsolete and worn out equipment.

The reserves were excellent but he didn't have a drilling rig to drill the proper kind of holes in the overburden so that ammonium nitrate explosives could be used. This greatly restricted the amount of coal that could be produced. Dad decided to deal with the problem by hiring a contractor to drill the holes and blast a large enough area to last for a whole year's worth of mining. It took three weeks to prepare the shot. The subsequent blast pulverized a body of rock approximately one-hundred acres in areal extent and about fifty feet thick, or what amounted to approximately twenty-million tons of earth material. It was the largest explosion I've ever seen in my life. It was like Hiroshima and Nagasaki revisited, except this time without the Japanese.

We were positioned about a mile upwind of the shot zone, parked on the county road in front of the mine entrance when the explosion occurred. The blast generated an enormous mushroom cloud that reached an altitude of approximately 35,000 feet in less than two minutes. Over the next half hour, under the influence of the jet stream, this plume of superheated gas and dust took the form of an anvil-shaped cloud approximately fifteen miles in length and two miles wide at the base.

The plume was reportedly observed on the radar screens of military bases in at least five states. Fearing a nuclear first strike by the Soviets was in progress, NORAD went to DEFCON-2 and scrambled a pair jet aircraft from the 123rd Tactical Reconnaissance Wing of the Kentucky Air National Guard. Dad quickly recognized them as Martin RB-57B Canberras. These planes made repeated passes over us as they took hundreds of high-resolution photographs of the ionized plasma core and its surrounding pulverized rock aerosol. At one point they flew over low enough that we could clearly see the pilots staring back at us. Everybody watched with great interest as these planes circled above.

In the meantime, as the others seemed to be watching the planes maneuver, I recall observing the blast cloud as it drifted to the northeast, toward a little country cafe that sat on a hill about a mile from the mine. The restaurant completely disappeared from sight as the roiling, dark mass encompassed it. Approximately ten minutes later, as the jets departed, we noticed a car coming up the county road at a high rate of speed. Anyone who has ever worked in the mining business is probably very familiar with the "old car coming up the county road at a high rate of speed routine." That is, the men seemed to suddenly get that "something evil this way comes" feeling and instinctively began to spread-out.

However, Dad stood his ground commendably as the automobile roared to a stop at the mine entrance. The car looked like it had just emerged from a volcanic disaster zone. The grille was crammed with fused silica. The driver had employed the windshield wipers in an attempt to clean the glass. All it did was make a few streaks in the thermally bonded pyroclastic veneer. A stream of rock flour poured from inside the car as the door opened. Then out stepped a waitress whose appearance and demeanor gave one the distinct impression that she was in fact the Spawn of Hell itself. Her body was covered entirely with a quarter-inch layer of durable ceramic foam. The only recognizable human characteristics were her eyes. They were like brilliant blue and white flowing oases on a dark and barren desert. The contrast was truly startling.

The dirt-waitress with human eyes looked around at everyone. Nobody said a word. She tried to stare down each man, and did, even me, and I was only nine-years old. She looked at me like she was going to rip my lungs out, stretch them over my head and suffocate me with them. I was genuinely traumatized. She then slammed the door of her car causing a dust cloud so thick we couldn't see her for a few seconds. As the dust cleared she lumbered toward us, leaning into her gait with fists clinched and jaw cocked. The men started to step back from the projected vector of her approach. As this happened, my father suddenly found himself isolated and cut-off, precariously vulnerable to this sooty creature.

"Are you the %&@!* pieces of $@&%^ that just shot that #!@$% dynamite?"

Dad was so utterly traumatized by the raw brutality of this initial salvo of ghastly invective that he was literally rendered speechless. He desperately struggled to make a verbal response but no words would come forth. The only sounds that emerged from his mouth were:
"Wha...wha...wha...wha..."
Just when he was about to get out a complete word she cut him off cold:
"Don't tell me that crap, I know you're the sumbitches who did it!"
This was about the time that she must of developed an itch inside of her substantial brassier because she suddenly reached under her stylish waitress blouse to make what seemed to be a very sober and urgent adjustment. However, when she did this the steel-reinforced butyl-nylon shoulder strap snapped back prematurely causing a cloud of dust to erupt from her cleavage area and rock chips to tumble from her armpits. When this happened, a mild but clearly perceptible shudder cascaded through the crowd of the by-now outwardly fidgety coal miners. Dad subsequently conjured up some of that incredible willpower that he was so famous for and made one last, Herculean effort to speak:
"You...you...you..."
The dirt-waitress glared at him and said:
"What are you looking at? Are you making fun of me?"
Finally, in a staggering exertion of gut-wrenching determination, he pulled together a measure of composure from that mysterious primal reservoir of the Human Will and managed to utter these words:
"...you have beautiful eyes!"
There was no response, other than disbelieving, stunned silence. She just stared at him as though she were waiting for some perverted, irreverent punch-line. One could literally have heard a proverbial pin drop. The coal miners remained both motionless and attentive, waiting in earnest to see what she would do next. A few meadowlarks chattering on the breeze were the only sounds punctuating the muteness of the moment. The whole time Dad kept bombarding her with that famous boyish smile

of his, never once breaking eye contact. This deep vision-lock between the two of them continued for some substantial interim.

The seconds ticked by, accruing into more than just a simple pregnant pause. Had it been a movie, this is where the mushy music would have started. Finally, surrendering a very subtle Mona Lisa-like smile, she spoke:

"Do you really think so?"

"Fair, fair lady, the most beautiful eyes any man could ever hope to behold."

"Well, my hair's a mess!" she replied, fluffing some shale chips from her dirt-packed scalp.

One fragment became lodged in her ear, requiring her to tilt her head sideways to get it to fall out, but she kept speaking and maintained eye contact with my father.

"So who's going to clean my bistro?" she asked, now in a sultry, or even provocative tone.

Dad must have picked up some primal sensory undercurrent in her question, because immediately after that he eased up to her, took her hand in his, and softly brushed some gravel from her forehead with his other hand. He then looked toward the by now stupefied crowd of coal miners and said:

"Okay men, everybody get some buckets and shovels and follow me. Clyde, drive up to the store and get a couple cases of detergent and a dozen mops. Buster, you and Lloyd fill up the water truck and meet us over at her cafe as quick as you can. Roy, you and Junior wash her car inside and out. I want it to look brand new – *and go ahead and change the oil and rotate the tires while you're at it."*

As Dad issued these commands she never took her eyes off of him. She seemed to be admiring the take-control-of-the-situation dash that he was exhibiting.

"I like the cut of your jib." she said.

"Thank you very much, ma'am."

Dad escorted the dirt waitress to his pickup truck and opened the door and helped her get in. He then drove her back to the cafe and the men followed. It took them an entire day to completely clean the place. In the meantime, over the next several days in fact, Dad lavished her with a motor tour of such area marvels as the Green River Lock & Dam at Rochester, the plywood factories over in Hockertown, the oil fields of Cumberland County, and the nightclubs of Dunlapburg, or that's what the official story was. They were gone for quite a while. I'm not sure if my mom ever knew about my father's highly evolved public relations techniques.

Two of my father's greatest talents were exhibited that day: 1, seeing beauty in places no one else would think to look, and 2, taking an almost hopeless situation and turning it completely around. Dad had a policy of always doing the right thing, right from the start; and if a new friendship could be cultivated in the process, then that was generally okay too, especially if she was a single gal. Dad was a true pioneer in American management techniques. Today, his Good Neighbor policy has come to be standard practice among many of America's top companies, successfully employed by corporate CEOs, managers, shift supervisors, Kentucky governors, and even by United States presidents.

It took me a while to figure it out, but I am now convinced that there is more than a pretty good chance that my entry into this world was an unanticipated collateral phenomenon directly attributable to my father's advanced management policies. I am not complaining, but I will save that story for another time.

Chapter 9

Trouble at the Railroad Office

My father was widely known as a very personable individual. He tried to get along with virtually everyone, not just waitresses. It was a passion with him. He had his own ethical paradigm that governed his conduct. It could perhaps be described as a cross between the *Golden Rule* of the Holy Bible and Immanuel Kant's *Categorical Imperative*. His version was simply:

"Always put yourself in the other fellow's shoes."

And he lived by it. He also believed that if everyone would just obey this one simple rule, the scourge of war would forever be wiped from the face of the earth. Dad also saw his rule as a statement about perspective in general. That is, a person should strive to expand their perspective, or widen their scope at all times. They should not allow self-imposed myopia or neglect to distort the quest for real truth. Problems should be examined from as many angles as possible. And above all, we should listen to the other guy. As hard as it is to believe, sometimes we are wrong, or have an incomplete picture. But Dad also knew that the world is copiously appointed with those who don't give a damn about the other fellow, or his apparel, foot or otherwise (shoe thieves notwithstanding). Such people would usually get one over on Dad the first go-around, or even two or three times.

But eventually Dad would disassociate himself from them. That is, my father always let thieves and con-artists have the first shot. He would give them the benefit of the doubt until they turned their hand. But he always avoided confrontations too. He would rather walk away without elaboration than to create a scene.

No one ever attributed this behavior to cowardice. Most people knew that he did it because he was a true gentleman. And also perhaps he knew that just a flick of his fist would kill most people. My father was a tremendously strong man. He stood six foot-three, and weighed around 250 pounds, very little of which was fat. Dad had such great strength because he worked so hard. When I used to watch him work I would shudder with fear because if that was what I was going to have to do when I grew up, then I never wanted to grow up.

I entertained many career options during this period. I would consider anything to save me from employment in the energy production industry. I realized very early that there had to be professions that did not require getting out of bed at four in the morning, seven days a week. There had to be career tracks that did not necessitate working until at least eleven every night, or frequently coming home bleeding, with broken bones, a sprained back, or third-degree burns. Surely there were jobs that did not demand commitment of all of one's cash to keep the business going, with no guarantee of success.

There must be some profession that does not involve going without even the most basic necessities others take for granted so replacement parts can be purchased for drilling rigs or bull dozers. There had to be a way of earning a living that did not entail constant abuse by officials who wielded their power unreasonably and arbitrarily.

One particular case of such arbitrary abuse occurred when my father was operating a small coal mine near Muskrat Lodge, Kentucky. Dad had managed to acquire a tract of land near the mine that possessed both highway frontage and a spur of the W&B (Wooten & Breeding) Railroad. Using little more than dilapidated equipment, he constructed a small but very efficient coal crushing and rail loading facility on this land.

Coal was brought to the facility from the mine in dump trucks. After it arrived, the coal was cleaned, crushed, and then loaded onto the railcars by a conveyor belt. Pretty straightforward stuff. But there was a catch: the supply of railcars was never adequate to handle the output of the mine. Whenever Dad would be promised a certain number of railcars on a certain day, they would always arrive late, sometimes days late, and only a fraction of the number promised.

Dad tolerated the situation the best he could, hoping it would get better. It only got worse. He had large stockpiles of coal laying around the mine and at the rail facility. He had a solid contract with a major utility. But since he couldn't get his coal delivered, the situation became critical. He finally had to idle the mine and send the men home.

Businesses fail every day, and Dad had his share of failures. But this was a case where he was doing everything right. The circumstances driving this failure were perplexing and beyond his control. Or at least that was what he thought.

Wooten & Breeding Railroad Corporation had been struggling financially since the end of WWII. But when the new environmental laws came into effect, the company began to decline at an alarming pace. Various remedies were attempted, mostly to no avail. By the late seventies, W&B had been through so many lawsuits, restructurings, and receiverships that stock brokers began referring to it as *Wounded and Bleeding.* However, its latest strategy of massive efficiency improvements and staff reassignments had begun to yield positive results, even though for some reason the company was failing to provide Dad with the service he required.

So he decided to pay a call on the W&B district office over in Har Megiddo, Kentucky. The office was manned by a single employee, a fellow by the name of Dusty Kuntz. He was the person solely responsible for the allocation of all railcars in Dad's district.

Dad informed Mr. Kuntz that because of the railcar shortage he was dangerously close to shutting down the mine, eliminating the jobs of fourteen men. Dusty informed Dad something to the effect of:

"I don't give a rat's ass about you, your stupid mine, or your pathetically ignorant, genetically-defective coal-mining employees. As far as I'm concerned, you can all just go and die somewhere."

"What is the reason for the car shortage." Dad asked.

"There is no shortage." Dusty replied.

"Why can't I get the cars I need?"

"Because I don't want you to have them."

"Would you mind explaining that?"

"Listen McCasoway, I am under no obligation to explain anything to you, or for that matter anyone else. All coal car distribution is up to my personal discretion and there's nothing that you or any other one-trunk-inheriting, mix hick can do about it. So if you know what's good for you, you'll get on down the road and leave me alone, because I have work to do."

"What am I supposed to do then?"

"Maybe you should get a job."

"What do you mean by that?"

"Everybody knows what crooks you coal men are. You ought to just snap out if it and quit ripping people off with your stupid coal mine. You ought to face reality and get over your addiction to coal. Your business is doomed and if I can have anything to do with it, I'll see you thrown in jail."

"Why are you acting this way?"

"Because I can."

Dad was becoming convinced that he was getting nowhere with this railroad man. Dad was not subject to rash or impulsive action. He was always able to control his anger. Yet this situation was both hopeless and infuriating. One man was arbitrarily determining the fate of Dad's business, his employees, and his family, with no apparent logic or purpose, and totally in the absence of accountability. If there had been a tangible reason, like perhaps a shortage due to the war effort, or if the coal was of inferior quality, etc., Dad would have swallowed his pride and walked away like a man.

But as he stood there he continued to consider his options. He was tempted to just kill the man outright. But no, he was not worth it. Plus there was the fact that he had encountered this sort of thing before, except not so pronounced. That is, he realized that this odd behavior could be some kind of machination designed to generate a kickback. Therefore, being desperate, he decided to forego his ethics and offer a bribe.

"I need fifty coal cars a week. I'll do whatever it takes, but I need those cars. If a contribution to the pension fund would help..."

For the first time since Dad had arrived, Dusty put down his pencil, leaned back in his chair, and looked my father in the eye, and said:

"I don't want your stinking money."

"Well what do you want then?"

"I just wanted to see you grovel you worthless bastard. And get it through your head once and for all, you will never get any cars from me, ever! In fact McCasoway, if you want my opinion, I hear Popsicle stands are a pretty hot item right now. What you ought to do is invest in one because after I'm done with you, that will be about all you're qualified for."

Dusty then reached into a drawer and produced a loaded revolver. He placed the weapon on the desk. Dad made eye-contact with him. Dusty smiled and said:

"You want some of this, come and get it then! Otherwise, march the hell out of here and never show your face in this office again!"

Now the cogs really turned in Dad's head. There was no sane reason for a representative of a major corporation to behave in such a manner. Some critical threshold of honor had been crossed. I suppose Dad's mental processing centers were crunching the variables, weighing the options one last time. Since the guy had obviously crossed that fine line of routine business deportment by brandishing a loaded firearm, Dad finally came to the conclusion that he had no choice other than to respond in a proportionate manner.

So, without any additional words or apparent warning, he abruptly stood up from his chair, reached out with his massive, rock-abraded hands and latched onto Dusty's scalp, dragging him harshly across the desk, propelling the pistol onto the floor and crushing a lamp in the process.

Dad instantly ushered him into an improvised variant of a half-Nelson and proceeded to grant him a particularly abusive, almost inhuman *Dutch-rub*. My father rubbed the man's head so hard that hair was dislodged in wads. Several large meat furrows became clearly visible in the railroad man's scalp where Dad's knuckles had macerated the flesh. Tufts of hair were scattered about the room. Dad then proceeded to take Dusty for a free tour around the office, rubbing his face with great unnecessary roughness upon every surface more or less at waist level in the room, and punching him repeatedly in the jaw, ears, and nose as he did this. The whole time also berating him with a barrage of coarse invective. Dad knew this was all probably very unwise, but he also felt that wisdom no longer applied in this situation because his coal mine was going to go broke no matter what he did. Dad finally released the headlock when he discovered that Dusty had soiled himself.

"There you sumbitch, how do you like that!" Dad said.

Dad reached down and took the pistol. Then he left, more or less walking through a heavy oak door without ever touching the knob. As Dad drove down the road, what he'd done started to sink in. He figured that he had gone too far this time. He fully expected the police to be waiting for him when he arrived home. But much to his surprise no such eventuality ever came to pass. Still he was faced with the bitter prospect that he was going to have to shut down the coal mine. He went into the house and prepared to call the employees and tell them the bad news. Then the phone rang. It was someone from W&B headquarters in Damascus, Kentucky. They sounded pretty mad. The person on the other end told Dad that he had better be at their office at 9:00 o'clock the next morning or a warrant for his arrest would be issued. He agreed to be there.

My father was uncharacteristically depressed as he arrived at the corporate headquarters of W&B Railroad. It was a huge and intimidating building. The receptionist told him, "Oh yes, they're expecting you." The office he had to go to was on the sixteenth floor. The higher the elevator went up, the lower his spirits sank. He walked off the elevator into a huge executive reception area, its twenty foot high walls were lined with Grecian marble. The closer he got to his destination, the smaller he felt.

The receptionist on this floor told Dad to have a seat, and someone would be with him shortly. About that time the elevator opened again and two Kentucky State Troopers walked out. They approached the receptionist and she directed them to Dad. They came up to Dad and told him to follow them. He figured that this was it. He had been set up. They were taking him straight to jail.

Instead however, they escorted him down a short hallway, through a pair of massive mahogany doors and into what appeared to be a large conference room. In the center of the room was an oval shaped table, around which were seated no fewer than twenty men, all dressed in expensive business suits. A box of fresh doughnuts occupied the middle the table. No one smiled. One of these men thanked the State Troopers and asked them to wait in the lobby. After the troopers left, this same man asked Dad to be seated. All twenty men around the table stared at him with unabashed contempt. No one spoke. A few of them jotted notes onto legal pads. Finally the man who had asked him to be seated addressed my father:

"Mr. McCasoway, obviously you understand the reason we called you here today."

"I think so."

"I presume that you also understand that physical attacks on our employees cannot be tolerated?"

"I do. But I'd like an opportunity to explain."

"With all due respect Mr. McCasoway, we're not interested in your reasons. As a matter of fact, we may just end this all right now by calling the troopers back in here and having you hauled away. Do you understand?"

"No."

"What don't you understand Mr. McCasoway?"

"Why nobody seems to be interested in my side of the story."

"Mr. McCasoway, with all due respect, W&B Railroad cannot afford to concern itself with the success or failure of every under-funded, one-horse coal mine in the state of Kentucky. The needs of our large customers must receive priority. If you can't sustain a few delays in rail access, maybe you should find another line of work."

Dad was stunned. His conception of American freedom didn't have room for such convolutions. And he certainly did not expect an outlook of that type among the Captains of Industry commanding this table. To him every business was sacred. Each entrepreneurial enterprise was graced by the laws of Nature, and of Nature's God, with its own inherent, real value, regardless of size. Dad believed that small businesses constituted the backbone of the American economy, human freedom, human happiness, and ultimately therefore, civilization itself. And in so many words that is what he told the W&B executives. He also quoted them a paragraph from *Reflections on the Revolution in France* by Edmund Burke:

"[Men]...have a right to the fruits of their industry, and to the means of making their industry fruitful. They have a right to the acquisitions of their parents, to the nourishment and improvement of their offspring, to instruction in life and to consolation in death. Whatever each man can separately do, without trespassing upon others, he has a right to do for himself; and he has a right to a fair portion of all which society, with all its combinations of skill and force, can do in his favor. In this partnership, all men have equal rights; but not to equal things."

The combination of his original ideas and the germane quotations he eloquently delivered, seemed to merge into a stunningly effective presentation. It was reminiscent perhaps of the famous *John Galt* speech from *Atlas Shrugged*. My ability to reproduce this remarkable proclamation is far too imperfect, so therefore I shall not trivialize it by attempting to. Following this impassioned oratory, the executives each exchanged glances, seemingly feigning detached disinterest, but still seriously impacted by his words. After a long silence, the main executive stood up and walked over to a bar in the back of the conference room and poured a cup of coffee.

"Would you like a cup of coffee, Adam?"

"No, thank you."

"Okay Mr. McCasoway, obviously you have given us a great deal to consider. Why don't you wait out in the lobby for a few minutes while we talk it over."

As Dad waited in the executive lobby, the State Troopers tried to stare him down. This was futile on their part. Dad had no fear. He had been shot at before. Literally thousands of Nazi soldiers had tried to kill him during the war, and had failed miserably. So it was going to take more than a few dirty looks from a pair of rent-a-cops to intimidate Adam McCasoway. He feared no man on this Earth. And he also knew he was right. He was actually far beyond fear or depression at this point.

In fact, as he later recounted this part of the story to me, his eyes lit up. Because as he sat there with the cops watching, he got the idea that he could acquire some trucks and haul the coal to the power plant himself and circumvent the railroad entirely. It would be terribly expensive, probably even impossible, but he could at least try it. He also got the idea that he could sell his coal at a reduced price to a business associate who did have good rail service. There were other ways to skin this cat. But a jail sentence could greatly complicate the whole affair. Just then, the mahogany doors swung open.

"Mr. McCasoway, would you come back in now?"

For an instant Dad hesitated. But he decided to go back in and hear what they had to say. In the meantime the executive whispered a few words to the state troopers. Curiously, the policemen walked over to the elevator and departed. But they did make a point to lavish Dad with a nasty glare as they passed him. Dad went into the conference room as the elevator descended.

"Please have a seat Adam."

Dad sat down.

"First Mr. McCasoway, we want you to know that as a direct result of your attack, Dusty Kuntz has submitted his resignation."

Dad decided to say what was on his mind. The way he looked at it, there was nothing to lose.

"With all due respect, I regret that I cannot say I am sorry about that." Dad said.

The executives exchanged glances with each other, but remained silent.

"Mr. McCasoway, to resolve this distasteful matter, without involving the authorities, the first thing you must do is pay for the door and the lamp that you destroyed. Will you do that?"

"Yes."

"Okay, if you will do that, we think we can supply you with 100 railcars a week for the next four years. Will that help you out?"

My father was dumbfounded. This was twice the number he needed to fill his contract, but he could certainly make use of them.

"Yes, that would be absolutely wonderful."

"However Adam, we are willing to do this only on three additional conditions. First, you must give us your word as a gentleman that you will never again threaten or attack an employee of W&B Railroad Corporation."

"I promise."

"Second, Mr. Kuntz has stated that he wishes to have his pistol returned."

"Sorry, I cannot do that."

"Why not?"

"Where I come from, if somebody pulls a gun on an unarmed man he forfeits the weapon."

"I see."

"Actually, he's lucky to be alive. By all rights of honor, it was my privilege to kill him. I chose to let him live. The pistol is mine sir."

"But he felt threatened Mr. McCasoway."

"I cannot in good conscience give the weapon to him. Frankly gentlemen, with all due respect, it comes down to who you believe more, him or me. If your offer hinges on the pistol, then I regret that I will unable to accept your terms."

The executives exchanged glances.

"We understand Mr. McCasoway. There's no need to let this one point derail the progress we've made here today. I'm sure that other arrangements can be made with respect to the handgun. Actually, I was simply keeping a promise."

A pregnant pause ensued. During this interim Dad looked at them each in turn. Finally he asked:

"You indicated that there was a third condition?"

"The last condition is purely voluntary Adam. It is our sincere hope however, that you do elect to accommodate us."

"How may I be of service?"

"We would like for you to answer a question."

"I will try."

The executives exchanged glances with one another and nodded almost imperceptibly.

"We were just curious, Adam: is it true that Old Dusty soiled his pants while you were giving him a *Dutch-Rub?*"

"Yes."

"It must have been one hell of a Dutch-Rub!"

"It was."

Dad held out his massive right hand, displaying the severe abrasions on his knuckles, most of which were still bleeding slightly. At this point every executive in the room broke out into a severe, arguably pathological species of laughter. The guffaws were so exaggerated that some of the men had to sit down to keep from hyperventilating, or fainting. Others seemed to spew saliva and fragments of partially chewed doughnuts in random directions.

One man, in the process of sipping his coffee, powerfully ejected a fan-shaped plume of the tepid leachate across the conference table, tipping an attractive arrangement of flowers. Eventually however, each executive regained sufficient outward composure to approach Dad and examine his hand in detail. Some were again brought to tears in their glee as they filed past him reception-style. Each man congratulated him, patted him on the shoulder and shook his hand, delicately no doubt, but shook it nonetheless.

"Adam, we just want you to know, that there's not a man in this room who wouldn't have paid good money to have been there."

It turned out that Dusty Kuntz was one of the most loathed employees who ever worked for W&B Railroad Corporation. He had never really committed an act serious enough for them to fire him. So supposedly, as a part of their massive restructuring program, he had been transferred to a remote district where he would help modernize their system. But they really transferred him to the most obscure location they had in an effort to make him quit. But he never did. He got mad. He got bitter. But he never quit. It took nearly a year for someone like Dad to come along and serve the role of catalyst.

"I think this calls for a celebration." said the main executive.

He walked to the bar and produced two bottles of expensive bourbon and some glasses. They all sat around the conference table and didn't get up until the bottles were empty. In this interim, at their request, Dad recounted the entire incident for them. He described in exhaustive detail how he had more or less dusted all of the furniture in the office with

Dusty's face and so forth, the whole time with the audience laughing, congratulating him, and offering supportive comments.

This lively discussion continued for over an hour. They even called a nurse to come in and wrap Dad's hand with a gauze dressing while he talked. By the time the bottles were empty, Dad had made twenty new life-long friends. He became an instant legend in the W&B family of companies.

Dad never had problems getting railcars ever again. It was one of the greatest victories of his life. Memos were distributed throughout the W&B corporate system, in all the district branches, detailing the demise of Dusty Kuntz, and lauding the hero responsible. To this day his name lives on in the collective consciousness of W&B Railroad Corporation.

The executives at W&B acted on Dad's advice. They began an intensive promotion in which they offered special prices and services to small businesses all over the state. The result was a resounding success. They became profitable again. The last anyone ever heard of Dusty Kuntz, was a legal notice in a major Damascus newspaper, where he had filed for bankruptcy in a failed Popsicle stand venture.

Chapter 10

The Cortez Transformation

Abandoned camping supplies were a common sight.

Around 1965, when my father was operating a small coal mine along the Upper Saline Peninsula of southern Butler County, our residence was located in Fort Higginbotham, which at that time was north of the Yazoo River in Muhlenburgh County. During this period he owned a 1962 Chevrolet pickup. It had a three-speed manual transmission with the shifter handle affixed to the steering column. This was the truck in which my father taught me the art of driving. Dad had me routinely operating motor vehicles by the time I was six years old.

My ability to shift the transmission was often less than satisfactory, but according to Dad, I could navigate, work the throttle, brakes, steering, and turn signals with at least as much skill as my mother. I usually drove when he got sleepy. After he dozed off I would be totally responsible for operating the vehicle. If I had a problem I would awaken him, or simply stop.

Since my legs were too short to reach the gas pedal while sitting in the seat, Dad rigged the truck with a hand throttle and brake. When the seat was scooted all the way back there was enough room for me to drive standing upright on the floorboard, thus resulting in an operational configuration not unlike that of the helmsman of a ship at sea. He even bought an admiral's jacket and *a hat of a Welch frigate captain* as he called it, for me to wear. He also procured a MacArthur-style corncob pipe for me to gum around on while driving. It is likely that I appeared quite rakish when fully outfitted with these nautical accoutrements.

Dad considered it stylish for me to chauffeur him around. And naturally, I thought it was the greatest thing in the world. Overall, it was a fairly successful endeavor. Dad was able to catch up on some badly needed sleep and I learned how to drive ten years before my contemporaries. However, there were some close calls. For example, once during this period, when I was driving in the *Welch Frigate* fashion, and wearing the hat, the jacket, and smoking the pipe, a Kentucky state trooper followed us for several miles, waiting for an opportunity to safely pass. When he finally did overtake us however, just as his high-performance police interceptor sedan drove past my window, he suddenly slowed down and observed me with immense interest. I could *feel* his gaze boring into the pores of the skin on my face. At first I panicked. Naturally, I wanted to act as casual as possible. But under the circumstances it was an immense challenge. I quickly became desperate to find a way to convey the illusion of normality.

For some reason it occurred to me that I should tap the bowl of my MacArthur pipe in the palm of my hand a couple times, and cast the ashes out the window. I noticed that when I did this, it seemed to relieve some of my tension. The policeman appeared to take curious note of it as well. Then I casually adjusted a few knobs on the dash and checked the throttle setting. This felt pretty good too. So after that I decided to hang a hygrometer out the window and take a reading of the relative humidity. I then casually jotted the results on a clipboard. Things were starting to really roll at this point. Finally, I took a couple of star readings with a sextant, checked the chronometer, and got a fix on our position, again jotting the results on the clipboard. Somewhere in the middle of all this I also managed to reload the pipe and light it. I took a long puff and then sipped a cup of tea.

During this entire exhibition I never looked directly at the policeman. My hope was that he would just think I was some kind of mutant, sea-faring Leprechaun. I envisioned him contemplating:

"Oh yes, just another friendly mutant Leprechaun operating a motor vehicle in the traditional Welch Frigate style."

Finally, in a masterful *coup de grâce* of total casualness, I walked around to the left side of the steering wheel, completely turning my back toward him. My epaulets were flapping in the wind. From this new position, I could now see his reflection in the rearview mirror on the passenger-side door. And since I was no longer blocking his view, he was now able to see Dad. The policeman seemed almost hypnotically captivated by how my father was spread out across the seat with his eyes closed and his mouth hanging open.

By this point I was out of options. There were no more maritime chores for me to perform short of sending an SOS in semaphore. Just when I thought we were sunk, an oncoming vehicle appeared ahead in the distance. As the car rapidly approached, the trooper looked at it intermittently while continuing to stay even with us, as if trying to decide whether to drop back behind us and pull us over, or to go ahead and pass us before the oncoming car got too close.

I obviously did not want him to drop back. I knew if he got behind us we would be dead in the water. So, before the oncoming car got so near that the policeman would have no choice but to drop back, I throttled the engine down to 1/3, signaled five shorts blasts with the fog-horn, and sounded the collision bell. Unable, or unwilling to slow down, the cop simply shook his head in apparent disgust and went on around us. He subsequently sped away without further incident.

It is possible that the policeman was en route to an emergency. Or he might have been running late for an appointment. It is also possible that he elected to avoid the distastefully laborious process of incarcerating my father and completing the hundred-some-odd pages of child-welfare paperwork that would be required to send me to *The Home*.

I rode to the coal mine with Dad almost every day that summer. While he was working I would pester the mechanics in the shop, shoot rats in the dynamite shed with the .38 caliber police revolver Dad bought me for my fifth birthday, or play with blasting caps that the miners gave me. When I ran out of ammunition and explosives, there were some creeks and ponds in the woods nearby where I could fish and swim and so forth. It was not that bad of a setup.

Quitting time was always right at dark. After work, Dad and I would get into the Chevy and drive home on State Route 26, also known as Mosquito Road. This highway passed through the edge of the *Great Red Chigger swamp* between Cottageburg and Midland City. This was no ordinary swamp. It was a virtual carbon copy of the coal swamps that existed in the region over 250 million years ago during the geologic time period known as the Pennsylvanian Age.

For example, the area was covered by a dense forest of moss-draped swamp trees extending for hundreds of square miles. There were sporadic groves of primitive ferns over fifty feet tall, and thousands of interconnected fetid bogs filled with willowy reeds and resurgence pools gurgling with gaseous hydrogen sulfide. There were also accounts of seething herds of carnivorous snapping turtles the size of car hoods, and swarms of giant dragonflies over three feet long that were said to prey on swamp gophers and small armadillos, but would also occasionally forage along the periphery of the marsh, taking chickens and puppies when the opportunity arose.

The chiggers that infested this swamp were not like regular chiggers. They were mutant. They were approximately the size and color of a ripe strawberry and resembled sea crabs in their outward appearance. However, these crab-like creatures did not walk sideways, they came straight at any endothermic animal. Entomologists tell us that the common cockroach is the fastest terrestrial insect in North America. However, the scientists who are encumbered by such a misconception are obviously unaware of this species of chigger. These chiggers could exceed 80 mph over short distances. Moreover, they did not simply burrow into the skin like a normal chigger, they constructed tunnels in their victims, sometimes up to a foot deep. Some people poured gasoline or used motor oil into these tunnels to try to flush out the chiggers. But this could cause problems, especially if the chigger died. The only way to effectively remove them was to bait a fish hook with a piece of bacon and lower it into the tunnel and hope that after snaring them they didn't burrow deeper and get tangled around a major artery or a tendon. It was a damn lousy deal from every angle.

In addition to its heightened level of pestilence, there was also something else about this swamp. It is difficult to put into words. It seemed to contain a darkness or a kind of evil that defies routine classification. Some malevolent force permeated the dim backwaters and cracking thickets. It could not be seen or touched, but still it could be felt. It surrounded a person the moment he or she entered the area. It faded away upon their departure. But traces of it could linger for hours, causing severe anxiety and abominable nightmares. It was as if all the foulness, hostility, mercilessness, and futility of nature were concentrated in one dismal place.

Obviously, I did not like for Dad to stop the vehicle in the swamp. As referenced above, the conventional senses seemed unable to gauge the evil. However, there was one normal sensory pathway that did give a clue of this foul background: the sense of hearing. The swamp had a voice. A coarse, raspy, incessant drone emanated from the depths of the bog. It was as if trillions of winged vermin were in the base throes of a vast carnal melee. This phenomenon could easily be heard from inside a moving vehicle, even with the windows rolled up. It was terrifying. But when the vehicle was stopped and the engine turned off, one could also detect all of the subtle nuances, gross inflections, and little layers of horror embedded within. It was enough to truly chill the soul.

Dad would often lecture me on the pure Darwinism of the swamp. He considered it to be his own personal living laboratory for observing the statistical elegance and ultimate futile indifference of nature. He taught me many things using examples from the swamp ecosystem. However, it ultimately boiled down to one basic axiom which Dad reiterated countless times:

"By trying to kill us, nature has created us."

"Like it or not, that is how we got here. The brutality and randomness of nature always pushes toward the destruction and disorder at the edge of chaos. It's tough love. But it is at this same edge where properties are both annihilated and multiplied. Fins are discarded for legs, gills are supplanted by lungs, and strength is given up for intelligence."

"The Standard Model is in fact so entirely elegant and beautiful that an underlying order is self-evident. That is, because the road of evolution has a direction and mileposts (species) along its way, some higher thing or purpose is inherently implied. Such a system must be going somewhere. Implied also, is some ultimate endpoint to the basic process of evolution."

"Are we it? No. But our mere existence proves the absolute possibility of a higher state. I do not believe we are the ultimate state. But I think that we may be only one or two steps from it. And that is the point after all: to make the realization that our own possibility is equal to the possibility of the higher state."

He also thought it was possible to use the mileposts of evolution to estimate what this next state might be like. His favorite analogy was the chimpanzee-human comparison:

"The differences that we can readily appreciate between ourselves and chimps, can be reasonably extrapolated to represent the gulf that exists between us and the next level. Chimps are to us as we are to the next state. We never see representatives of the next level for the same reason a troop of chimps never really encounter suburbanites. Even though we share the same general space, we have moved on to a different realm. So have those of the next level."

"We can watch the monkeys and be glad we are not them. The monkeys however, cannot watch us. Nor do they ponder the possibility of our state. They do not envision a greater thing. Our gift, and a key piece of the puzzle, is that we do *envision*."

This is what Dad believed. And he saw the evidence in the natural environment. It is likely that anyone with a scientific mind who ventures into such swamps on a daily basis would eventually formulate many of the same theories. Today however, a person does not have to leave their home to experience such epiphanies. That is, the same educational effects of a field trip into the unclean, vermin-seething foulness of a reptilian swamp can be obtained simply by observing an episode of *Howard Stern*.

Needless to say, the mosquitoes were indescribably thick in this swamp. They were bad everywhere back then. But in this swamp the mosquitoes were physically overwhelming. It is difficult to imagine how any land animal could have survived. The mosquitoes were so numerous that the air often gave the appearance of a black blizzard. Perhaps that is why only turtles, armadillos, and burrowing animals could live there.

Every night that we drove through the swamp, which was about fifteen miles across, the windshield became completely blackened with millions of splattered mosquitoes. The windows of the vehicle had to be kept rolled up or the cab would fill with an opaque, bloodsucking fog. The radiator often became clogged with mosquito carcasses making the engine run hot. This had to be cleaned out or the motor would be ruined.

To address this problem most motorists simply wired a large piece of window screen over their grille to help filter out the mosquitoes but this too would become matted in a short time. The engine air cleaner would become sealed with mosquito goo and cause the motor to loose power or quit altogether. The front of the truck would be completely coated with a slimy mat of mosquito debris. It was shocking to behold. At first Dad turned on the windshield wipers and that worked for a little while until they were so glommed up that he would finally have to pull over and pour soapy water onto the glass from a jug he kept in the bed of the truck, then peel the mosquitoes off with an ice-scraper.

Trucks didn't have automatic windshield washers on them back then so it all had to be done manually. Dad would have to stop no fewer than three times to clean the windshield every night just to get through the swamp. Everybody that drove through there did. There were always cars pulled over along this stretch of highway. And every time Dad would get out of the truck the mosquitoes would jump on him like ugly on an ape and absolutely bite the living hell out of him. He would curse and yell and be swatting with one hand while scraping the windshield with the other. Then he would rush back into the truck and off we'd go and he would be cursing "...those @----------!!%&*! mosquitoes!" all the way.

Mosquitoes weren't much better in town. Aerosol mosquito repellant, known locally as *Mosquito Dope,* was so popular that some supermarkets dedicated an entire isle to such products. Our family purchased so much of the substance that it constituted a sizeable fraction of our monthly household budget. My mother used to literally soak us in the obnoxious compound. This was totally useless of course. In fact, the pungent aroma of the repellant seemed to actually attract the pesky vermin. Despite any countermeasure tried, I still felt like an all-you-can-eat super buffet for them for most of the formative years of my life. And they considered my little sister Bronte, their own personal mobile snack bar as well. There were times when every square inch of her body contained at least ten bites.

Our neighbor, Mrs. Garbecker, forgot to leave the door unlatched for her Mexican Hairless one evening. The next morning she woke up my parents banging on their bedroom window. She was utterly hysterical. While Mom tried to console her, Dad and I frantically combed the neighborhood looking for the little dog. We found what was left of *Cortez* at the edge of the woods in our back yard. It looked like about two pounds of premium beef jerky. Had it not been for the eyes and the little red collar, I would have stuffed it in my kit bag for later, thinking that some city-slicker campers were being a little careless with their provisions again.

Things were getting out of control. One day when people started dropping dead from encephalitis, the government finally brought in airplanes to spray the swamps. But to do any good they eventually had to spray everywhere. I remember sitting out in the yard at home many times and seeing the mosquito plane fly over on its weekly rounds. The poison had a strong petroleum odor and I often felt the droplets landing on my face. Little specks of the pesticide could be seen on everything in town, particularly on the exterior surfaces of automobiles.

Nobody ever complained too much though. Those who cared enough just parked their cars in a garage or covered them with a tarp on spray days (every Wednesday afternoon in our town). It was a little extra trouble but anything was better than being sucked dry by infinite legions of mosquitoes. In fact, some of my peers' moms deliberately made them stand outside when the plane flew over. In their way of looking at things, it was just a free application of mosquito dope.

Chapter 11

How the Burr Haircut Conquered Communism

My critical formative years during the late fifties and early sixties were mostly unencumbered by societal controversy. It was a time of order, predictability, and conformity. People wanted it that way. After the chaos, uncertainty, and horror of World War II, a conflict responsible for the deaths of at least 56,000,000 human beings, including 413,000 Americans, the welcome reprieve of such order was considered truly precious. And it was no doubt most appreciated by those who had suffered the greatest.

One of the many manifestations of this order was the unassailable notion that women should have long hair and men should have short hair. Pursuant to this idea, my father was the natural arbiter with respect to all permissible hair grooming specifications at our house. Dad performed his hair management duties with great sobriety and discipline. His interpretation of scalp grooming protocol was very simple: no hair on my head could exceed 3.2 millimeters (about 1/8 inch) in length. To maintain such a rigorous standard, we visited our hometown barber, a grizzled old fellow named Claude, at least once a week.

Claude was no ordinary barber. He was perhaps the only one-armed barber in Kentucky at that time. He lost his other arm while serving in the Navy. A shark had bitten it off after the ship he was on was sunk by a Japanese torpedo during the Battle of the Coral Sea back in 1942. Claude had a few other problems too. In the name of charity and good will, they will not be expanded upon other than to say that of all of them, probably the second most conspicuous thing about Claude after his arm deficiency was his proclivity for unsolicited emissions of hydrocarbons.

Everybody knows about methane, how biological organisms, from termites to mammals (particularly those species that prey on burritos), generate this most natural of gasses as a part of their normal metabolic processes. However, Claude must of had a more advanced system because accompanying his copious output of methane, were apparently other gasses including: propane, butane, and acetylene.

In fact, with properly calibrated spectrographic analytical equipment, perhaps even jet fuel could have been identified within the foul and pestilent congregation of vapors typically wafting through Claude's shop. Claude never opened the windows in the barber shop because he had a 1940's vintage air conditioner in the cloak room that was supposed to keep the place cool. He took great pride in informing anyone who cared to ask, that the old air conditioner had been running non-stop since June of 1947. The problem was that it ran out of Freon around 1951 and had been blowing hot air ever since. If it got too hot or stuffy in the shop and someone asked Claude to open a window, he'd just point at the air conditioner and say:

"The air conditioner is running."

It could be hot enough to melt lead, or smell like the lavatory in an oil refinery, but Claude would always point to the air conditioner and say it was running and that would be that.

Today we would consider haircut prices of the early 1960's to be quite affordable. Claude charged seventy-five cents for a standard haircut. The standard haircut of course, was *the burr*. It was a simple cut, straightforward, elegant, and clean. There is a particular economy to the organic lines of the burr that transcend the mercurial fickleness of mainstream trends.

When I was about seven years old, some of the boys in our town started sporting a new and totally revolutionary kind of haircut: *the flat-top*. As far as I was concerned, this new style was a quantum-leap beyond anything I'd ever seen. It was radical. It was fresh. It was cool.

The theory behind the flat-top was simple: the barber had to sculpt the dorsal surface of the cranium so that it resembled the flight deck of a World War II aircraft carrier, without the planes. But because of his arm problem, Claude was forced to use a carpenter's square and a bubble-level to help align the scalp to within the 0.01-percent of perfect flatness that was required at that time by the *Midwest College of Barber Procedures* guidance documents. He was an artist at this. Before long, every guy in town had a flat-top and they all came to Claude to get it. Everyone that is, except my father, and of course me.

Dad considered the flat-top to be just another classic example of how a bunch of sissies got together every so often in Paris, France, and came up with ways to make ordinary men more distracted and vain. Dad believed that a man should never concern himself with the style of his hair. That's why guys like Claude were paid outrageous fees to cut it off. The theory is that something that's not there never needs the brain to devote processing time to it. Therefore, men with short hair have a whole section of brain available for other applications.

That is, the part of their brain ordinarily dedicated to hair vanity can be made available for more important problems: things like improving the design of cantilever-truss bridges, the optimization of titanium alloy mixtures, or new methods of enhancing the sensitivity of radar.

According to Dad, the diesel engine, the automatic transmission, and synthetic plywood, were all invented by men with exceedingly short hair. He knew that Western civilization would be in a major bind without these and similar inventions. So to him the burr was not only a matter of personal pride, but was the ultimate guarantor of freedom and technological superiority in a world packed with anarchists and communists.

Dad didn't believe in shampoo either. He figured that if a man needed more than water and a bar of soap to take a bath then there was just something wrong with him. In addressing the merits of this argument, he always fell back on two principal evidentiary points: 1, they didn't have shampoo in the army, and 2, *girls use shampoo*. These two irrefutable facts usually were sufficient in their impact to cause me to dispense of any further silliness with regard to my hair-care products.

There eventually came a time however, when I convinced myself that I needed a flat-top and no amount of arguing was going to change my mind. Armed with this knowledge in advance, in a noble effort to mitigate familial disharmony, Dad evidently spoke to Claude about the issue prior to arriving for our weekly trim. Upon my ascent of the chair and subsequent cavalier request for a modern flat-top, Claude informed me that, sadly, I had the wrong kind of hair for a successful deployment of the flat-top. He said that a flat-top on my head would not be flat at all, but instead would be more of a cone-top, or maybe even Heaven-forbid, the nefarious slope-top style seen on so many sissy-boys down Leningrad-way. Still, if I really wanted one, he was willing to take a blind stab at it.

He just wanted me to understand that since my hair was so genetically deformed it was going to require the use of not just one, but two carpenter's squares and a plumb-bob, each secured with absolute precision for the duration of the cut, while at the same time my cranium was immobilized with a special *shearing jig*, this final step being entirely for safety purposes because if my head were to slip during the main sculpting phase of the procedure, it could cause him to accidentally lop-off my ears, or maybe even a nostril.

The catch was he claimed, that the performance of this feat of hair-wizardry would require the use of not only his chin, teeth, gums, and one remaining good arm, but also, unfortunately, a second arm, like the one he lost in 1942. So, if I really had to have a flat-top, somebody in the room was going to have to swim to New Guinea and get the damn thing back. Claude then looked at Dad, who remained silent, and at the only other person in the shop at the time, an old fellow named Thurman, who always seemed to be carrying on a lively conversation with himself, but seldom spoke meaningfully to others.

Obviously, I was completely devastated. Not only was I biologically unfit for a flat-top, but now I was allegedly exhibiting the signs of a latent communist too. And what about poor Claude's missing arm? I was definitely conflicted. I stepped down from the barber chair that day with a morbid fear of sharks, a deep distrust of pretty much all countries lying east of the Danube, and another burr haircut, all of which curiously, I still possess to this day.

Two major watershed events were brewing in the hair world however, that would ultimately lead to the annihilation of virtually all manifestations of this type of traditional collusion between guys like Claude and my father. The first occurred on January 28, 1964. That's the day when the price of a haircut raised from seventy-five cents to a dollar. It was a major, revolutionary upheaval of essentially Biblical proportions. In conversations at places like truck stops, tractor factories, and post offices, all across this great nation, men of every class, ethnic and racial background, religion, creed, marital status, and beer preference, were expressing their strong contempt for this most recent milepost on the road to inflationary recession and ultimate Soviet domination.

There were magazine articles addressing the topic. Elected officials joined into the fray with their partisan spin. There were calls for congressional hearings and special prosecutors. Late night talk-show hosts predictably exploited the issue gratuitously, unfortunately all to no avail. The price remained at a dollar for a while and then spiraled upward from there. But then it stabilized around 1970 at about $3.50. By 1990 the price was about $6.00 in most small-town barber shops. Sometime around 1995 the price was floating at approximately $7.50, ten times what it had been when I was a kid. These days a standard haircut from a barber with two arms, will run around $14.00. A haircut from a woman in a beauty shop will cost between $20.00 and $50.00, and most don't do burrs. Half don't even know what a burr is. If it's a young woman, just tell her to cut it in the style like *Sinead O'Connor* wears her's, and chances are she'll understand. For an older lady, the name *Yul Brynner* may be employed for the same basic result.

The second earth-shattering milestone that changed the hair-scape forever of course occurred less than two weeks later on the evening of February 9, 1964. That's when the *Beatles* made their first appearance on the *Ed Sullivan Show*. Dad popped a spring. There was more hair on each Beatle than Claude would see in a month of burrs. To my father, it was the last nail in the coffin of America. Years later, when *whatever happened to America* conversations would spontaneously erupt, Dad still subscribed to and promoted the following theory:

"It all started to go to hell the day the Beatles set foot on American soil."

In the immediate months following the Beatles' appearance, we started visiting Claude at least twice a week. The dollar price, although still quite steep, was no longer an issue with Dad. In fact, Claude was now suddenly doing a booming business as other concerned dads were also taking their sons to get haircuts at an ever-increasing frequency. The flat-top, as a fashion statement, was essentially dead now. Some men even blamed the liberal lines of the flat-top for being the ultimate cause of the Beatles phenomenon, like the camel's nose under the tent analogy. And Claude played right along too. I remember him glaring down at me as I cowered in the chair. His one good arm brandishing a massive, chrome-plated electric hair trimmer. Back in those days a typical barber's electric hair trimmer was about the size of a modern microwave oven and weighed around forty pounds.

The noise generated by such an instrument was not unlike that made by a fully-loaded DC-3 running up its engines just before take-off. When he switched it on, the lights in the room would dim, the plate-glass windows would resonate, and the dirty combs in Claude's complimentary jar of blue liquid would dance around wildly. If Claude was cutting some particularly wiry hair, the old air conditioner would start blowing black smoke in addition to its copious volume of hot air.

When he'd unleash this horrible device onto my skull it would absolutely decimate each and every hair follicle. Sometimes the carbide-tipped blades would bite into my scalp and bog down the motor until it locked up. It once blew a fuse when this happened. To get the teeth dislodged, he would have to pull back hard on the special chrome-plated hydraulic levers that controlled the cutter elevation. After getting the carbide-tipped blades removed from my scalp he would take a pair of needle-nose pliers from his shirt pocket and extract any hair, skin, and chunks of meat that were caught in the blades and flick it en masse into the spittoon sitting by the water fountain.

He would then dress the lacerations in my scalp with some of the blue liquid from the comb jug, or paint on a little styptic pencil. Alcohol simply didn't burn hot enough for Claude. So he often deployed a styptic pencil to cauterize and weld-shut any arteries or major veins that had been ruptured by the teeth of the trimmer.

Around 1975, after we moved to another town, we heard through the grapevine that Claude had met with a tragic end. An electrical short-circuit in the antique hair trimmer had apparently ignited a sizeable volume of combustible gas trapped within the shop, resulting in a powerful explosion. All they found of Claude in the rubble was his one good arm, with the trimmer still clutched in the hand. Curiously, according to official government records on the incident, the old air conditioner was still running.

Upon receiving this news Dad had a sea-change of sorts. He grew his hair out into a kind of abbreviated pompadour, complete with a set of complex, serpentine sideburns running down to the bottom of his jowls. He took up wearing what was considered at the time to be the centerpiece of the stylish polyester line, *the Leisure Suit*. He also bought a huge diamond ring for himself. He even began using shampoo.

About this same period I also grew a thick head of hair and started using shampoo as well. Dad was going for the leisure suit w/diamond ring look, while I was into the hippie/back-packer look. Dad bought a yellow Mark-IV and I was driving a green Jeep. Dad also backed-off a little on the Beatles. That is, he finally did recognize their *right to exist*, but continued to categorically and unequivocally hate their music. Despite these slight departures from the straight and narrow however, we still always saw eye-to-eye on the sharks and the communists.

Chapter 12

South Pacific Romance

A little bit of Dingo Bango goes a long way.

When Dad was about eleven years old his parents sent him to spend a month with his uncle Aesop in Phlegmingsburg. Aesop Uriah McCasoway was a retired Navy engineer who also fancied himself a self-made investment expert. After he left the Navy in 1924, he moved to New York City where he dabbled in various Wall Street ventures and managed to assemble a fairly impressive portfolio. After the Crash of 1929, he moved back to Indiana and took a job as a machinist. He worked in several area factories before retiring in 1953.

While serving in the Navy, Aesop was stationed at a number of bases in and around the Solomon Islands. The Solomons are a chain of hundreds of small volcanic islands located east and south of Papua New Guinea, separating the Coral Sea from the Pacific Ocean. It was on one of the tiniest of these primitive islands, *Dingo Bango,* that Aesop met and fell in love with the woman who would become his wife: *Cheu Dong.*

Dingo Bango was an unremarkable island, noted only for its strategic location relative to certain navigable waters. The island had very few natural resources. There were no trees to speak of. There was no arable land. It consisted of little more than a platform of volcanic rock covered with a dense mantle of cogon grass *(Imperata cylindrica)* and a few rat-infested marshes. Correspondingly, the island's human population was quite small, perhaps less than 500, when missionaries first arrived there in 1871. Other than the marsh rats and a few migratory birds, the only other notable animal life on the island was a species of wild dog *(Canis familiaris dingo)* with an estimated population of one-million.

At the time when Dad came to stay, Aesop was employed at a pulley factory in Hymenoptera. Dad stayed with Cheu Dong during the day while Aesop was at work. Aesop was a real nice fellow, everybody knew that. But Cheu Dong was crazier than a wedge.

Aesop however, must have loved his wife a lot because he was always bragging on her. For example, he often articulated detailed anecdotal accounts about how Cheu Dong saved enormous sums of money with her island-tempered frugality and keen eye for a bargain. He seemed to be particularly proud of the fact that ever since they started keeping house together, his grocery bill had dropped to less than 25% of what it was when he was single.

But as Dad explained, the reason Cheu Dong was so good at saving money was because she was more than just a little frugal, she was tighter than a gnat's ass stretched over a rain barrel. She was the kind of tight that had not been practiced in most parts of the world since the Bronze Age.

Moreover, her skills were not simply limited to extraordinary feats of budgetary management. For example, one day Aesop noticed a small leak in the roof that needed to be repaired. After mentioning it in passing to Cheu Dong, he made a mental note to himself to stop at the hardware store after work the next day and buy a bucket of roofing tar. The next day he was almost home before he realized that he had forgotten to buy the roofing tar. He thought about turning around and driving back to the hardware store but decided he would put it off until the following day.

But just as he pulled into his driveway it started raining. He found himself becoming depressed. One can appreciate his profound surprise therefore, when he suddenly discovered that the modern clay-tile roof of his suburban bungalow had been completely covered over by what appeared to be a jungle-style thatched roof. For a fleeting moment, he thought he was back on Dingo Bango again. Since there were no dense stands of *Imperata cylindrica* in the Phlegmingsburg area, Cheu Dong had conveniently utilized similar locally available materials. The only suitable plant species she could find in sufficient quantity however, was corn *(Zea mays)*. She had subsequently and painstakingly acquired several hundred fresh stalks from nearby cropland, leaving a two-acre void in a local farmer's field.

Aesop immediately located and settled-up with the farmer before the authorities became involved. When he returned home he tried handle the situation with Cheu Dong as delicately as possible. And after much measured discussion, he was finally able to convey to her the absolute necessity of obtaining his consent before proceeding with major renovation projects, or before exploiting locally available materials of any kind, for any application whatsoever. She promised to comply.

Cheu Dong did not like Dad, he was reasonably certain of that. At dinner she fed him like he was a two-year old. When Dad would try to get a normal helping of food she would make him put it back, telling him that he did not need so much, and upbraiding him severely at the same time.

A typical meal she served to my father consisted of half a slice of bread and a bowl of stewed rutabaga, or fried rutabaga, depending on the day of the week. Dad hated rutabaga. But because he was starving he forced himself to eat it. What little meat was offered, Dad considered wholly unpalatable. There was something curious about it. Purely out of concern for his own mental well being, he elected not to cogitate the ramifications. Dad was too proud to say anything to Aesop so he just endured the situation, hoping that it would get better.

As the days went by, Dad started losing weight and getting weak. Whenever he would try to sneak some real food out of the kitchen Cheu Dong would come down on him like a sack of bricks. Dad was powerless to get food for himself because squirrel hunting was not really practical in town. After about two weeks Dad finally had endured all he wanted of this little love nest and decided to make a run for it. So he slipped out one morning after Aesop left for work. He had three dollars that he saved from selling possums earlier that spring. He found an old bike with no tires somewhere in town and bought it for two bucks. He spent the remaining dollar on Twinkies and then hit the dusty trail.

It was a pretty good haul from Phlegmingsburg to New Hope and on bare metal rims it seemed even farther. But he took off riding with a level of determination that perhaps only a starving man can fully appreciate. He rode like the wind all day. Finally towards dark a car came up along side him. The metal rims of the old bike were screaming because he was really pounding those pedals trying to make some time. The car cut him off and stopped. It was Aesop.

"What in the world are you doing Adam?"

"I'm going home...so I can get something to eat!"

"What do you mean?"

"What I mean is that crazy gal you're married to has been feeding me nothing but stinking rutabaga for the last two weeks! *I hate rutabaga!* I've always hated rutabaga! And I always will hate rutabaga, now more than ever! The silly woman is trying to starve me to death. I'm not going to take it anymore!"

It was clear that Dad was extremely agitated. Aesop responded with a kindness fitting for the situation.

"Rutabaga? I hate rutabaga too! Come on son, lets go home."

Aesop helped my father to put his bike into the car and then they drove back to Phlegmingsburg. When they arrived Aesop read the Riot Act to Cheu Dong. He made her cook Dad a hot meal, without rutabaga, and then sat there and ate with him. Cheu Dong claimed she didn't know, that she was only trying to save money. She said that she liked rutabaga and she thought Dad did too. Dad was livid.

Dad was very happy when he finally got to go home. Even though the chores were admittedly difficult, at least he could eat. For a few weeks after that when Dad went hunting, he killed thirty squirrels at a time instead of his usual dozen or so. By the start of school he had regained most of his weight. Aesop apologized many times over the years. He always felt bad about having been the cause of Dad nearly starving to death.

Aesop and Cheu Dong finally split in 1941. Aesop supposedly filed for divorce when he discovered the true secret behind her grocery budget artistry. That is, he learned that she was exploiting local materials without his consent again: since November of 1929, virtually all meat products served by Cheu Dong at the family table had been courtesy of the Phlegmingsburg area stray dog population.

Chapter 13

A Bad Day in Hurlington

There usually comes a time in the career of a successful businessman when he must make the transition to a more effective mode of transportation in order to accommodate the growing demands of his schedule. That is, he finds himself continually needing to be in two or more places at the same time. The traditional American approach has been to take the step up to business-class aircraft. By the time my father had reached the age of forty, he and many of his associates were either at or approaching such a juncture.

Eventually most of them acquired airplanes of various configurations, generally starting with a modest single-engine plane like a Cessna 172. If they survived this stage, within a few years they might have graduated to a Beech Bonanza or a twin-engine plane in the Cessna 310 class. My father tested many of these technologies as well. However, after much deliberation he ultimately concluded that aircraft were an impractical transportation platform for his particular business application. Their capabilities were formidable, yet too specialized. Airplanes were good at getting somewhere far away quickly. However, after arrival they were essentially useless. That is, they excelled at going from one airport to another, but nowhere else. Plus they were expensive to operate and required constant maintenance. He needed a vehicle with the reliability and flexibility to be useful for all destinations. He needed the kind of mobility that could only be achieved with an automobile. But he still had to get there quickly.

Dad finally decided that the most fitting choice for his transportation requirements was the *high-performance sedan*. In reaching this conclusion he conducted exhaustive research of the literature. He talked to engineers. He wrote letters to car companies. He test drove scores of vehicles. Then, in the spring of 1967 he decided to purchase a brand-new, highly-modified Ford police sedan, equipped with a special 427-cubic inch V8-engine capable of generating at least 850 horsepower. The car had a maximum speed of approximately 225 miles per hour. Dad didn't want me to tell my mother, but we had this car *floated-out* on the turnpike many times.

An automobile is said to be floated-out when it reaches what can only be described as *take-off velocity*. This highly technical engineering term, also known as *stall speed,* refers to a critical point in the performance envelope of an aeronautical vehicle. It is the velocity at which air striking a body produces a lifting force exactly equal to the weight of said body. Below stall speed airplanes stay on the runway. Above stall speed they fly. The same general idea applies to cars as well, except the process is slightly more complicated.

Cars are not supposed to fly. They are supposed to roll. Propulsion is dependent upon the transfer of power to the road through the drive wheels. The transfer of power is a function of friction. The wheels must be firmly in contact with the road for friction to occur. As an automobile approaches take-off velocity, contact with the road, and thus friction, are reduced and the transfer of power becomes incomplete, causing a decrease in velocity. When this happens friction and velocity increase and the cycle is thus repeated in a positive-negative feedback loop as long as power is applied. It is an unavoidable chaotic property of automotive propulsion. To make a long story short, as a car reaches this critical speed it begins to surge and hop. If this phenomenon is handled improperly it can lead to catastrophe. But when managed appropriately, the car reaches a metastable point halfway between being airborne and spinning out of control. It is at this stage that the automobile is said to be *floated-out.*

According to retired law enforcement officers who wish to remain anonymous, they were aware of the car at the time, but they never learned the make, model, or even the color of the vehicle until the year 2000, via sealed records obtained under the *Freedom-of-Information Act* (curiously, the records were resealed after passage of the *Homeland Security Act*).

Dad was obviously very proud of this car. And he was also very passionate about its care. He meticulously maintained each and every mechanical component. He had to. At the speeds he normally operated the vehicle, it was essential for survival. One of the items of paramount concern was the routine changing of the engine oil. He changed oil at one-thousand mile intervals. Dad was a specialist in engine lubrication. However, just simply changing the oil was not enough. To truly optimize the process, the fresh oil had to be *driven-in* after each change.

This involved operating the vehicle in a complex series of stepped power levels for approximately one hour, and subsequently allowing the engine to cool completely by shutting it down for no fewer than eight hours. This procedure supposedly conditioned both the new oil and the metal surfaces within the engine. The theory was that by operating the engine under a specific pattern of loads, microfractures in the metal could be forced to expand and contract in a predicable way. When this happened, the last traces of the old oil would be *driven-out* and the new oil *driven-in*. As an added benefit, accumulated microscopic stresses in the metal, at the molecular level, would also be eliminated.

Driving-in a fresh change of oil eventually became a tremendous pleasure for Dad. It was how he relieved his own stress as well. It became something of a ritual that we both looked forward to. Over the course of an hour we would take the car from a slow idle around the suburbs to speeds in excess of 200 miles per hour on the turnpike. Afterwards, we would sometimes just drive around for hours on back roads in the country without any particular destination. Once I remember asking him where we were going. He replied:

"*Hopetown.*"

"Hopetown. Where's that?"

"See where the road goes out of sight over that hill up ahead?"

"Yes sir."

"It's beyond that."

A few minutes later, as we topped the referenced high point, I was expecting to observe houses, side streets, pedestrians, gas stations, grocery stores and so forth. Instead, there was just another rural scene. At first I was confused, but I soon caught on. I knew Dad was kidding in one way, but still, he was serious too.

"I thought you said we would be in Hopetown by now."

"No, I said that it was beyond this hill. Do you think we should keep on going? Or should we turn around and head for the house?"

"Well, how far is it to Hopetown?"

"Nobody knows."

"Have you ever been there?"

"No, not yet."

"Then why do you want to go there?"

"Everybody wants to go to Hopetown son."

"How long have you been looking for it?"

"For as long as I can remember."

"If you've never been there, how will you know what it looks like, how will you know if you're even there?"

"They say all you have to do is get close to it and you'll know."

"How close?"

"Ten miles. If you can get within ten miles of Hopetown, it is the same as being there."

"I guess we better keep going then."

"Good boy."

My father was so particular with his car that he categorically refused to allow anyone to work on it. He performed all routine maintenance and mechanical repairs himself. However, one day when it was raining, he took the car to a garage in Hurlington, Kentucky, to have the oil changed. That was literally all that they were supposed to do. Mom dropped us off later that afternoon to pick up the vehicle. But when we went into the shop there were four teenagers working on the car. They had the engine almost completely disassembled. The cylinder heads and intake manifold were laying in a pile on the greasy concrete floor. Understand that this was essentially a brand new, high-performance car. It had less than 6,000 miles on it. Dad said something to the effect of:

"What in the world are you doing to my car?" The boys were mute. The shop owner came out and claimed that he was a teacher at the local vocational school and these boys were in effect, in the middle of their final exam.

"But all I wanted was the oil changed." Dad said.

The shop owner reassured Dad that they would have the car back together in a couple of hours and for him not to worry, just come back later and everything would be okay. Since Mom had already left we just walked around for about three hours. When we got back to the shop, the car was finished and parked out in front. Dad went in to pay and the bill was over $150.00. He almost freaked out.

"All I wanted was the oil changed!" Dad repeatedly emphasized.

"Yes, I know, but we had to put on new head gaskets."

The details of how they settled up are unclear, but we finally got into the car and headed for home. But when we got to the edge of town the car started getting hot. It got real hot. Steam was blowing out of every conceivable place that it could on the engine. The hotter the car got the hotter Dad got. To the day he died, I never saw him as angry. Finally, he whipped the car around right in the middle of U.S. 41 and headed back to the garage, cursing and getting madder the entire way.

As we rounded the first curve on U.S. 41 in downtown Hurlington and closed in on the shop (which was on the second curve), with steam billowing from the car, and the engine barely running, the mechanic suddenly looked up and saw us coming. The guy immediately dropped his monkey wrench and ran around to the back of the station in a panic. Dad saw him do this so he adjusted the course of the automobile to cut him off. Inexplicably however, just as we pulled onto the lot, he screeched to halt and jumped out of the car and started chasing the guy around the station. The mechanic was a little weasely-looking guy but he was pretty quick. But I suppose anybody would be quick if they had a screaming, 250-pound, enraged, veins-popping-out-all-over-his-face, wild-man chasing them.

Onlookers quickly began to filter in from the ambient urban environment and loosely assemble around the station, moving with the unfolding spectacle as Dad chased the guy. Dad was screaming profanities and utterances that to this day I've never heard again, even in a modern PG-13 Hollywood movie. The mechanic was probably seeing his whole life flash before him. He ran into the garage and tried to pull the overhead door down but Dad was too cunning to be repelled by that. So the guy darted into the station again but quickly found himself pinned between the gum machine and the water fountain. He flitted around for several more seconds, narrowly eluding Dad's extremely robust, vice-like grip. It was truly a chase scene from Hell.

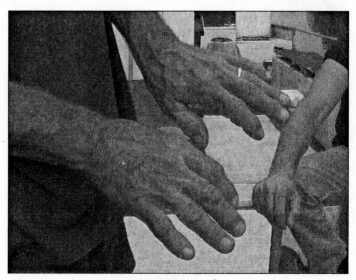

A grip to avoid.

Finally trapped between the brake fluid dispenser and the pneumatic tire changer, in desperation the mechanic picked up an empty Coke bottle and wielded it in a threatening manner. But this was a pathetic gesture because it was clear to all the witnesses that the guy would get said bottle rammed down his throat if he actually struck Dad with it. Ultimately however, Dad backed-off as his rationality returned to him. He assertively demanded that his money be refunded immediately and that his car be repaired correctly. The mechanic just nodded and kept saying "Okay...okay...no problem...okay..." The guy then launched into a ten-minute, teary confessional about how his life had been falling apart ever since he discovered that his wife was sneaking around with the nightshift foreman at the rubber factory. Dad just got a disgusted look on his face and then continued to taunt and demean the fellow for a protracted period, calling him a wide variety of unflattering terms, some of which I cannot remember, some I can, but all too coarse for this narrative.

The trade school teacher-mechanic and his students had ruined the engine by putting the head gaskets on backwards during the reassembly process. As a result, the engine got hot enough to fuse the pistons to the cylinder walls. Dad subsequently had a brand new engine installed in the car by a factory certified technician and the trade school teacher had to pay many ducats, all by court order. I've always wondered what kind of grade the students got on their exam. It was another valuable life lesson for me because I learned how helpful a well-drafted letter from your lawyer can be. I also learned that it's probably better to just directly run somebody over with a car than to try to jump out and chase them down on foot.

Chapter 14

The Deer Problem

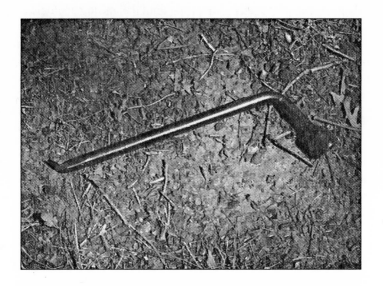

Back in the early-sixties a few White-Tailed deer *(Odocoileus virginianus)* started to appear in some parts of western Kentucky. Before that there were essentially no deer in the area. This was because in most parts of the Midwest, virtually all deer, and about every other palatable species of wildlife, had been devoured by hungry people prior to the beginning of the 20th century.

Presumably with the only best of intentions in mind, the Department of Fish & Wildlife started releasing deer in selected areas in the years following World War II. But it took decades for the deer to multiply and disperse sufficiently to be seen by average people.

My father visited forests nearly every day in the pursuit of squirrels or other game starting in 1923 at the age of four. Additionally, because of his career in the energy production industry, he continued to visit wildlife inhabited areas practically every day until 1996. This being because coal mines and oil fields are located mostly in rural areas.

However, he never actually encountered a deer until he was forty-seven years old. That is, for a substantial fraction of his hunting life, encounters with meteors were probably more common than with deer. So when a sighting did occur in the area it was tantamount in both rarity and socio-cultural impact perhaps to a train-wreck, an appearance by a former governor, or even an Elvis drive-by.

Rumors of sporadic deer sightings started to filter into the collective folklore of Kentucky huntsmen in the early- to mid-sixties. These accounts slowly increased in frequency and detail until the phenomenological lines crossed for Dad and I in the spring of 1966. That's when we had our first sighting. It occurred on State Highway 26, near Hubnerville. We came to a place where dozens of vehicles were stopped on the side of the road. All of the motorists were out of their cars standing next to the guardrail, apparently looking at something in a field. Back then it was no big deal for people to pull over their automobiles and start aggressively gawking at some random phenomenon, especially if other motorists were doing the same.

It was as if America was one giant nature park and it was just understood that we each possessed the unalienable right to obstruct traffic and generate opportunities for personal injury lawyers. Dad stopped the car and we got out. There were three deer grazing in a field about 300 yards from the highway. They were so far away it was quite difficult to see them. Still, it was such a phenomenal sight for the period that the people were not only in absolute total amazement, but also willing to risk severe traffic-related mutilation along a congested major highway to experience it.

The deer were near enough however, for me to be able to see their faces when they were staring back at us. I thought about the movie *Bambi*. I recall being curious about what they were thinking. I have often wondered if they had any idea that they were going to be the progenitors of the millions of deer that now infest virtually the entire North American continent. Who can say? Chances are that they probably did not contemplate this or any other meaningful concept, at least none that we would be able to significantly appreciate. Likewise, they also probably never stopped to consider the thousands of human fatalities, millions of personal injuries, and hundreds of billions of dollars in property damage that was going to be caused by their offspring in the years ahead.

After about 1968, unplanned encounters between automobiles and re-introduced deer started to become increasingly common. However, during this initial transitional period, deer were still a tremendous novelty to many people. In fact, it was considered a windfall of the highest order to actually strike and kill one with an automobile.

Any deer that got ran over back then never remained on the roadway for more than a few minutes before some ambitious citizen would come along and snatch it up. I am not sure if this phenomenon was purely a function of the novelty of the deer, or if it was a manifestation of the pervasive Old-School mentality still firmly rooted in the general population. It probably was a combination of the two. Times have changed however. These days virtually no one harvests road kill deer, nor do most people consider it fortuitous to collide with one.

Dad often elatedly discussed the biological merits of deer and professed his goal to eventually procure a suitable specimen when the circumstances allowed, his expressed motivation being related to the irrefutable fact that deer represented a level of culinary delicacy far in excess of any other domestic wildlife species. He also made repeated reference to the idea that a deer constituted at least one-hundred squirrels in equivalent crude tissue mass. That is, a single deer could render the sustenance represented by a month's worth of squirrel hunting. The savings in ammunition alone amounted to a staggering sum.

The problem was however, finding the necessary time to hunt down the shy creatures. This situation was frustrating for Dad. That is, unlike squirrels, deer were extremely scarce, ran away when approached, and never climbed trees, making hunting them a completely different proposition than what he was accustomed to. In squirrel hunting the denominations were admittedly smaller with respect to the prey, but the time investment required per hunt was correspondingly less rigorous. So Dad continued to focus his efforts solely on squirrels because his on-the-go lifestyle was unsuited to deer hunting. But fortune's fickle wheel eventually presented him with an unexpected opportunity late one night when he was driving home from Elizabethtown on the Western Kentucky Parkway.

As he was forging his way through the foggy night, he suddenly encountered a semi-tractor trailer that was stopped along the shoulder. It had struck a deer. There were several other vehicles stopped and the drivers were standing around debating over how the meat should be divided.

As Dad walked up to them, it was apparent that a mildly disorganized ado was in the process of evolving into a full-blown impasse. This all ended rather abruptly once Dad got a whiff of the blood however. Because when he did it triggered some primal instinct within him ultimately resulting in his receiving the major share of the meat.

That is, as the other drivers exchanged their crude gestures of forensic posturing, he simply dragged the mutilated carcass off the road and started dismantling it workmanlike, in what amounted to total darkness. He arrived home just before dawn. In his possession was a large, irregularly shaped mass of venison wrapped in a blood-soaked grocery sack. The dark red meat was generously supplemented with gravel, soil, hair, bone fragments, and a faint odor of diesel fuel. And Dad didn't look much different. He too was covered in blood and had what appeared to be fragments of raw sausage stuck in his hair and on his eyebrows. His hands were scratched up and his fingernails were packed with macerated cartilage and bone spall.

But he was absolutely beaming with pride. That sack of meat was the greatest thing he had ever seen. Dad then avidly recounted every detail of how he had argued with nine other travelers to achieve the lion's share. No one present at the scene had a knife so Dad ultimately was responsible for what is arguably the single greatest *thinking outside the box* incident to ever occur at a deer road kill site.

That is, he is now widely considered by those who keep up with such things, to be the first person in history to skin, gut, and pry a deer carcass into easily manageable pieces using a lug wrench from a 1965 Ford Galaxy. The unparalleled genius of this act was apparently not lost on the witnesses that night either. Because for his contribution he received approximately half of the meat. This included a front quarter, a rear quarter, and the tenderloin. Segments of the head, neck, ribs, and remaining quarters were distributed to the other motorists.

Once he got home, Dad spent the rest of the morning cleaning the dirt and hair out of the meat. Then as requiring failed, he did compel my mother to cook it. First she fried it (it was awful). Then he made her pressure cook some (ditto). Then she broiled some in the oven (no help either). But Dad ate it all.

However, he eventually freely admitted that he had been encumbered with a significant misconception in his belief that *Odocoileus virginianus* was the most palatable species on the North American continent. His summary appraisal was that venison seemed equivalent in taste and general edibility to the boar meat that was sometimes served at the family table during his childhood. In other words, it was the bottom of the barrel, the lowest of the low. It was better left alone (boar meat is noted for its extraordinarily pungent, repulsive, gamy aroma and flavor).

Of the fifty pounds of meat that Dad brought home that morning, our dog Sparky, ended up dining on approximately forty-eight. And he wasn't that wild about it either. Needless to say, this was the last time Dad ever experimented with deer or the cuisine associated therewith.

Ironically, despite the fact that most domestic venison tastes like hell, by the early seventies deer hunting had become a widespread pursuit among the male population of the Midwest. Today, the burgeoning deer population has driven the evolution of a fantastic variety of socio-cultural phenomena and propagated a broad spectrum economic and commercial spin-off effects. Chief among these being a multi-billion dollar sport-hunting industry, and a ten-fold increase in the number of automotive body repair shops.

Chapter 15

The Dynamiter

Back in the days when we were all still on the same side, my father maintained an extensive and completely legal inventory of high explosives that he deployed in a variety of mining and energy-recovery applications. One of these endeavors was the "shooting" of oil wells. Typically, Dad and his highly proficient team of oil well technicians would perform such a procedure on at least one well per week. And like many of Dad's pursuits, it was an art that was continually evolving as he made new discoveries almost on a daily basis. Oil well shooting was an established method used to loosen-up the rock formation in a new oil well, or to revitalize an older well, both scenarios intended to stimulate production. The theory was that by fracturing the natural rock formation, the rate at which the oil flows from the reservoir into the well could be increased. It is analogous perhaps to the difference in the rate of blood loss one would expect between a simple stab wound to the neck and the same wound after having a firecracker shoved into it and detonated.

Liquid nitroglycerin was used for oil well shooting by those who originally invented the practice. Containers of the substance would be lowered into the well on a cable and then set off with a blasting cap. Obviously this practice had some problems. The slightest slip-up could, and often did, result in instant death for those involved. After all the liquid nitroglycerin users were killed or mutilated, someone got the bright idea of trying gelatin explosives to do the job. Gelatin explosives consist of a solid, clay-like material wrapped with a paper casing. Gelatin explosives are at least an order of magnitude safer than nitroglycerin. Translation: they generally never detonate until you want them to.

This was a major improvement, in that nitroglycerin would generally *always* detonate when you didn't want it to. This often happened at the most inopportune times as well, say, like when it was in the trunk of your Studebaker Hawk while you were driving over to your girlfriend's house. And even when you did survive, it was never easy explaining to your date why there was a spare tire hanging out of your ass.

Gelatin explosives are generally referred to as *dynamite*. But the sticks they used on oil wells were four feet long and six inches in diameter. These would be lowered into the well with a fuse and primer attached. After they were put into place at the exact depth, small chunks of lead wool would be dropped on top of the charge to provide confinement, thereby concentrating more of the explosive energy into the rock formation instead of up the pipe.

Lead wool looks a lot like steel wool. It has a consistency similar to heavy modeling clay and is surprisingly workable. It comes in big bundles and it must be ripped off and formed into manageable masses that can be dropped down the well. This was a task in which Dad often let me participate. We would sometimes spend hours putting the lead wool into the well, making sure everything was perfect. After the lead wool was in place, Dad would light the fuse and we would all run away. Because the fuse could be hundreds of feet in length, it sometimes took several minutes for the shot to finally detonate. This was the most suspenseful part of the endeavor.

Firing explosives in an oil well (which is a hole in solid rock that has been lined with steel pipe), in principle is no different than firing a cannon. Any material in the hole above the charge becomes a projectile. This material typically consists of, you guessed it, lead wool, but there would be ample supplies of rock fragments, crude oil, and salt water ejected also. So what's the catch? If the pipe lining the well was improperly bonded to the surrounding bedrock, it could sometimes be propelled out of the hole at a very high velocity, like a missile, potentially up to several hundred feet in length.

If any part of this ballistically energetic pipe were to land on you, or your friends, it could be very problematical, with results not unlike the spare tire analogy referenced above. Out in an open field it was a pretty straightforward affair. If the pipe was propelled from the hole one could see it coming and get out of its way. But in the woods one couldn't see where it was going to come down. The only recourse was to crawl under the nearest truck or bulldozer and cringe. When a shot went right however, the well took on the appearance of a geyser for a few seconds.

The spray would go at least 200 to 300 feet high and would be shaded in varying degrees of white or black depending on ratio of oil to water in the well. For several seconds after the shot there would be a rain of debris for a substantial radius around the well. We got hit by something nearly every time.

The Demonstration

After an oil well shot there would always be a few sticks of dynamite left over. If there was not another well to shoot immediately, these had to be stored in a refrigerator or they could become unstable. If they could not be stored they had to be disposed of. Disposal of course meant blowing the living hell out of something just for the fun of it. Dad tried to share the experience as much as possible. He would often conduct seminars on exploding techniques for friends and associates. This would typically involve moving a large boulder a specified distance or uprooting an old stump, both intended to demonstrate the power of dynamite. However, one time in the middle of the woods somewhere in Muhlenburgh County, Kentucky, he was unable to conveniently locate a distinct object worthy of dynamiting, so he simply placed the explosives directly on the surface of the ground.

Some of the region's most influential entrepreneurs were present that day. It was like a Who's Who of the Golden Age of Interior Basin petroleum exploration history. The Midwestern oil business has always attracted talented people from a wide range of professions. The oil business may be their second, third, or fourth major career. They are often highly educated and very successful in other fields. People who have called themselves oilmen include doctors, lawyers, engineers, scientists, politicians, industrialists, salesmen, journalists, educators, and clergymen. As diverse as their backgrounds are, they all share one very important characteristic: a fascination with petroleum, and the art of finding and selling it for a profit.

Among the players present that day was one of Kentucky's most famous Country & Western singers, *Starke Howell;* also in attendance was the world-renowned chiropractor *Sharpe Polk*; the highly celebrated anti-trust prosecutor *Peerce Tervale*; the celebrated Hollywood dermatologist, *Wyatt Scales*; and a no-nonsense old fellow, *Hart Knox*, who was said to have been the founder of an innovative business school bearing his name. They were all good friends of my father.

After Dad got the charge prepared, everyone gathered around and there was a moment of silence. Then he lit the fuse and we all ran away. The rowdy laughter of these oil magnates echoed through the woods as they ran (with the exception of Mr. Knox). I was too scared to laugh, perhaps rightfully so, because the charge detonated far sooner than planned. It was the loudest noise I've ever heard in my life. Huge tree trunks, limbs, root masses, and clumps of soil fell all around us (thank God there was no lead wool this time). We didn't stop running until we reached the trucks. The men grabbed some homemade corn liquor, and we returned to ground zero. What we discovered was shocking. A grove of sycamore trees had been transformed into a debris plain of fractured wood and clay balls. There were some shattered trunks still upright farther back, but the inner hundred yards was total devastation.

At the center of this zone we found an elevated ring of heaved earth. Beyond that was a crater about forty feet across and about perhaps eight feet deep, with a little bit of muddy water in the bottom. A vaporous cloud of superheated ionized plasma lingered above the water. Limbs in the canopy around the perimeter of the crater were broken and twisted. Roots hung in tree tops. Trees as far as seventy-five feet away from the rim of the crater were leaning. The men just stood around for over an hour and vigorously drank moonshine. Between sips they stared at the crater and told war stories.

It was very educational for me. The explosion kicked up a spectrum of geological oddities and everybody also seemed intrigued by the richness of the otherwise invisible subterranean biology that had been exposed in the crater. Dad theorized that since it was in a swampy area, the crater would become a small pond and therefore strengthen the health and diversity of the local ecosystem.

This was the general gist of the collective thought on the subject, except for one detractor, Peerce Tervale I think, who cautioned that a common opossum, *Didelphis virginianus,* walking along at night might accidentally fall into the crater pond and drown, a misfortune that otherwise would not have occurred, thus constituting *a bad thing.* But this proposition was sharply countered by the argument that opossums are essentially the lowest form of multicellular life on the planet and should be drowned anyway. Ultimately however, they all concurred on the notion that despite the drowning risk ramifications, overall the crater *was a good thing.* It was a special moment. Dad was proud of this magnificent crater he had created. So was I.

Shooting dynamite in the woods however, can have at least one major problem associated with it, creating water hazards for inattentive possums notwithstanding: it makes squirrel hunting more difficult for a few days afterwards. If Dad knew he was going to shoot some dynamite in a patch of woods, he would always try to go in a day beforehand and aggressively harvest each and every squirrel. He would then store the meat in a refrigerator or icebox until he was ready to cook it. When everything was right, he would build a fire at a convenient blast crater, then cook the squirrels and eat them.

It was a great time to be alive and Dad knew it. It was a time when a man could go out and drill an oil well, kill a few bushels of squirrels, blow a hell of a big hole in the ground, and then sit around, get drunk, tell war stories, eat to his heart's content, and nobody would bother him: no Police SWAT teams, no Hazardous Materials squads, no EPA enforcement teams; no ATF, no FBI. Just freedom. Pure human freedom. Those were the days. And think of it, out there today, so many decades later, there are vast numbers of fish, frogs, ducks, and other aquatic organisms thriving in Dad's blast crater ponds, perhaps watching an opossum in the terminal throes of drowning, that otherwise would never have been able to do so.

McCasoway Pond, somewhere in Kentucky

Chapter 16

Valley of the Bloodsuckers

In the summer of 1967, Dad was working on a major coal deal in Butler County, Kentucky. The most challenging part of this enterprise, logistically and economically, was the effort to conduct a core drilling program to accurately determine the amount of coal reserves in the two-thousand acre project area. The land in question was covered by thick hardwood forest and located in one of the more geographically treacherous parts of the state.

The absence of sizeable towns, the inordinate topographic relief, and poor quality of access roads, among other things, made conducting drilling operations there difficult at best, and virtually impossible at worst. The extreme remoteness of the area also attracted a variety of rugged individualists, loners, and homesteaders who pursued happiness in sporadic little pockets amid the hills and draws, most of whom did so without even the most basic amenities, not to mention the ubiquitous absence of indoor plumbing, electricity, and telephones.

One of these hearty individuals was a character by the name of Milo Falconbridge. Butler County has always been known for its rugged country and rugged people. But even the salty citizens of Butler County tended to afford Milo Falconbridge a wide berth. Not only was Milo no ordinary individual, but he was also hitched to a full-blooded Cherokee gal who was wilder than a bobcat. Milo never explained how this betrothal came to be, but anyone who ever cared to think about it would surely conclude that it was a match made in Heaven. She went by the name Cool Breeze, or at least that's what Milo called her. Since they were husband and wife in accordance with all applicable statutes in the Commonwealth of

Kentucky, presumably her full legal name would have been *Cool Breeze Falconbridge.*

Cool Breeze was anything but like what her name suggested. She was hot-blooded as a mink. She had coal-black hair, fiery brown eyes, and her skin was hued like polished hickory heart. She was beautiful. She was as beautiful as a twenty-eight year old wild woman could be. Her beauty was comparable to that of some of the ladies that used to be featured in *Irrational Geographic Magazine* before it became Environmentally Correct.

Her beauty was only part of the story. She was rough too. She was the wiry kind of rough. Back in those days it was called *being rougher than a cob.* She weighed around 110 pounds and stood about five-foot-four.

Pound for pound, she could probably have whipped the living hell out of about six out of ten men on the planet. In my estimation, only the most determined and seasoned men of her weight class would have been able to weather her for more than a few rounds of regulation sparring. She had no illusions concerning her appearance either. Never did I observe her wearing makeup, jewelry, or fancy clothes. Her wardrobe seemed to consist of little more than a few pairs of blue jeans and some old army shirts.

She always wore cowboy boots and had a Bowie knife in a scabbard strapped on her hip. She kept the cows milked, the traps checked, the trot lines ran, and all the game gutted. She attended the farm chores, kept the sawmill going, and could rebuild a Mack transmission about as easily as other women might powder their noses, or adjust their brassiere straps.

Dad first met Milo Falconbridge purely by chance while squirrel hunting near Milo's forest compound. Dad was about five miles from the nearest road when he heard what he thought was an old John Deere tractor coming up the draw. It was Milo Falconbridge dragging a log back to cut up for firewood. But it soon became clear that he was not driving a John Deere tractor.

Dad quickly recognized it as an improvised motor vehicle fabricated from an airplane engine (with the propeller removed), a war-surplus Sherman tank, and a few other odds-and-ends, all held together with welded billet and strong nylon rope. Positioned directly behind the turret was a Pratt & Whitney R-2800 air cooled radial engine. Dad immediately recognized it as the standard powerplant of the Republic P-47 (an American World War-II fighter plane). Milo was sitting in a plush Captain's chair welded to the side of the tank. Dad was instantly fascinated by this extraordinary machine and the person operating it.

It turned out that Milo was an undiscovered mechanical genius. But he had no formal education of any kind. The closest thing to schooling in his experience was the mechanic training he'd received in the army during the Korean War. Milo lived with his Native American wife, in a log cabin nestled on a knoll surrounded by woods as far as the eye could see in every direction.

It was miles to the nearest improved road. The only way in to Milo's homestead was along a precarious, muddy logging trail that wound over hill and dale, crossed numerous creeks, ran for better than a mile up the middle of one creek, and switched-back at least ten times along the way in order to negotiate the formidable, jutty mountains.

Human beings were evidently such a rarity in those parts back then that when two people crossed paths in the woods it was generally deemed sufficient justification for an impromptu celebration, or at least a pause. They would always cease and desist with their hunting, or laboring, or whatever they were doing, and engage in animated conversation for a while. Typically, at some point in the dialog, one or both parties would produce a container of strong spirits, invariantly decanted from previously-owned half-gallon glass orange-juice jars, and toasts would be exchanged. This is the probable scenario when Dad and Milo first met.

Milo informed Dad that his wife was preparing breakfast back at the ranch and offered him a plate, if he didn't mind riding on the improvised log-dragger. Dad thanked him and climbed onto the tank, bringing with him his shotgun and sack full of freshly slain squirrels. When they arrived at Milo's house, Dad was instantly overwhelmed by the spectacle that lay before him. He stood in rapt silence for several minutes, trying to take it all in. Milo never said a word. He just watched Dad and the reaction he was having.

Milo didn't get many visitors. Perhaps a few in-laws would occasionally filter in from the ambient ecology, stay until the fatback and buttermilk ran out, and then drift off as suddenly as they had arrived, never seeming to even notice, much-less actually appreciate Milo's enduring passion. So it was a special treat for him to be able to share the sum total of his life's labor with a kindred spirit.

What was it that Milo was so proud of and my father so fascinated by? Filling nearly all of the cleared space around Milo's compound were scores of bizarre mechanical apparatus of various configurations. Some were clearly intended to be mobile. Others conveyed the absolute static nature of their habit, if not their precise function. Still others seemed to occupy a queer transitional state between the potential for locomotion and perhaps what seemed almost like a pathological obsession to remain sessile.

The only thread of commonality coursing through this remarkable collection was that each individual item was a more-or-less jury-rigged hulk assembled from assorted cannibalized components encompassing a wide range of domestic technologies. Perhaps a scientist would have viewed it as a kind of junkyard universe that had given rise to life by random self-assembly of available parts. Yet most people would have probably perceived it more as a Frankenstein's menagerie of the mechanically macabre. But what ever one would have called it, Dad was profoundly impressed.

It is likely that Dad, who was a trained petroleum geologist possessing an understanding of both the practical and technical merits of the theory of biological evolution, recognized an undercurrent of Darwinism resonating in this freakish metallic pageant. There were many devices that seemed to have been interesting ideas initially, but had not stood the test of time, so to speak, and therefore could be viewed as evolutionary dead-ends.

One of the contraptions that easily warranted inclusion in this class of *aberrant mutations* was what appeared to be an old wrecker, also with a Pratt & Whitney R-2800 airplane engine mounted on it. But this is where the similarity to the log-dragger ended, the primary difference being that the airplane engine on the wrecker still had its propeller. A cursory summing-up of the situation left little doubt to a reasonable person: this device was intended to be at least in principle, a propeller-driven wrecker, but for one reason or another it had been somewhat less than successful. As it was later recounted to Dad, extreme triaxial vibration of a brutal, almost inhuman degree, during the test phase, was the principal reason that the propeller-wrecker had never been able to move significantly under its own power; this notwithstanding the fact that operating such a device in the middle of a forest obviously had some inescapable, although understandably as-yet unvocalized ramifications in terms of practicality.

After all, the four-bladed propeller was at least twelve feet in diameter. It would have been suicide to have even tried to start the damn thing, much less taxi it anywhere near Milo's place, driveway or no driveway. There wasn't a twelve-foot wide space between any trees, anyplace, this side of U.S. 41. And to top it off, if a person were actually going to use it to tow a car, well, let's put it this way: have you ever seen what a beer can looks like after it has been ran over by a lawn mower?

Another glaring evolutionary dead-end seemed to be some kind of a marine vessel conformed from the stripped-down chassis of an early-to mid-fifties Buick. Fifty-five gallon steel drums were welded to the automobile undercarriage, ostensibly to provide the necessary floatation. Paddle wheels were attached to the rear axel in lieu of conventional automobile wheels. Steering was the courtesy of a pair of tailfins from a 1957 Packard that had been retrofitted onto the front axel, replacing the factory wheels.

Again, it seemed to be a completely logical, even inevitable marriage of propulsion concepts, whose time may have indeed come. Yet equally manifest was the cruel reality that should anyone ever be foolish enough to attempt to operate this device in a body of water, that person would undoubtedly be exposing themselves to extreme peril at best and certain death (with a high potential for severe post-mortem mutilation) at worst.

As my father toured this graveyard of the Industrial Revolution from a Parallel Universe, a very subtle but clearly recognizable pattern slowly became emergent. That is, in the overall view of Milo's collection, there appeared to be a sporadic, yet consistent progression toward greater sophistication and functionality through time. Near the end of the line Dad noted a fully operational sawmill that had been fabricated from parts of an old farm tractor, some refrigerators, and a dump truck.

Just past the sawmill was a fully operational trash compactor assembled from a bulldozer blade, a Packard engine, and two Russian phone booths. But parked at the very end of the line off to itself, was a fairly neat looking one-ton International truck with what appeared to be a drilling rig set-up mounted on the bed. Dad was amazed by what he was told about the device.

Milo had serendipitously constructed a more-or-less state-of-the-art, compressed-air rotary drilling rig utilizing scrap components he had collected from every war-surplus depot, junkyard, and municipal landfill this side of the Ozarks. It had a rear differential from a 1947 Mercury as a power head. The deck engine was from a 1961 Bonneville. The air compressor had been salvaged from a Swordfish-class submarine.

Overall, it was a very trim and straightforward setup. Milo claimed that he built it expressly to explore for water on his farm. A dependable supply of potable water had been chronically elusive so he constructed the drilling rig to help expedite the endeavor. The rig had enabled him to narrow the search for the best spot to install a permanent well. He and Cool Breeze had subsequently dug a well over 30-feet deep using shovels and pick-axes.

Milo continued the tour by leading Dad on a leisurely pass through the barn and environs appurtenant thereto. A couple of cows were in there, but most of the space was consumed by even more techno-industrial contrivances of various species. These included many smaller devices, or what appeared to be various household appliances, striking electronic mechanisms, or items more or less solely intended to enhance life's pleasure.

The most obvious of these was a fully operational, two-story high distillery/brewery set-up. Cool Breeze was attending it even as Dad passed. Perhaps for convenience, or some other reason, there was also a fully functional grill set-up mounted on the side of the main boiler for the distillery. Cool Breeze was filling a carboy of ale from one of the vats and cooking a rasher of sammin patties at the same time. Of all the sensory overloading that occurred in my many subsequent visits to the distillery/ barn, the one thing that stood out most was its poignant aromatic signature. It seemed to be the combined odors of fermenting grain, burning sugar, deep-fried onion rings, spilled diesel fuel, and day-old cow manure, a pungent mixture not that dissimilar to what one encounters near the midway at the annual 4-H fair.

In the back corner of the barn were several hundred 55-gallon steel drums, stacked two and three-high. Some were marked with alphanumeric character combinations like "SAE 30" and "SAE 90," clearly indicating their contents to be highly-refined petroleum products for various applications. But the majority of the barrels were marked only with the letters "DDT." When asked about this, Milo indicated that he had swerved into a good deal on the DDT and just couldn't pass it up. He claimed that because their expiration dates were up, he was able to acquire 608 drums of the insecticide from an Alabama jobber for what amounted to seven-cents per barrel. He had emptied the contents into some old semi trailers behind the barn so that he could have the barrels available for his sundry research projects. He said he really didn't care about the DDT, he just wanted the drums.

They made excellent general-purpose containers. They also of course played a very important roie in the fermentation of organic matter used in the production of various strong spirits. Traces of DDT left in the drums helped cut down on maggot infestations, something that evidently can be a major problem for farmstead distilling/brewing operations. Dad just nodded as this was explained.

It was like he was taking it all in routinely, as though he understood and was totally familiar with the concept as a whole:

"...maggot infestation, oh yeah, been there, done that, um hmm, go on..."

What was really going on is that the cogs in my father's head were turning. This was exactly what he had needed for his Butler County project: a local guy who was familiar with the territory, whose expertise spanned a wide range of disciplines, who was a good trouble-shooter, and could get the job done quickly and cheaply (and could spot a good deal on surplus pesticides when he saw it). Sure he was a little eccentric, but hey, nobody's perfect. Again, it was like a match made in Heaven.

Dad asked Milo if he'd like to hire-out the drilling rig to explore for coal. Milo admitted he'd never considered it before, but that he was willing to at least try it. Without ever seeing the rig operate, Dad cut a deal with him right there on the spot, they shook on it and the game was afoot. It turned out to be a resounding success. The rig was fast and worked more or less flawlessly. Together, Dad and Milo proceeded to drill hundreds of test holes over the course of the summer.

Since I was out of school on summer break, Mom made Dad take me with him to Butler County each day. I spent a lot of time there, sometimes from dawn till midnight, six days a week. After dark we'd build a bonfire in an effort to dissuade the hordes of poisonous snakes, annoying packs of coyotes, and the ubiquitous legions of bloodsucking mosquitoes.

Bufo americanas

During the day when my father and Milo were operating the rig, I'd go hunting with my .22 rifle, shoot frogs in a creek with my bow and arrow, or do all kinds of other things that a typical 11-year old boy found interesting. That is, there were always plenty of rock cliffs to explore, bird nests to rob, and crawdad holes into which I could to drop firecrackers.

If Dad could keep me supplied with ammo and a couple of packs of Twinkies, I would stay out of everybody's hair for hours at a time. We also had this system going where I would bag a couple squirrels when possible before showing up back at the rig around 11:00 a.m. If I got some squirrels Dad would skin them out and toss them on the fire. If I didn't get any, he would still have time to stroll out and pop off a few with his shotgun, then get back and cook them for lunch. Therefore, the majority of the squirrels we ate were provided by Dad. This was because my success at squirrel hunting was generally marginal at best. First, I was not exactly as graceful as I needed to be, and second, squirrel hunting with a .22 is somewhat challenging, even for a good marksman. The squirrels must be sitting almost perfectly still for a .22 to be effectively deployed against them.

Squirrels only sit that still if the hunter exercises stealth of the most rigorous degree. Stealth of that intensity requires extreme patience and temperament, virtues generally not always as highly developed in pre-teen males as we would like, and for me personally, remain more than a little problematical even to this day. When my ammo supply started to get low I would generally fall back to my bow and arrow. This protocol eventually helped me to acquire a reasonable degree of skill at striking bird-sized targets inside a fifty-foot radius. In fact, I was far more successful at shooting frogs or fish with a bow and arrow than I was at squirrel hunting with a rifle. Since there were miles of creeks surrounding the Falconbridge compound, aquatic fauna ultimately constituted a significant fraction of the total seared animal tissues that we consumed that summer.

At other times when I was low on ammunition, I would remain at the compound and assist Cool Breeze with various routine farm chores. That summer I slopped pigs, fed chickens, watered horses, hoed potatoes, harvested rutabagas, scraped floating slag off vats of fermenting beer, and used a crowbar to pry mutilated cow femurs out of an industrial meat grinder, as well as an extensive assortment of other exciting and highly educational tasks.

Actually, I found most of these remarkable endeavors to be quite enjoyable. Each day seemed to bring new and interesting challenges. My efforts did not go unnoticed. The reduction in workload for Cool Breeze was both significant and greatly appreciated. Somewhere along the way, she and I began to cultivate a genuine rapport. She eventually took a deep, maternal-liking to me. And naturally, I liked her as well.

As our friendship grew stronger she began to open up and become less stoic in her outward formalities. For example, she told me her family just called her "Breezy." And her sense of humor soon started to emerge as well, because she kidded me frequently about how I must have Indian blood in my veins, saying my budding skills with the bow and arrow could be explained in no other way.

With my labor now making a measurable difference, the chores became sufficiently caught up such that there was a little spare time each day for pursuing some of the rugged felicities of country living. Breezy seemed to particularly enjoy using this time to help me improve my sporting skills. For example, she often conducted highly spirited archery seminars that always seemed to culminate in frantic, go-for-broke shooting matches.

These basically consisted of seeing who could kill the most toads (species: *Bufo americanas*) in the barn lot via a sporadic series of very intensive five-minute heats, carefully metered by a stopwatch she carried with her everywhere. Breezy was pretty good at this, easily dispatching the lumpy vermin at distances of up to forty feet and sometimes beyond. Slowly over the summer however, with her sagacious coaching, she helped me to refine my skills to the point that I surpassed her.

This being outwardly manifested in my ability to handily prevail in total toad casualties inflicted. The climax occurred the day I filled a two-gallon bucket with the unattractive amphibians in only 19 minutes and 7 seconds. It was one of her proudest moments, and mine too. These heady days seemed to bring a dimension to her life that she needed desperately. And most importantly, it made her happy.

Sometime during this magical period, as a gesture of true friendship, she painstakingly hand-crafted for me an authentic Cherokee warrior's knife scabbard, quiver, moccasins, headband, and snakeskin loincloth. However, there was a singular condition attached to their bestowment. She would not allow me to simply keep them as mere curiosities. That is, in order to posses them permanently, I had to wear them. *I had to wear them for her.*

Therefore, purely as a courtesy of respect (and to make her happy), I did this unhesitantly, and proudly. With my Bowie knife in the scabbard, my arrows in the quiver, and my trusty bow clutched in my hand, I became a fully operational instrument of Indian mayhem. Just about the time that I was starting to genuinely appreciate how good I appeared in these cool new Indian garments, much to my surprise, and ultimate profound fascination, I found myself instantly distracted.

Apparently, when Breezy finally observed me freshly outfitted in the authentic Native American fashions, she became irresistibly compelled to adorn herself in traditional attire as well. She quickly stole away to the cabin and returned less than two minutes later. Not unexpectedly, I was literally rendered speechless by the sheer scope of her sudden transformation. And naturally, I couldn't help noticing how much better she looked in her Indian outfit than I did in mine.

Over the days and weeks ahead I wore my special attire both in a practical capacity during hunting expeditions, and also while prosecuting a rich array of antic presentations expressly created for her entertainment. These latter theatrics took many arcane forms. Some involved little more than me prowling madly around the compound scouting for mock buffalo. Others employed demonstrations of complex engineering theory, such as a pair of dugout canoes upon which I intermittently toiled with great fervor. I also recall performing both an eclectic suite of traditional Native American ritual medicine dances, and a few avant garde interpretations of my own composition.

However, the irrepressible influence of modern Hollywood cinema and television eventually propelled an unanticipated collateral intertwinement of the ambient Native American context with the motifs of *Tarzan of the Apes, Jungle Jim,* and *Mutual of Omaha's Wild Kingdom,* to produce a revolutionary new species of abstract, hybrid wilderness character: *Wild Monkey-Boy of the Trees.*

Breezy found this soubriquet quite compelling, even quaint, but ultimately preferred to call me *Kills Many Toads.* I remember scurrying through the arboreal canopy over the compound, cavorting, swinging, pouncing, and leaping like a wild juvenile primate as she watched with concentrated interest from below, continually cheering and chanting optimistic slogans. I also recall how I wrestled a pig in the pond, tied a rope around it, dragged it onto the shore with an old Land Rover, loaded it into a wooden crate, and affixed a radio transmitter to its neck.

Breezy seemed particularly fond of my rendition of Tarzan's famous jungle yell. This was totally outside of her experience and she found it strangely compelling, quickly mastering the subtleties of its harmonic nuance far more keenly than I, and eventually adding novel eurhythmic elements of her own improvisation. Suddenly the forest was alive with a rare genre of melodious, Utopian resonance that cannot be described purely via the written word.

As time went by, the subject matter of my impromptu boondock-vignettes became more sophisticated and historically correct, eventually culminating in detailed reenactments of many important events of Indian societal significance, such as the signing of the *Treaty of Tellico* on October 27, 1805, and *Custer's Last Stand*, among others. The phenomenon took on a unique and untranslatable intercultural-thespian gestalt that probably will never occur again in the history of mankind. And I was there. I lived it. If a committee of alien historians from the future ever come back to clarify certain cultural mysteries of the human race, I am sure that I will be thoroughly deposed on this matter.

Breezy and I continued to enjoy these special sessions unabated until one afternoon when Dad and Milo returned a little early from the project site. My father was suddenly and profoundly surprised when he observed me as I was stalking around the compound fully regaled in the nifty Indian gear, including war paint, trying to kill rats with my Bowie knife.

I guess for a moment he thought it was an uprising. He immediately commanded me to put on my regular clothes. He said something to the effect of:

"Get your damn pants back on before the chiggers eat you alive!" and, *"Boy, don't you know better than to be running around in the woods with nothing but a rag on your ass?"*

So after that, I only wore the *Little Brave* outfit when I knew Dad wasn't going to be around for a while. I still have the outfit in my possession. It even fits, it just doesn't cover as much as it used to. To this day, Dad and Breezy are the only two people who have ever seen me wearing it. I hope to keep it that way. Curiously however, Dad didn't seem to mind seeing Breezy wearing her outfit. In fact, he was so enthused by the design that he contracted her to fabricate a dozen or more for him to take home.

On the days when I wasn't helping Breezy, I would roam the wilderness until mid-day and head back to the rig for lunch. Dad and I would either dine on sandwiches brought from home, fresh game cooked on the grill, or a combination of the two. These items would be supplemented with a copious inventory of cookies and assorted other confectionary paraphernalia. We were able to assemble a fairly nutritionally robust dietary ensemble that suited our overall purposes and palates well enough.

Milo Falconbridge however, had an entirely different dining arrangement than Dad and I. Depending on the severity of what is known today as the heat index, Breezy would bring him provisions at various intervals throughout the day. On the really hot days she visited about every two hours, starting at around nine in the morning. This pattern would continue until we called it quits. On normal days she'd just come at noon and four. But if we were working past dark she'd also arrive at dusk, set up a field kitchen and tend the fire.

Every time she visited she would bring at a minimum, three gallons of *Falconbridge Lager* and a couple of gallons of cow's milk, freshly squeezed from the animal, all contained in second-hand, ½-gallon orange juice jars, neatly arranged in wooden crates. After being filled, these were lowered into the well to chill and then subsequently ferried out to the work site by Breezy. Milo didn't sip from a jar incrementally like most people. Instead, he would pour down the entire contents of a jar in one protracted run, breaking it into anywhere from 10 to 20 seamless gulps. Typically he would drink two jars of home brew per jar of milk, or roughly between 1½- and 2½-gallons every two hours depending on the heat index. For his noon meal, Breezy also offered up a whole spectrum of prepared meat dishes, generally loosely based on seared, or pulverized and seared members of the rodent, pigeon, or carp families, or some combination thereof, and of course copious quantities of salad generously enriched with her home-made dressing.

This amalgamation of earthy concoctions evidently worked greatly to preserve Milo's endurance, and presumably to give him that can-do-anything zest needed to perform at the level demanded. That's all well and good, but I'm glad now, and I was glad then, that it was him and not me. For example, one of Milo's favorite dishes was baked pig stomach stuffed with roasted chicken-livers, onions, rutabagas, duck-eggs, and molasses. I have never heard of anything like it before, or since.

When the pig stomach inventory was running low, evidently any old stomach would do. I've seen Milo gnawing on the stuffed stomachs of rabbits, squirrels, geese, possums, raccoons, and beavers. When stuffed and fully cooked, these smaller stomachs often resembled rude sausages of a sort, perhaps like the kind they serve at pancake houses in Hell. The composition of the stuffing varied between the species of stomach used but was almost always richly anointed with rutabagas and onions, two ubiquitous staples of the Falconbridge experience. But other than that, it was anything goes.

One rule strongly adhered to however, at the behest of Breezy it is said, was that no stomach could be stuffed with the meat of its own species. It was okay to eat a rabbit stomach stuffed with pig brains and diced carp gills, but it better not have any rabbit in it or Breezy would go on the warpath (and nobody wanted that).

Milo offered me sprigs of these haute concoctions once or twice a day, and of course I declined every time, respectfully. But Dad had to occasionally sample selected tidbits of the odd fare offered up just to be sociable: the chance rabbit stomach here, the sundry possum sandwich there. But he never really ate more than what he thought could kill him. In modern environmental lingo, he never exceeded what he estimated the *LD-50* (Lethal Dosage-50%) to be for a particular cuisine item. That is, he would limit his intake to an amount that statistically would be lethal to exactly 50% of a test population consuming an equal amount. Another way of putting it is to say that he would eat just enough to where he had no less than a fifty/fifty chance of making it to the next sunrise.

This logic being predicated on the assumption that his constitution was undoubtedly in the stronger percentile class. For the most part he handled it pretty good. I did see him turn green one day though when he discovered that the *spices* in the home-made butter were blowfly thoraxes. But he never let on like there was anything wrong. He went ahead and finished the bean muffin that Breezy made for him. But after that, Dad got to be pretty attentive about the types of items he would accept. He just took more care to not let himself get in a position to be offered the food.

To Dad, being so cautious was a form of sandbagging and he didn't like it because it made him feel like he was turning snooty. But he really had no choice. He could not afford to get sick. It's not that Dad was afraid of the meat in terms of species or palatability, he'd eaten exotic foods too (except for the baked stomach dishes). No, it was something more.

Dad finally admitted to me that his temporary, apparent elitist behavior was only the result of the overwhelmingly obvious fact that the Falconbridges had not yet adequately mastered all of the intricacies of modern kitchen hygiene procedures. As he described it, they were still a bit casual with their attention to the little things that helped their guests have confidence they were not ingesting foreign matter, pathogens, and undesirable mesofauna with the offered food. So dining with them was not only awkward, but also dangerous in a very real sense.

And as far as the native lager and the fresh milk were concerned, Dad and I graciously declined to indulge in these rugged beverages as well. First, the so-called beer, produced in the barn by Breezy in multiple-gallon quantities daily, looked more like rusty brown tomato juice than it did any kind of ale I've encountered in my travels across the globe. One couldn't help but notice that instead of having an amber-colored, transparent, watery consistency like the human conception of beer, this substance was more akin to an opaque stew of sorts, or light gravy perhaps, replete with undifferentiated lumps, random bits of flotsam, and immiscible linear inclusions.

It's anybody's guess what the stuff was actually made from, but I've always firmly believed that whatever parent materials were amassed to generate the ruddy leachate Milo was funneling, it was certainly uncontaminated by barley or hops. Dad always seemed to think they made it mostly from soybeans, with a pinch of corn and sorghum. The red color was theorized to be an incidental byproduct of the iron plumbing of Milo's custom built, diesel-powered microbrewery.

Second, I've never been able to get behind any liquid *fresh squeezed* from anything, unless it involves oranges. Farm fresh milk to me borders on the gross. I'm sorry, but there's some kind of a psychological buffering effect, however minimal, associated with the industrial pasteurization and refrigeration process that seems to diminish the impact of knowing you're drinking an unstable emulsion of lard and perspiration that has been filtered from the blood of a cow by a cluster of hyperactive sweat glands located in the animal's crotch. So to more perfectly circumvent the awkwardness of having to decline Milo's endless invitations to share his beverages, Dad always made sure we had plenty of water, sodas, and store-bought beer on hand.

Then there was the salad. What possibly could somebody do to screw up a salad? Lettuce is lettuce, the world over. Like laughter, it's the same in all languages, among all the races, throughout all the generations of humanity back into the darkness of prehistory. So are lettuce, cabbage, carrots, and celery, and so on. But leave it to Breezy to find a way to make it more interesting. She came up with a unique recipe for salad dressing that she produced in quantities almost as great as she did beer, whose flavor, like that of the beer, cannot be honestly described in a family publication.

They put it on everything. They put it on the salad. They put it on the meat. They used it as a marinade, as a sauce, as a gravy, as a soup stock, and they even slathered it on the dog to treat a skin disorder (and it worked). It made the dog quit licking the sore spot, thereby helping it heal faster. Breezy liked to call this concoction her *Ranch* dressing.

But her strong, French missionary-influenced Cherokee accent made it come out more like *Raunch*. All I could think was: "It's raunch alright, as in made from fresh raunch. Or as in *raunchy*. Because it looks raunchy, it tastes raunchy, and above all, it smells raunchy."

Most people probably wouldn't understand; the dictionary says one thing about raunchy, but to me it means that and much more too. Raunchy, to me, means a quality of being like something that is supposed to be harmless, colorless, odorless, and smooth, but is really threatening, coarse, yellowish green with gray streaks, and smells like rotten fish mixed with garbage. In the background there's the buzz of blowflies. That's what raunchy means to me.

All of this rampant, epidemic weirdness finally started to build up to some kind of a critical mass. It came to a head one day in mid-August. It started like a typical Butler County day. Dad and I arrived at the Falconbridge compound before sunrise as usual. Like most mornings, Dad and Milo started going through the routine maintenance checklist for the drilling rig. This was always done immediately prior to our departure for the project site.

When Dad and I arrived at Milo's that morning I couldn't help noticing what appeared to be a Holstein calf of approximately 500 pounds in weight, tied to a post in front of the barn. Since this was not remarkable I never gave it much additional thought. I stayed with Dad and Milo while they worked on the rig that morning, part of which involved running up the deck engine and the truck motor, both being unmuffled. The noise was so great that vocal communication was reduced to a kind of semaphore shouting match, looking more like a dialog between Marine drill instructors than conventional civilized speech. In about half an hour however, just as the sun was starting to rise, the rig was finally checked-out and ready to go, so we saddled up.

As we taxied through the compound in the prosecution of our timely departure, I noticed that where there had been an entire calf tied to the post just minutes before, there now remained only the dangling head of the animal, delicately suspended by a strong rope lashed about its muzzle. The purplish tongue of the creature lay spradled across the earth beneath the cedar fencepost from which the head hung. The balance of the cow was nowhere to be seen. I recall being captivated by the spectacle, but not mesmerized. Sure, in my home town we didn't get many cow heads hanging from fence posts, cedar or otherwise. But this was out in the country. And they have cows out in the country.

And no matter what you've been told, cows just don't voluntarily hand over the hamburger. It has to be coaxed from them. And coaxing of that degree, like it or not, unfortunately often requires rigorous and deliberate separation of the hamburger-rich sections from those regions less encumbered by burger deposits. So a cow's head here or there every so often should be expected. I mean hell, as an inhabitant of the suburbs I must have been leading a pretty sheltered life, having never to stumble over them in the street.

The way I was figuring it, if it weren't for modern hamburger factories, we'd be up to our necks in cow heads all the time. So it now suddenly seemed perfectly normal, even expected, to run across a cow head. As our car came past the cow head, I recall Dad making visual reckoning of the object. I also remember seeking intelligence regarding the meaning of this rude sign via a barrage of pointed queries and that Dad's responses seemed at best cryptic to me. He seemed to utter a few words below my hearing threshold and then laughed out loud. He told me that:

"The Indian..." (as he liked to call her), "...is quite a gal."

He shook his head in seeming disbelief, then smiled as we drove on with Milo following us in the drilling rig.

On this day we were continuing with our exploration of an area about eight miles from Milo's farm. We had drilled several holes tracing a pretty good seam of No. 11 Coal and it was holding all the way down the slope. So when we got to the bottom of the hill we turned downstream and followed the creek looking for where the crop line crossed. After two more holes the coal kept holding good at around five feet thick and about thirty-five feet deep, because it was dipping with the valley.

It was a perfect set up for mining. But as we got closer and closer to the river bottoms we couldn't help but notice that the density and ferocity of the resident mosquitoes were rapidly approaching a degree of plague-like criticality. Milo always worked shirtless and before long he was enduring a bloodsucking assault of epic proportions. I climbed into the cab of the drilling rig early on and rolled up the windows. Please understand that this was happening on a sunny morning at about eight o'clock, but the mosquitoes were suddenly so thick that there was a marked reduction in the light outside. It was a blizzard of mosquitoes. I could hear a soft rush as waves of their bodies collided with the windshield and body metal of the vehicle. It sounded like an effervescent drizzle. It was at about this point that my father and Milo decided to join me in the truck, letting in with them perhaps five-thousand mosquitoes.

They were engaged in the recitation of some of the most eloquent invective I believe I have ever heard. They were mad as hell and laughing at the same time. Their faces and bodies were smeared with gray, slimy mosquito guts from where their energetic swats had been more like desperate coarse wipes or mortal gouges, thus smiting countless mosquito carcasses at once, yet amassing their collective biomass into random moraines of putrid goo that covered virtually every square inch of their bodies.

Together they elected to wait out the swarm, while also recognizing the necessity of exterminating the remaining vermin within the truck. So we waited and we swatted. And we waited and swatted some more. Finally after an hour of waiting and swatting, and no let up in the swarm outside, Dad and Milo decided to go out and disconnect the drilling steel so we could drive the rig out of there. It was hopeless. The mosquitoes were so thick in the air by then that the men were breathing them into their lungs and gagging. Their eyes were getting so full of them there was no way they could even find the tools, much less perform any meaningful tasks.

After about fifteen or twenty seconds of this hell they made a desperate dash for the truck again. And when they opened the doors to get in, approximately 1,000,000 mosquitoes entered with them. They told me to fold up on the floor, which I was already doing out of pure gut survival instinct alone. Then they used pieces of cardboard to smite the airborne vermin. It was one of the most brutal expressions of the human will I've ever had to witness.

Dad and Milo thrashed those damn mosquitoes almost into another dimension. About the time that we started to get a pretty good handle on the population of mosquitoes inside the truck, we noticed that outside they were becoming so thick that visibility was down to under 50 feet. We watched in horrified amazement as the visibility degraded even further to 25 feet. Finally, it went to zero. All that was visible that morning was pure grayish-black washout. It was dark enough inside the truck that Milo had to turn on the dome light so we could see. Dad and Milo just looked at each other blankly. They were not laughing anymore. That's when I started to get scared.

About this time we heard the sound of the log dragger – it was Breezy showing up for her regularly scheduled nine-o'clock supply drop. Dad and Milo wrapped a piece of cardboard around me and we all together made a dash for the tank. It was like running through a vat of electricity. They shoved me through the portal first then came Milo and finally Dad, who slammed the door. Breezy had been operating the tank combat style, locked in and protected from the mosquitoes. In the tank we finally got to stand back for a moment and take accounting of our situation.

The first item of order was to retreat from the area. Second was to ascertain our condition. It was determined that aside from approximately three-thousand bites each, Dad and Milo were okay. They estimated that I had suffered maybe three-hundred bites. But when they took a look at Breezy they were shocked. She didn't have any bites, but she was covered with blood from head to foot.

She also looked a little pale. Upon closer examination they discovered a cut that ran at an angle from just below her left nostril to the end of her top lip, coming out about half way between the center of the lip and the corner of her mouth on the right side. The cut went all the way through, separating the tissue completely. It was as if her upper lip had been cut with scissors all the way to her nose. It was horrible. I cringe to this day when I think about it.

They asked her what had happened. She kind of hung her head down and recounted the series of terrible events that had led her to this juncture. It seems that she was using her Bowie knife to remove a tick from the face of the cow that was tied by the barn. But the animal reared its head unexpectedly and knocked the blade into Breezy's face, causing the laceration. She became enraged and subsequently murdered the cow with the same knife.

This all happened while we were preparing the rig. After she killed the cow, she dressed it out in the barn and got it ready to put into the well house. She had lost enough blood by this time that she was starting to get a little weak. She still did not know how badly she had been cut.

While she was hanging the meat in the well house she got dizzy and fell a distance of about 15 feet down to the water level. As she was climbing out she encountered a copperhead worked into the stones lining the well. She grabbed the snake with her right hand while holding onto the wall with her left. She then transferred her weight to the right hand using it to hold the snake's head against the stone.

She reached into her pocket with her other hand and produced a Barlow jack knife, extended the blade by grabbing it in her teeth, then shoved the point through the snake's head and dragged the blade toward her, splitting its skull from the neck to the nose. The snake was firmly coiled around her arm but was no real threat now. She then folded the knife against the wall, placed it neatly back into her pocket and resumed her climb out (taking the copperhead with her), and still bleeding from the gash on her face.

We were all deeply captivated by this incredible account of heroism, but what is more amazing to me is that as she detailed this dark affair I suddenly realized that the terrible cut on her lip had in fact been carefully stitched as if by a trained medical professional. When queried about this Breezy acknowledged that after she climbed out of the well she had hung a mirror on a nail on the side of the barn and used it to inspect the cut. After deliberating about it she decided that she might as well sew it up herself. So she did, while standing upright, looking into the mirror, without any trace of anesthesia, using the same needle and thread that she uses to fix their clothes. Upon hearing this, my father smiled warmly, reached out and patted her on the shoulder, and said: *"God bless you Mrs. Falconbridge."*

Then he sat back and took a deep breath and peered out the gun-sight, never saying another word. Milo smiled too and reached out and took her in his arms and held her. She just rested her head on his shoulder. It was a special moment. Milo was proud of his woman and he let her know it. He was giving her the rest of the day off. He sat her on the floor and covered her with a blanket and had me to hold her head in my lap.

When we finally broke out of the mosquitoes it was a bright sunny day. We drove ahead a few hundred feet more and stopped. We climbed out of the tank and beheld the spectacle before us. The entire valley below was a churning black fog. There had to be thousands of tons of the bastards. If there were any animals or people caught in there, they were dead now. But as we watched, it became quickly apparent that the mosquitoes were on the move and they were approaching our position. So we climbed back into the tank and headed out. But it was at least an hour back to the compound. In a matter of minutes the mosquitoes overtook us and attempted to harass us on and off for the rest of the trip. In the meantime Dad and Milo brainstormed on what they could do to get the rig back. But it soon became apparent that this just wasn't about the rig anymore, it had become a question of survival.

Our situation was starting to look pretty grave by now. We were all sore and bleeding, the log dragger was running low on fuel, the Indian was down, and we were starting to stray off course because of poor-visibility. Then, just when it looked like it might be curtains for us, my father calmly leaned forward and broke the silence by asking Milo if the P-47 engine on the wrecker would still start. Dad had an eager look on his face as he spoke. Milo started to remind Dad that the wrecker couldn't move under its own power. He suddenly froze in mid-sentence however, stared blankly for a moment, and then with renewed enthusiasm informed my father that with a couple of shots of ether and a little throttling, the sonofabitch would fire right up. Dad then shared the rest of his plan with us.

It took us about two hours to get all of the necessary equipment moved into place on a hilltop up wind from the *Valley of the Bloodsuckers*. This included the propeller-wrecker which had to be towed by the log-dragger, Dad's 1967 Ford LTD, and a total of six 40-foot dump-bed semi trailers loaded with DDT. These were pulled to the site by Milo's 1953 Mack truck. Each trailer was methodically positioned approximately 25 feet behind the wrecker, directly in line with the propeller, and its contents were dumped. By the time all of the trailers were empty, there was a single cone shaped pile containing approximately 152 tons of pure, concentrated DDT powder, located in line with the propeller. Into this Dad carefully placed approximately four pounds of nitrogelatin high-explosives, this being intended to give the DDT a "jump start." The final step came when they secured the wrecker to nearby trees with several large chains and steel cables.

When everything was in place they stopped and took one last look at the seething horde filling the valley below. The cloud was moving closer at a frightening pace. There was a moment of silence as they both looked at each other, then at me. Between the three of us there was a mutual, attenuated nod: it was time. Milo donned an aviator's cap and goggles, climbed onto the superstructure of the wrecker, and began making adjustments to various engine components in preparation for the ignition sequence.

Meanwhile, Dad connected the jumper cables between the LTD and the wrecker. I climbed into the cab of the wrecker where it was my job to operate the fuel mix lever and actuate the handle that controlled the variable pitch, paddle-blade propeller when the engine reached maximum speed. When everything was ready, Dad revved the 427-Ford up to about five-thousand r.p.m. Milo looked toward Dad, then at me. Dad gave the thumb's-up gesture and Milo followed-suit, as did I. Then Dad yelled *CONTACT* and Milo stuck a screwdriver between the leads on the starter, shot a slug of ether into the turbo intake, and the giant engine rumbled to life.

The smoke was so thick we couldn't see anything at first. Then it suddenly was blown away as the engine smoothed out. About this same time the DDT started being picked up and blowing everywhere. It was now or never. Milo looked toward Dad through his DDT-covered goggles. There was another of those subtle nods and then Milo throttled the engine up as high as it would go. He gave me the signal to pull the pitch lever causing the propeller blades to rotate to maximum cut, like putting it in overdrive. This instantly quadrupled the force of the air coming from the propeller. At that instant, Dad hit the plunger on the detonator.

"He lives! Kills Many Toads lives!"

Hearing the above words is the first thing I remember after pulling the lever. She kept saying them over and over. That sweet voice of her's was like music. I remember watching a blur that slowly focused into her big brown eyes blinking back at me. She was smiling.

Then the three of them were suddenly hovering over me. Breezy was in the center now, her swollen lip hanging from the top of her grin, but at least her hair was its normal color. On either side were Dad and Milo. Their hair was literally snow-white with matted globs of DDT.

They had it in their ears, in their noses, under their eyelids and stuck in the cracks of their teeth. I know this because they were smiling. And they had a good reason to smile: because making up a plausible story to explain my death would not be necessary after all, not to mention the mountain of paperwork they just avoided in one fell swoop. As my senses started to return I found myself suddenly realizing that not only did my head hurt like crazy, but oddly, I also seemed to have a remarkable variety of unexpected objects positioned on and around my person.

There were a pair of falcon feathers crossed on my chest, a pine cone stuffed into my shirt pocket, and some walnut hulls, corn kernels, and soybeans on the pillow on either side on my head. Just when I was starting to think that there was some kind of smart-alec chipmunk on the loose, I suddenly became aware that attached to my forehead with masking tape, was a necklace composed of approximately twenty rat stomachs, each meticulously stuffed with fragrant herbs and dried flowers. I panicked. I of course instinctively reached to try to take leave of these foreign objects and in doing so sat-up abruptly, dashing my head on an ammo canister.

Because I had been comatose, Dad and Milo figured it wouldn't hurt anything to let Breezy perform an impromptu Native American healing ceremony. The rat stomach-incense necklace was part of this methodology, as well as all of the other items.

Evidently when the explosives detonated, there was so much DDT thrown into the air at once that cavitation was induced in the propeller which in turn caused the wrecker to bounce violently. I must have struck my head on the roof of the cab when this happened. The shock was so violent it threw Milo a distance of over twenty feet. By the time he found his way back onto the wrecker, all of the DDT was gone. He killed the engine and then they brought me back to the cabin.

After we got cleaned up, and I finally allowed Breezy strap a piece of jowl-bacon onto the knot on my scalp (but I categorically refused the raunch dressing), we all got into the log-dragger and headed back to the drilling rig. It was a pretty rough ride and early on Breezy got to feeling bad so we wrapped her in a blanket and made a spot for her on the floor.

As we entered the impact area it became clear that this was a phenomenon unlike anything we had ever witnessed before, or would be likely to again. It reminded me of a how a winter day might be - a winter day in Hell that is. It was 103 degrees in the shade and an odd, acrid, organic stench lingered in the air. There was what appeared to be anywhere from two to six inches of sooty snow on everything as far as the eye could see. In places there were immense drifts of this pestilent matter upwards of a foot thick. On the steeper reaches of the draws, or along the breaks of ridges, there were stretches where landslides of the fetid calculus had heaped up into broad fans and lobes. At the bases of many trees lay rings of the material sloughed-outward three feet or more.

As our welded plate-steel dreadnaught lumbered indifferently into this coarse organic theater, Milo suddenly elbowed me in the ribs and enthusiastically queried:

"How long do you think it will be before you ever see anything like this again?"

I remember my reply being simply:

"Many moons."

Curiously, when I said that, Breezy lifted back her blanket just enough to make eye contact with me. Then she reached out and took my hand and held it.

Steadily we trudged onward through this dipteran Armageddon. When we finally arrived at the marooned drilling rig we immediately climbed out of the log-dragger to investigate the scene. Wading through the greasy detritus, knee-deep in places, was a distinctly unsavory experience. Upon closer examination it was discovered that the layered material, as suspected, was composed of unimaginable numbers of deceased mosquitoes intermixed with DDT grains.

Dad used his trusty ten-power geologist's hand lens to microscopically examine random samples of the material. What he saw completely stunned and amazed him. Each view through the magnifier revealed a scene of absolute and utter devastation beyond the comprehension of civilized humans. The mosquitoes were interlocked in a limitless framework of horrific death. Their tiny faces seemed frozen in mute agony. Their little eyes were bugged-out as if capturing for all time their total shock and surprise at the overwhelming finality of the attack. Had they had mouths, they would most likely have been agape, still trying to scream in abject terror. Perhaps some sensitive people would have felt sorry for the mosquitoes. Well I say let these people give the mosquitoes a hand: a hand to suck blood out of that is! It was war. No pity could be expected, nor was any given.

In humanity's struggle against the bloodsuckers, there is no place for mercy, quarter, or misguided soul-searching sensitivity. It's us or them. And on August 9, 1967, the day was ours. Considering the broad areal extent of the battle debris, strictly from a biomass standpoint, it was clear that the material constituted thousands of tons. It was an extraordinary phenomenon that defies description. The operation had been more than just successful - it was genocide.

The two-thousand-plus horsepower airplane engine, the coordinated detonation of high-explosives, the favorable prevailing winds above the forest, and the relatively static ground level wind, all worked together to produce what is now widely considered to be the single largest privately-funded mosquito extermination event in the history of the United States.

Chapter 17

The Anti-Waitress

Because of my father's enduring presence on the nation's highways chasing opportunities in the energy production industry, at one time or another he conducted commerce at practically every motel, steakhouse, truck-stop, drive-in, dairy-whip, burger-grill, chicken-place, and barbecue-joint in a three-state wide swath from Alabama to Michigan.

Not coincidentally, he knew or had knowledge of virtually every waitress, car-hop, barmaid, concierge, towel-lady, and hat-check-girl staffing each of these varied establishments at all points between. My father's extraordinary charisma, grace, sincerity, and stunning good-looks won him the respect and admiration of thousands of people throughout his life. Perhaps fully half of these were female employees of the retail food service and motor lodging industries. Moreover, many waitresses considered my father to be Kentucky's answer to Peter O'Toole in terms of pure, raw good looks. He was continually propositioned by these women. And being a gentleman, he never discussed the details of said liaisons, or if they even occurred. He left it up to me to figure it out. By the time I was six years old I had fleshed-out the fundamental connection between Dad's roadhouse popularity and the fact he first met my mother when she was a car-hop at a dairy-whip in Baroquesville.

Dad was the superlative customer. He was friendly, courteous, patient, ate anything put in front of him and lauded those who prepared it; and of course he always tendered a handsome gratuity. So everywhere he dined it was only natural that he was fawned over and doted on by the waitresses. Some of his peers and associates expressed their concern that the waitresses' gestures were merely thinly veiled antics intended to take advantage of his misguided generosity – as though they were playing him like a flute, courting the big tip.

These criticisms he would always sharply rebut with the forensic agility of a trained logician. His counter argument would be couched as a simple question: "Am I receiving superior service or not?" To this his critics could only concede. As a result he made many converts. Modern restaurant workers probably owe a great debt to my father in that he helped set into motion a new sensibility concerning the art of tipping that today has spread throughout the civilized world.

Dad was an advocate for all waitresses, regardless of their race, religion, national origin, dress size, or marital status. Dad had a great empathy for these women and was not ashamed to explain it to his peers. For example, whenever his associates complained about the poor service or bad attitude of a waitress, Dad would encourage them to imagine being in her place.

"These old gals come in here and work twelve - fourteen hours a day for sixty cents an hour plus tips. Most of them probably have two or three kids laid up in a house trailer somewhere. Their husbands, if they have one, are generally worthless, or alcoholics, or both. And besides, how friendly could anyone be if they had to look at faces like yours all day?"

During the early- to mid-sixties, the typical gratuity was between a dime and a quarter, depending on the tab. Dad always left at least a dollar, even for glass of tea. He espoused the philosophy that if he treated waitresses (or anybody) with respect, talked to them, and bestowed a worthwhile reward, it would go a long way in helping to improve their attitude, and thus they would naturally reciprocate accordingly. So great was his confidence that he zealously declared that there wasn't a waitress alive from which he could not at least evoke a smile. So, with cocky dash my father often boasted the universal applicability of his *Friendly Customer* methodology. Understandably however, he was constantly chastised by his more cynical associates for this apparent provincial naïveté. Still, he stood his ground. It was inevitable therefore, that his claim would be formally challenged.

One of my father's oil promoter friends, Cleston Pickett I believe, claimed that he knew a waitress who would categorically and unequivocally be immune to the Friendly Customer method – that no one could make her smile. A casual wager was then effected upon this precise conditionality, for the consideration of the subject lunch tab for the three of us and two impartial observers; and a case of beer. Handshakes were exchanged and the game was afoot.

After the bet was secured, Dad requested more information about the waitress that would be his adversary.

"So tell me a little bit about this gal. What's her name?"

"Payne."

"Payne?"

"May H."

"May H. Payne...hmm...nothing too sinister there. What does the *'H'* stand for?"

"Hammond."

"I see."

"She works at a fish-hut south of Hockertown on Route 721."

"I know where that restaurant is but I don't recall ever dining there." Dad confessed.

Cleston then proceeded to enumerate a variety of anecdotal instances intended to help my father more perfectly appreciate the character of said waitress and the true nature of the task that he had agreed to undertake. Cleston was careful to not omit any detail.

The evidentiary items presented included accounting of how the subject often spoke extremely harshly to customers, how truck drivers had been overheard referring to her as the *Waitress from Hell,* how she reportedly had once drop-kicked a customer's pet Dachshund with such harshness that the unfortunate, elongate canine was literally broken in the middle, taking on the shape of an "L," and subsequently cavorted wildly in a macabre series of frantic zig zags before it expired in a misshapened, quivering wad on the cold, nasty linoleum. And of course Cleston seemed particularly gratified revealing the widely accepted rumor that *she never smiled.*

Cleston Pickett's other job was as a Holiness preacher. So it was perhaps only natural for him to couch his ultimate synopsis in religious idioms. He summed up the briefing by informing Dad that it was his professional opinion that she was the very incarnation of what could only be described as *The Anti-Waitress.*

He then went on to confess that every do-gooder high-tipper from Winchester to Moline had tried to conquer her, and how they had all failed miserably. She chewed them up and spit them out like they were childish amateurs. Dad just smiled and nodded. As far as he was concerned it was sauce for the goose.

The following day Dad and I, Cleston Pickett, Luther Fouts, and a fellow named Hans Mullenbach, made a special trip over to Hockertown in a high-stakes ploy to see if my father could make the fish-hut waitress smile. Before we arrived it was agreed among all participants that no one would do anything to make Dad's job more difficult. In the spirit of fair play, everyone would stay cool so as to afford Dad with a reasonable chance to succeed. At precisely 11:23 a.m., as we rounded a tree lined curve, a marquee came into view.

MAY & CLYDE'S
FISH HUT
- *HOME STYLE DINING* –

We walked in and surveyed the greater scene. The only other patrons there at the time were an elderly couple and their pre-schooler grandson sitting at a booth near the juke box. As we took our seats I saw the cook pop in and out of view a couple of times when he walked past the serving window. There was a very large aquarium in the back of the room containing lobsters and other marine fauna. I also noted a curious untidiness associated with the establishment. There appeared to be pieces of partially eaten bread products, some stepped on, some not, strewn across the floor and most of the horizontal surfaces in the dining area. We chose a table near the center of the room and sat down.

About the time the air stopped whistling from the foam cushions of our chairs, the kitchen doors abruptly swung open and out came the subject of our research: *May Hammond Payne*. We immediately looked toward her. Cleston nudged Dad's ankle under the table as though there could be some lingering trace of doubt that the creature now on an apparent collision course with us was anything less than the true, one and only Waitress from Hell. Dad felt a cold chill run up his neck, as did everyone in the room I'm sure.

She swaggered up to our table with a gait not entirely unlike that of John Wayne (John Wayne after an extended program of intravenous testosterone therapy, that is). She was around fifty, stood about five-foot nine, weighed approximately 175, and had an imposing countenance more like what one might traditionally associate with a North Korean prison guard rather than with someone expected to have formal contact with the public. She was dressed in a white waitress outfit with a light green apron.

She sported a pair of black, horn-rimmed glasses and her ebony hair was arranged in a classic bun style. There was a no. 2 pencil behind her right ear, with about 40% of its operational life trimmed away. And as it was later recounted by those present that day, her face could have been described as Modern Art, this being perhaps related to her Picasso-style cubistic looks. There was just something unconventional about the symmetry of her facial structure. There was a certain angle at which she could hold her head that it seemed as though it were possible to see both of her eyes, both ears, and the back of her neck all at the same time. As she approached us she had a suspicious look on her face as though she completely expected one or more of us at any moment to spring up and slit her throat. Upon reaching us, she extracted a chrome-plated .38 revolver from her apron and laid it on the table. She then made eye contact with all of us *at the same time*. There was a moment of silence, a very discordant, aberrant, and distasteful silence, but silence nonetheless. Then, just as Dad was preparing to brag on her, she spoke first:

"What in the hell do you piss-gummed-looking clowns want?"

Everyone seemed stunned by the direct rudeness of the question and the brusqueness of its delivery. But it didn't even register with Dad. He saw right past it as he kept his eye on the prize.

"Could we see a menu please?"

Dad replied, smiling and positively beaming charm. He was laying it on so thick it was splattering back onto the table. She pointed toward a large marquee-style menu over the kitchen serving window.

MENU

ADMIRAL'S BARGE	2.25	OYSTER SKIFF	2.10	COD SCHOONER	1.95
SHRIMP BOAT	1.90	MACKEREL SCOW	1.80	CRAB CANOE	1.75
FIDDLER FRIGATE	1.65	FIDDLER KAYAK	1.45	TUNA TUG	1.05
CARP BOX	1.00	MULLET FLIP	85	CLAM CHOWDER	75
FISH SANDWICH	70	RUDDER BURGER	60	PAIN-CAKES	50
TURTLE SOUP	40	COLE SLAW	35	BEET	20
SAMMIN PATTY	25	FRENCH FRIES	25	POKE	20
BAKED BEANS	15	COFFEE	15	POP	10
TEA	10	BUTTERMILK	10	PUNCH	10
GIN	85	WHISKY	95	KICK	10
HUSHPUPPY	5	CHICKEN NECKS	5	ROLL	5

NO SUBSTITUTIONS
DON'T ASK

"You can see that, *can't you?* That's the menu. If you can't see it, then you can move over to one of the tables by those old bastards, it's closer from there."

"No, we can see it fine from here thank you."

"Then make up your minds, I've got work to do."

"I'll take... the Cod Schooner and a large tea - and that's a lovely hairdo. Did you fix it yourself or is there a professional Hollywood hairdresser in this town?" Dad cheerfully queried.

There was a long silence. She just stared at him like he was insane. Her look was reptilian. It seemed to be intended to convey the absolute invulnerability of her dark, humorless soul. And this it did very well. So horrible was her gaze that not even Dad could withstand it. He had to turn away after about twenty seconds. Dad later recounted:

"...it was like looking into the very pit of Hell itself. Her eyes seemed to suck my soul right out of my body. Breaking eye-contact was not so much fearfulness, as it was self-preservation."

"Cod truck didn't show up today, pick something else – and keep your ignorant comments to yourself." she finally replied.

Dad was plainly shaken. Still, he recovered quickly and made a cunning lateral:

"Do you own this place, or do you just work here?"

"If you're hungry, then order. Otherwise, get the hell out!"

"Uh...give me a Shrimp Boat then."

"Hushpuppies or rolls?"

"Rolls."

"What are you going to drink with it?"

"Tea please."

"Sweetened or unsweetened?"

"Sweetened please."

Looking at Cleston she gruffly asked:

"You want something four-eyes?"

"Yeah, what's in a *Carp Box?*"

"One carp patty, one hushpuppy or roll, and a choice of baked beans or slaw."

"Where do the carp come from? Did you get them out of the crick out there, or what?"

"Farm raised in Louisiana. If you don't like the stinking carp, don't get it. Now order or go somewhere else."

"I'll have a Fiddler Kayak and a glass of gin."

"Large gin or small?"

"Large."

"Hushpuppies or rolls?"

"Hushpuppies."

"What for you ass-crack?" she said, looking toward Luther Fouts.

"Give me the Oyster Skiff, a large whisky, and a pitcher of buttermilk."

"Hushpuppies or rolls."

"Two orders of Hushpuppies."

There was a pause. Her stress accumulated until she broke the pencil lead on her ticket pad.

"Okay smarty pants, I'll bring you a double order, but you're going to eat every single hushpuppy – we don't waste food around here mister."

"What if I can't eat them all?" asked Luther.

"Then I'll ram the greasy sumbitches down your throat!"

I had up until this point been a passive observer. I was shocked certainly, but unperturbed nor so motivated or inclined to proceed, act, or respond in any capacity or complexion. I was a little dazed but unscathed. So therefore, like a fawn perhaps, I remained quiescent as the predator ambled nearby. However, after she finished noting Luther's order on her waitress ticket-book, she then turned her attention toward me. When this occurred, suddenly, instinctively, inexplicably, my primary overriding mission in life became to somehow remove her attention from me as quickly as possible.

"See anything you like you mutant-looking little brat, or can you even read?"

Her words seemed to tweak a little spark buried deep in my DNA. My fear had now been supplanted by a curious sensation that I later determined to be rage. I remember looking at Dad, as if seeking approval to respond in kind, but Dad winked and smiled. So I placed my order instead:

"Fish sandwich, small order of fries, and a large gin, *please*."

My emphatic "please" seemed to offend the delicate sensibilities of the waitress. Consequently, she rotated her deviant countenance approximately fifteen degrees on its major axis thereby aligning the virtual plane of her vision field with mine. She then engaged her by-now dreaded stare-down subroutine. I could feel fragments of my soul being sucked away like iron filings rushing to a magnet. I knew I had to look away before she turned me into a salt pillar. When I did I looked toward my father. He gave me one of those *at-a-boy* nods and smiled.

"I can't bring you a large gin."

"Okay, a small glass of gin then."

"Hushpuppies or rolls?"

"Rolls."

Finally, she got around to Hans Mullenbach. Now Hans was a pretty good old boy, it's just that for one reason or another he hadn't enjoyed as many educational opportunities as most of the rest of us. The bottom line was that he couldn't read. He always got along in restaurants by either ordering what somebody else did or by ad-libbing.

Also, being from the old school, he'd never really mastered the concept of so-called, *theme restaurants*. Somewhere along the path of life he had become encumbered with the misconception that there were two, and only two, species of dining establishments in the known universe. He ostensibly classified a certain fraction of eateries as conventional restaurants. Everything else to him was a *barbecue joint*. So, as the waitress' patience approached criticality, Hans rubbed his chin, leaned back in his chair, and uttered something to the effect of:

"Gimme a mutton plate, order of kraut, pitcher of whisky, and I'll have the hushpuppies, please..."

"MUTTON PLATE! We ain't got no damn mutton plate. Did you see a big sign out front that said 'MUTTON-HUT?' And who in the hell ever heard of eating hushpuppies with mutton? What kind of crackpot are you anyway? If you punks give me any trouble, I'm calling the cops. Now order something with fish in it or get the hell out."

Sensing an opportunity to apply diplomacy, Dad weighed in:

"Hans, go easy on this wonderful, charming lady. Why don't you help her out and try a shrimp boat?"

"I don't like no damn shrimp. They remind me of crawdads. Me and my little brother Fergus used to have to eat crawdads when we was kids to keep from starving to death."

Luther Fouts made his pitch:

"Go for the oysters Hans."

"I don't like no damn oysters..."

Hans was preparing to educate us about why he didn't like oysters. God only knows what they reminded him of and what he and his little brother Fergus used to have to do with them. But just as he was about to start down this anecdotal trail, Cleston interrupted and offered his menu item suggestion:

"The fiddlers sound pretty good Hans."

"All right then, give me the fiddlers."

"Fiddler Frigate or Fiddler Kayak?"

"Frigate I reckon."

"Cole slaw or baked beans?"

"Ain't you got no *kraut?*"

The waitress got a look on her face like she was getting ready to ask him if he saw a sign out front that said: KRAUT-HUT, but Hans cut her off:

"All right, okay, slaw then."

"What are you chasing it with?"

"Pitcher of whisky."

"Hushpuppies or rolls?"

"Hushpuppies. Can I have extra hushpuppies instead of the slaw?"

Everyone in our party cringed. Cleston kicked Hans under the table.

"CAN'T YOU READ?" the waitress screamed, pointing at the sign with her pencil.

"Read what?"

"What it says up there, right below 'CHICKEN NECKS'?"

"Oh yeah, sorry...I guess I overlooked that. Alright then, can I have *chicken necks* instead of slaw?"

It took a whole lot of explaining and diplomatic maneuvering to bring closure to this unfortunate misunderstanding. Dad was in his element. He finally agreed to personally pay for one extra side-order each of chicken necks *and* hushpuppies to get the waitress to stop screaming. But to compel her to put the revolver back in her apron, he had to make Cleston promise to eat Hans' slaw. Finally, upon conclusion of this awkward affair, the waitress headed for the serving window and yelled:

"CLYDE...GET OUT HERE."

In the meantime, everyone at our table exchanged glances and smiles. For a second there was a whole lot of eyeball rolling going on. It was at this point that Luther Fouts, via a loaded query, sought more intelligence regarding the shrimp-crayfish phenomenon alluded to earlier by Hans.

"Hans, how did you and your brother catch all those crawdads anyway?"

"Most of the time we gigged them with a pick-ax handle with a nail drove in the end of it."

"Where did you gig them at?"

"There was a ditch behind the old plywood mill where they were usually pretty thick. We got into a nest of them in there a couple of times and filled up a five-gallon bucket."

"I know that ditch. I never saw any crawdads in there, only those big green bullfrog tadpoles, you know, the kind that look like day-old chicken livers with tails. *Rana catesbeiana*, I believe, is the species name."

"That is correct." commented Dad.

"Yeah, we ate plenty of them too. *The little bastards remind me of oysters you know.*" continued Hans.

Just as the conversation was starting to show signs of developing a pleasant gestalt, with the promise of captivating intrigue implied, the essence of the moment was abruptly shattered by a noisy commotion at a nearby table. It was our waitress apparently addressing other customers.

Upon closer observation we discovered that she apparently had the previously-alluded-to child's cranium firmly secured in what could arguably be described as an Eastern-Bloc variant of a half-Nelson headlock. And as if this weren't enough, she also appeared to be energetically forcing objects of some kind into the child's mouth, much to his and his grandparent's displeasure.

"You didn't eat your hushpuppies you little freak. Did you even try them? No, probably not. Well here then, let me help you. See how easy they fit into your mouth?"

Not only was this scene disturbing outright, but it was made even more dreadful when one considered the size of the hushpuppies she was shoving into the child's mouth. These were no ordinary hushpuppies. They were mutant hushpuppies. They were roughly the size of tennis balls. The onion chunks were not little either. They were sufficiently large that they formed finger-sized spikes where they protruded from the surface of the hushpuppy. These spikes, having been carbonized by the superheated lard in the deep fryer, presented a grievous puncture wound hazard. Overall, May's Fish Hut hushpuppies resembled medieval mace balls, sans chains and handles. I had heard of *Home Style* dining before, but I never envisioned that it would be this realistic. I was glad that I had ordered rolls. When the child began to purge the compressed hushpuppies back onto his highchair, Linda Blair style, the grandparents' protestations took on a renewed sense of urgency.

Only after threatening protracted litigation were they finally able to persuade the overzealous waitress to cease and desist. But by the time they got her stopped she had already force fed the child at least three fish sticks, two hushpuppies, and a partially-eaten crab cake, the latter being sourced from the excess of his grandpa's *Admiral's Barge*. But even after she let loose of the child's head, she still lingered near the scene, apparently trying the stare them down. The tension of the impasse was suddenly broken by the toll of a bell and the words: "ORDER'S UP!" Not long after that everyone at our table was stuffing their maws with sundry preparations of aquatic and/or marine fauna.

At least initially, this phase of the Fish Hut experience seemed to be completely unremarkable. But suddenly Luther Fouts noticed that he had received rolls in lieu of the specified hushpuppies. Then, upon more careful survey of the scene as a whole, he ultimately discovered that there was a conspicuous absence of hushpuppies from the table in general. Just as suddenly, ostensibly instinctively, or by some Freudian-short circuit of his panic response, he yelled "HUSHPUPPIES!" at a volume far greater than one ordinarily would in a fish hut, unless of course one were attempting to get the attention of a waitress at a fish hut in a neighboring county. A pregnant pause followed as everyone froze. Not only did we each stop chewing our food, we even stopped breathing. About two seconds later we heard the kitchen door swing open.

"WHO SAID THAT?"

"I did!" replied Luther.

"What, you don't like the damned hushpuppies?"

"No, I ain't got no damned hushpuppies."

"Don't give me that crap! The floor is covered with them. Are you too good to bend over and pick the sumbitches up or do you need me to come out there and make you do it?"

This was an exclusively Luther Fouts v. May Hammond Payne exchange at this point because the rest of us were still frozen with our mouthfuls of incompletely chewed food.

"The ones on the floor are cold and all smashed up. I want some hot ones."

"Well why in the hell didn't you say so? I ain't no damned mind-reader you know. CLYDE, GIVE ME A BUCKET OF HUSHPUPPIES."

The complex series of events that followed are difficult to fully translate purely via the written word. The episode registers in my mind more like a slow-motion replay of a 80-millimeter mortar assault. The first hushpuppy came in fast at a low trajectory and landed squarely in an open dish of tartar sauce in the middle of the table. After that they mostly came in at a considerably higher trajectory, more or less randomly striking each of us multiple times in the head, neck, face, and upper torso. It was a hail of hushpuppies colliding with such fury and relentlessness that we were completely overwhelmed. Within the first two seconds, Luther endured no fewer than eight hushpuppies to the head, including a direct hit in the right eye. Meanwhile, Cleston Pickett got his bifocals knocked completely off of his face, and sustained several impacts in his left ear as he tried to shield himself by looking away from the primary fire direction. One hushpuppy struck with sufficient force to produce a nasty looking welt on his temple.

The main phase of this high-cholesterol artillery barrage probably lasted about ten seconds, but it seemed like an eternity. From the beginning I had instinctively tilted my head forward thus avoiding any hits to my face. However, by the time the bombardment had ended, my scalp was generously appointed with a coarse mantle of fragmented hushpuppies bonded together with tartar sauce, buttermilk, and gin. Because he was sitting with his back toward the kitchen, Dad was the only person at our table, except me, whose eyes were not encrusted with cornbread and onion shrapnel.

Once the onslaught ceased there followed a strange and curious silence. The gagging noises of Hans, Luther, and Cleston were the only sounds in the room. All three had been rendered effectively blind by the robustness of the hushpuppy debris caked in and around their eyes. At the peak of this silence was when Cleston, having held back as long as he could, finally unexpectedly expelled onto the floor the food that had been in his mouth ever since Luther had yelled "Hushpuppies." After approximately 50 milliseconds Hans followed suit. When this happened I saw my father get that look on his face like he always did right before he ripped the femurs out of something. It was about this time the waitress yelled from behind the counter:

"Is that enough, or do you *momma's boys* want some more?"

That's when we heard the distinctive sound of a pistol being cocked.

At this point, Dad leaned forward and whispered to Cleston:

"I'll be right back."

Still hacking up catfish chunks and unable to speak, Cleston simply nodded affirmatively. Dad then looked at me. I looked back. Instinctively, I inched my hand toward a nearby hushpuppy but stopped short of picking it up. Then Dad looked at my hand without moving his head – just his eyes moved. Then we made eye contact again. He gave me an almost imperceptible nod. Exactly 1.25 seconds later we both stood up simultaneously and started flinging hushpuppies toward the waitress with all the might and power we could muster. Dad's first three caught her dead on. One hit her in the forehead, one on her cheek below the right eye, and the third was a direct line drive right down her throat. That's when the pistol fired, with the bullet striking and shattering the aquarium. Luckily, the recoil caused the gun to be propelled from her hand and it fell to the floor.

During this interval, I managed to get two hushpuppies launched. The first one struck her in the chin and the second missed her entirely, but it did graze the pie display case and was deflected through the pickup window causing "Clyde" to respond with a surprised-sounding "Hey!" We quickly exhausted all the easily available hushpuppies lying on the table. So Dad started throwing anything he could find. He thumped her in the forehead with a fiddler. He nailed her one in the nose with a pepper shaker. He clipped her in the knee with a napkin dispenser. It was quickly becoming clear to me that this had evolved into more than just an ordinary food-fight. This was a food-fight at the Gates of Hell.

Finally, Dad grazed her skull with a full bottle of ketchup, sending her to the floor like a sack of toads. That's when he made his move. While she scrambled for the pistol on the floor, Dad grabbed up the remains of Luther Fouts' oyster skiff and started his advance on her position. As he approached her he began to lay down a merciless barrage of deep-fried oysters. He threw them with such force that they exploded on contact, leaving large welts on her face and neck. Meanwhile, I provided cover fire via sporadic, high-velocity bursts of chicken necks. This final assault had so stunned his adversary that she lay in a state of near shock. But Dad had the bit between his teeth and wasn't about to break off the attack. He leaped down onto her quivering body, coming to rest in a sitting position on her abdomen, with his knees crammed under her armpits. He had two oysters remaining. He delicately inserted one into each of her formidable nostrils and then with great prejudice, simultaneously shoved them home with his Arnold Schwartzenegger-looking thumbs.

He hurriedly surveyed the immediate area as though seeking other objects capable of inflicting severe tissue damage. In frustration he finally picked up a squirt bottle of mustard laying next to her head and much to her displeasure, began to apply ad hoc modern designs to her face and jowls using the mustard bottle as a makeshift paint brush. Just as he was starting to get really creative, the cook came charging out of the kitchen wielding a pipe wrench. Dad caught him under the chin with a jar of pickled eggs before he even made it through the doors. The impact was so strong that it knocked him out cold in mid-step, causing his limp frame to tumble backwards into the kitchen.

Dad then returned his attention to the unholy creature beneath him. It was like a scene right out of *The Exorcist*. Even though hopelessly trapped, May Hammond Payne continued to spew forth coarse invective of unconscionable severity. Her face was distorted with martial rage of an order one would expect only if supernatural agents were at work. But Dad responded simply by taunting her with rude slogans:

"I want a Mullet Flip with my Carp Box! And what the hell are *pancakes* anyway? What kind of den of inequity are you people running here? And whoever told you it was okay to point a pistol at customers?"

Then, somewhere in the debris field, Dad miraculously managed to locate a fully intact fiddler and a complete, undamaged chicken neck. Once he had them in his hands, curiously, she made eye contact with him. There was a pause. He did not know what it meant, but he picked up on it instantly. She then began to look intermittently at him and the objects in his hands. He made note of this. His mind raced. Logic circuits crunched. Then she watched with fanatical fervor as Dad slowly brought the two artifacts together before her. Suddenly, he held them in the sign of a cross in front of her face and screamed:

"SMILE!"

He placed the makeshift crucifix on her bosom. He then stood up, made a crossing gesture with his right hand, and stepped away. By this time Cleston, Luther, Hans, myself, and all the other patrons in the restaurant had gathered around the scene. As everyone watched, the waitress seemed to shift her gaze about the crowd, for a moment making eye contact with each of us. Slowly, cautiously, her lips started to quiver. The quiver gradually became organized, sporadically at first, but eventually stabilizing into a series of short-lived micro-sighs. These miniature spasms then slowly congealed into a what can only be described as a very slight, Mona Lisa-like smile.

The degree of this smile increased until her hushpuppy-caked teeth became clearly visible. Bits of onion could easily be discerned jutting from the corn meal packed spaces between her powerful incisors. It was at this point that the toddler let out a spontaneous, loud chuckle. Then everyone in the room began to laugh, including the waitress herself. Like her smile, her laughter built from a mere snicker up to a painful guffaw. In the midst of this progression she finally was able to raise up onto one elbow into a semi-reclining position. Her laughter started to become almost pathological in its intensity. But after a couple of minutes she regained a tenuous degree of composure. An almost unnatural silence seemed to prevail for about two seconds as everybody stopped laughing simultaneously to take a breath. In this pause, a presumably recently emancipated crab came strolling proudly through the debris field, defiantly nabbed a hushpuppy and then scurried under the jukebox.

May Hammond Payne became hysterical with laughter again. It was so severe that she collapsed on the floor and started thrashing like an eel in a possum's mouth. Her breathing was driven with such terrific force that cavitation in the flow of air past her lips was generating a low frequency resonance in the room, probably in the 10 to 15 hertz range. Bits of paper, cornbread, needle-sized fish bones, and basically anything on the floor within a four-foot radius was being sucked in with each breath. The resonance hurt my ears. Finally, the pressure exceeded some unpredictable critical threshold. The result was her suddenly blowing the oysters out of her nostrils in a gigantic, cataclysmic sneeze of utter devastation and destruction. So much energy was released that a sinusoidal whiplash traveled down her right leg with sufficient force to jettison the tightly-laced waitress shoe from her foot. Out of respect for human dignity, the reader will be spared additional details of this event, or to borrow words of Mark Twain: *"Let us draw the curtain of charity over the rest of the scene."*

Just accept it when I say that it was by a significant margin, the most horrible manifestation of human agony I have ever witnessed in my entire life. She quit laughing at this point and started to emit a subdued, semiconscious moan. Everyone in our party seemed to take this as a sign and began to inconspicuously filter toward the exit. On the way out, Dad placed a dollar on the table. After unloading the bullets, he laid her .38 revolver on the bill to hold it in place.

As we drove back up Route 721 that afternoon in my father's 1965 Galaxy 500, Luther and Cleston looked pretty rough. Their faces were greasy and their hair was very messy. Small children and the faint hearted would have at best been uncomfortable in their presence. Hans really didn't appear all that different from his standard look, other than the ketchup stains on his forehead. Cleston was still extracting bits of onion from his ear canal when he suddenly made a comment:

"Adam, I didn't know that you were a Catholic."

"Who said I was?"

"Well, I mean with all the crossing stuff back there I..."

"Oh that, no, I saw the Pope do it on T.V."

Cleston was using a match stick to gouge wafers of compacted cornbread from under his eyelids when he asked the question for which Dad had been waiting:

"Why did you leave the dollar Adam?"

Everyone else in the car chimed in at this point:

"Yeah, I wouldn't have left her a damned thing." commented Luther Fouts.

"Me either, unless it was a hand grenade." added Hans Mullenbach.

"Or a *bitch-seeking missile*." said Cleston.

Then everybody seemed to suddenly gleefully concur, a bitch-seeking missile would have been a just gratuity for the Anti-Waitress. Everybody except Dad that is. Instead he simply sat there and waited for us to stop laughing.

"I left the tip because she smiled. That means I am the victor. Therefore Cleston owes me the beer."

"We didn't even get to eat our food." Luther observed.

"Nobody paid for the food either. But it looks like you got your fill of hushpuppies just the same. Is there anyone in this car who is still hungry?" Dad said.

No one uttered a word. Dad was truly the victor and everyone in the car knew it. A few minutes later Dad pulled up to a liquor store drive-thru window. Instead of just one case of beer though, he got eight, and four quarts of gin, and a gallon of wine. Cleston paid for it all. After only about twenty or thirty miles, two of the cases of beer and a quart of gin were history. I managed to put away three beers myself, and I was only nine years old. Suddenly, after a long silence, and about ten beers, Hans spoke up:

"Adam, I didn't want to say anything back there, but I'm still hungry. You threw both of my fiddlers at the stupid waitress you know. Take the next left."

To this navigational request Dad quickly complied. After a few more turns, a more few miles, and a few more beers we came to a creek in the woods. We spent the next two hours gigging tadpoles and crawdads until we had at least five gallons of the bastards. We then built a fire, spitted the mud-puppy looking sumbitches on willow sticks, and roasted them like marshmallows. Cleston whipped up some kind of a marinade out of beer, gin, and wine. Hans and Luther got an assembly line type thing going on gutting the prey. My father always kept a mess kit in the trunk of his car so we had salt and pepper, toothpicks, and some gasoline-contaminated peanut butter. In the overall context of the day, it wasn't that bad of a set-up.

The crawdads tasted amazingly like shrimp: muddy, gritty, stinking, rancid shrimp that is. And it turned out that Hans was right about the tadpoles too. They are reminiscent of oysters. That is, they had all the qualities of the crawdads, plus a few more of their own. Mostly however, like oysters, they seemed better when not vigorously chewed. Indeed, it was eventually discovered that when consuming a roasted tadpole, one was far, far ahead to just swallow it whole in one smooth motion and then chase it with a slug of gin to attenuate the harsh aftertaste. Using this method, everyone put away at least a quart of the tadpoles and roughly an equal amount of crawdads. It was a culinary experience that linked all the ages of mankind from time immemorial to the very present. And I was there, I lived it. By the time all the booze and wild hors d'oeuvres were gone, everyone was too drunk and too sick to move. Everybody except me that is – because I had not been chasing mine with gin. I drove the Galaxy all the way back to Har Megiddo that night, a distance of over 180 miles.

The sun was just starting to rise when we pulled into town. Instinctively, I looked for a spot down by the river to park the car. Back in those days it was no big deal to see four grown men passed out drunk in a late model sedan pulled over on the side of the road in broad daylight. But I wanted to do everything I could to reduce the chance of us being found in this vulnerable state, because I had been burdened all night with the thought that the fish hut waitress may not have survived.

Cleston called a few days later to inform us that as a result of the events that transpired during our visit, the Fish Hut waitress had required hospitalization. But aside from a troublesome chronic sinus infection and slight elevation in the pitch of her voice, she suffered no other visible permanent damage. The Kentucky State Police were called in to investigate but they had no solid leads to pursue. And the truth of the matter was that their hearts weren't really in it.

They knew all about the Anti-Waitress. Over the years numerous complaints were received from a wide variety of individuals, including a former governor, but they could never really come up with enough evidence for a conviction. Still, they had been expecting something like this to happen for years. They eventually logged the incident as an unsolved case of assault and filed it away somewhere. But it was also rumored that if they ever found the person responsible they were going to give him a medal and probably let him get his picture made with the current governor.

The story of Dad's encounter spread like wildfire through the restaurant circuit. As a result, his reputation among waitresses everywhere was instantly catapulted to celebrity status. The Anti-Waitress had been a chronic dark blotch on the collective image of all waitresses. So to them, it seemed both ironic and fitting that the Ultimate Customer would be the one who did her in.

A few weeks later Dad and I were cruising down Highway 721. We were starting to get pretty hungry by the time we approached the outskirts of Hockertown. As we neared the city we did so with an unspoken anticipation, watching for the site of the alleged incident. But we discovered that since our last visit there must have been some changes in the ownership structure of the establishment. At least that's what we figured, because much to our surprise, the marquee had been replaced by a new one that read as follows:

CLYDE'S MUTTON HUT
- AND -
KRAUT BAR

Hans Mullenbach would have been proud. Although it looked extremely tempting, Dad and I decided to pass it up. We opted for a nearby dairy-whip instead.

Adam McCasoway poses with two lovely waitresses in Kentucky, c. 1957.

Chapter 18

The Chamber Test

During the oil-boom decades of the 1950's and 1960's my father's hectic pursuit of business ventures involved extensive travel throughout the Midwest. It was common for him to drive a thousand miles or more per week, a great deal of which was done at night. On these trips he would sometimes fall asleep and have traffic accidents.

State Route 91 - 10:47 p.m.

One night in the spring of 1959 when my father was driving a pickup truck on a narrow winding road in the hills of Kentucky, he fell asleep at the wheel and drove off a cliff at least two hundred feet high at a place called Bear Creek Mountain. Fortunately, his truck was caught in the canopy of a huge oak tree at the bottom of the escarpment. However, the truck came to rest in the tree upside down, approximately thirty-feet above the ground. He subsequently fell from the cab of the truck and was knocked unconscious.

Two oil business associates of his, an ex-card player called Blackjack Higgins and a semi-retired taxidermist named Gustav Blount, who were following him in a drilling rig and an army surplus 6x6 truck, respectively, stopped their vehicles and climbed down the cliff to look for what they assumed would be my father's dead and mutilated body. They found him lying directly under the precariously entangled truck. The entire contents of the truck which included hundreds of pounds of tools, spare parts, sacks of cement, gas cans, and a variety of other objects, had fallen also and lay scattered on the forest floor in a swath immediately around him.

One of these fallen cargo items, a drilling bit, had apparently struck him causing a severe injury to the area around his left eye. The bone beneath his temple was crushed and his eye had been popped out of its socket and was dangling by the cord on his cheek. When their flashlight illuminated this horrific sight, both men more or less panicked. Blackjack Higgins supposedly almost fainted and had to sit down on the ground to regain his composure. They thought Dad was a goner. But when Gustav held the flashlight beam directly on Dad's face, he suddenly stirred back to vivid consciousness. He immediately stood up and began to survey the situation.

Dad later recounted how he couldn't figure out what was going on at first because when he looked at Gustav Blount, who was standing, he also saw the face of Blackjack Higgins, who was sitting. When queried about this optical curiosity, they reluctantly presented my father with the unpleasant details of the severity of his eye injury. Dad said something to the effect of "Okay, no problem." and reached up and carefully snugged the rogue organ back into its conventional storage area. He then brushed the dust from his clothes and began to formulate a plan.

The nearest public telephone was at least thirty-five narrow, winding, mountain road miles away, and the closest modern hospital another hundred. Dad told the men that other than the eye thing he felt perfectly fine. They were insistent however, that he seek medical attention immediately. He reminded them that the drilling rig and the water truck were impractical for deployment as emergency transport vehicles. Subsequently, via a series of very subtle logical feints and stunning forensic maneuvers, he ultimately convinced them to climb back up to the rig and lower down the winch cable, to which he would connect the pickup truck. But several times during this presentation, when he would make emphatic gestures, or other overtures involving certain facial muscles, his eye would again set itself free upon the wide range of his ruddy cheek.

His reaction to this would be a seamless recovery and re-implantation of the unruly spheroid as though it were a completely natural act, never missing a word in his delivery. After about the fifth time however, he decided something needed to be done to cinch up the wound so as to acquire some modicum of authority over the rebellious eyeball.

Together the three of them searched in the debris field for something, anything to temporarily bind the wound. They looked for a piece of wire, string, even a rubber band. The closest thing they found was a clamp from an old set of jumper cables. But Dad was reluctant to use it because it was Gustav's catfish skinning tool. Even with only one good eye, my father could easily see the bits of fermented epidermal tissue encrusted around the tips of the clamp. Finally, Blackjack found a roll of electrical tape and the day was saved. Dad used several strips of the tape to effectively fence in the eyeball. Once this was done, they proceeded with their plan to recover the truck. Dad connected the cable to the pickup truck and Blackjack engaged the winch and started reeling it up. Everything seemed to be working normally. But as the truck got almost to the top of the cliff, the clutch started slipping on the winch at which point all progress ceased. That's when Gustav Blount grabbed the line with his bare hands and started to pull.

Gustav was an avid tug-of-war enthusiast. He had been on several championship farm league tug-of-war teams during his career. He had also spent some time as a free agent doing solo work throughout the south, and he did exhibitions at county fairs, church gatherings and so forth. Once Gustav got a good grip on the cable and a solid spot to plant his feet, his input started to make a difference. Within ten-minutes they had the truck on the pavement and righted. They filled the engine with oil, poured some water in the battery, and tried the best they could to clean out the gallon or so of spilled moonshine inside the cab. After a couple of shots of ether, the truck fired up like nothing had ever happened.

So down the road they went, behind schedule by less than an hour. They arrived at the project site, got the rig parked and then pitched their field tent. Back in those days, on remote drilling sites, it was common to pitch one or more field tents. These would serve both the function of quarters for the crew and a place to keep equipment and tools protected from the elements. This was necessary because it often took weeks to drill a well. Field tents were typically sixteen feet square, but sometimes smaller. During the day the sides could be rolled up to let air flow through.

All the ancillary amenities would typically be present. That is, there were cots to sleep on, a couple tables or so, some chairs, a stove for both warmth and food preparation, various cookware items, lanterns, bathing supplies, an ice box, a first-aid kit, some shotguns and rifles, and usually a couple of guitars to pick around on during the many tedious hours of waiting that usually accompanies the drilling of an oil well (there always seemed to be a Gibson ES-355 and a Fender Stratocaster laying around in the bed of Dad's pickup truck, scattered in amongst the other tools).

For businesses today the utility tent has universally been replaced by the portable office trailer. They come in all sizes and price ranges, upwards of a million dollars. Dad forked out fifty bucks a pop for his war surplus tents, and at the time that was a tremendous investment, but necessary.

Today, no self-respecting oil company, construction firm, etc., anywhere, would be caught dead pitching tents (excepting perhaps businesses based in regions where camels remain a principal means of transport).

Once everything was unpacked, Dad found a mirror and sat down to inspect his wound by lantern light. After some protracted discussion it was agreed that Gustav would treat the wound and Blackjack would serve the function of medical assistant. Dad stretched out on his back on one of the cots, the tape was removed and the cleaning process commenced.

After only a couple of minutes however, they determined that the only way to properly attend the injury was to remove the eyeball and clean out the socket behind it as well. Pursuant to this, Dad flexed the muscles that would ordinarily result in a wink and the eyeball popped out, subsequently dangling down over the side of his cheek. Blackjack immediately lost his guile and was compelled to look away. But commendably, he continued to pass medical supplies to Gustav as they were requested. At one point however, when Gustav asked for the box of cotton swabs, Blackjack was unable to comply because they seemed to have gone missing.

Dad asked them what was the color of the missing box. Blackjack told him that it was blue and white with red lettering. Dad then informed him that the missing box was in fact located on the ground next to Gustav's left boot – which needed polishing by the way. It took a couple of hours to get all the broken glass, paint chips, flakes of tree bark, termite thoraxes, and various other foreign matter evacuated from the wound. At one point during the procedure, a rattlesnake came slithering through the tent. Of course Dad was the only one to see it.

It just happened to occur at a juncture when Gustav was using a pocket knife to scrape some limestone chips from Dad's eye socket. As Gustav executed this delicate operation, Dad watched every movement of his hand with his good eye while monitoring the progress of the snake with the other. After earnest reflection, he chose to delay notifying Blackjack and Gustav because the snake never made any threatening gestures and because he didn't want to introduce unwarranted distraction at such a critical phase of the procedure. It turned out that the snake had trailed a mouse into the tent. The snake eventually tracked down the unsuspecting rodent and dispatched it cleanly. Dad watched the whole thing unfold. He later described the experience as being like a trip to an optometrist's office/deer head stuffing station and watching the Discovery Channel at the same time, not unlike perhaps my father's conception of what a visit to a North Korean optometrist might be like.

Gustav Blount's considerable experience as a freelance taxidermist was a really big plus in this whole deal. He carefully cleaned and reconstructed every element of the damaged region to near-natural perfection. If he'd had a spare set of antlers to graft to Dad's head, it would have been perfection. After the restoration was complete the whole area was copiously saturated with Listerine, the general-purpose disinfectant that Dad kept on hand for all his medicinal needs, large and small. Gustav then cinched up the freshened wound with a pair of clothes pins and a few inches of electrical tape and Dad was more or less good as new. He handed Dad the mirror.

"What do you think?"

"Looks good!"

After the operation they were feeling a little too edgy to simply go straight to work on the drilling rig, so they decided instead that a restorative libation would be in order. They got cleaned up, put on their night life attire, grabbed the guitars, and hit the trail. The closest licensed tavern was across the state line in Tennessee, less than five miles away as the crow flies. It was a secluded little inn owned by a long-time friend of Blackjack's by the name of Thaddeus Dalton Burns. Mr. Burns proudly boasted genetic heritage with both the Scottish poet Robert Burns, and the infamous William "Bill" Dalton of the so-called Doolin-Dalton gang.

Through the course of his rich and complex life, T.D. Burns had been known by many aliases. Chief among these was *Crash*, a name he supposedly acquired during his tenure as a race car driver back in the late forties. To supplement his racing income, he eventually had to take a job driving a fuel truck for Substandard Oil of Mississippi. But after a terrible job-related traffic accident he quit and moved up north and opened a pub. The sign out in front read as follows:

CRASH BURNS'
HIGHWAY 349 TAVERN
BEER – WHISKY
- NO PARKING IN REAR –

On the way to the tavern somebody (no one seems to remember who exactly) got the sterling notion that within the rowdy milieu of their intended destination, Dad's special condition presented a tremendous opportunity for the pursuit of some perverse antics of sport and amusement. A general plan was subsequently promulgated between the three of them.

Conveniently, by the time they arrived a tentative crust had developed sufficiently over the wound so as to provide some minimal degree of confinement to the eyeball. Therefore, in pursuit of their good-natured machination, the electrical tape and clothes pins were removed immediately prior to arrival.

Although Dad's injury would probably have stood out fairly prominently in broad daylight, within the sooty recesses of the tavern his countenance appeared to reside comfortably within the statistical range of human morphological variation one might commonly expect to be present in such an establishment. So, not unexpectedly, they were able to enter rather unremarkably, garnering only a minimum of disinterested glances in the process. At first the three of them just stood in the threshold with the door unlatched behind them. The smoke in the room was so thick it was almost stifling.

Dad thought the place was on fire. But no one in the room seemed to be too excited about it. Presumably it was just another typical night at the Highway 349 Tavern. Or maybe it was *Tobacco Night*. But what ever the reason, the smoke was very effective at making Dad's injury less conspicuous. Then, just as Dad thought they were going to slip in without being noticed, Blackjack Higgins shouted:

"Gawd bless every soul in this establishment!"

"Amen!" several voices called back.

They secured a table at the far end of the room and awaited the bartender. Dad later recounted that after he got settled in he began to notice an array of unusual artifacts liberally displayed throughout the room. Among these were a partially combusted car tire hanging on the wall behind the bar, a grille from a Mack truck suspended from the ceiling, several hubcaps containing popcorn on various tables in the room. And most enigmatically, mounted on the side of the cash register was a block of clear acetate containing what appeared to be a slice of charred bologna.

As Blackjack explained, perhaps the single most significant event in the life of Crash Burns occurred on the day he had a head-on collision with a semi tractor-trailer from a competing oil company. He was pulling a 6,400 gallon load of naphtha from Moline to Arkoma when he got cross-ways with a Hexaco rig pulling a equivalent load of methyl ethyl ketone in the opposite direction.

The resulting conflagration burned for three days and effectively shut down U.S. 79 between Johnson City and the Mississippi state line for a week. When they pulled Crash from the wreckage the only skin he had that wasn't burned to a crisp was on the soles of his feet and lining his armpits. By necessity therefore, this paucity of tissue ultimately constituted the foundation for a complex series of grafts and pioneering tissue regeneration experiments by the U.S. Veteran's Administration and the Hoosier University Agricultural Extension Office that ultimately facilitated his complete recovery to an essentially normal life. The bottom line is they used skin from both his own body and from special pigs raised in Indiana to re-build Thaddeus Dalton, a.k.a. *Crash* Burns. It was cutting edge stuff for the time. Finally, from an unspecified location in the crowd a voice called out:

"What can I get for you fellows?"

"We'll take a round of the house brew." answered Blackjack.

"How many?"

"There's three of us."

"Alright then."

A few minutes later Crash hobbled up to their table and carefully put down three quarts of beer. The mugs were metal oil cans. The tops appeared to have been cut out with a butcher knife, leaving a perilously jagged edge around the circumference of the can. Blackjack's can was a Quaker State 10W-40. Gustav received a Phillips-66 in SAE 30, and Dad got a Sinclair power steering fluid can. The paint was starting to wear off a little bit on a couple of the cans.

"Darn, Crash, you're going to have to find some new cans, these sumbitches are getting faded!" commented Blackjack.

"Yeah, I know it. They don't make 'em like these anymore. They switched to those crappy cardboard jobs a couple of years ago. We tried to make 'em work but they're just too flimsy – you can't wash 'em. But come to think of it, we don't wash the metal ones either."

Everyone at the table exchanged glances.

"Just kidding!"

While Crash was speaking, Dad took the opportunity to get a good look at his face. As Dad's scope widened to encompass the greater emerging spectacle, he carefully undertook methodical reckoning of Crash's mottled and deeply furrowed complexion. He carefully observed his inordinately diminutive facial features, like his apparently atrophied ears and nose. He made special note of Crash's unusually thick, bushy, dark eyebrows. They looked more like mutton chop sideburns turned sideways, or chic, Bohemian goatee's than they did any eyebrows Dad had ever seen. From an orthogonal perspective, within the dim, smoky atmosphere, it appeared almost like a pair of Fidel Castro jowls were protruding from Crash's forehead.

Dad carefully noted how Crash's lips were afflicted with a what appeared to be dozens of tiny razor cuts. Some were healed, some not, and two or three seemed to glisten with fresh blood. Reconstructive surgery or not, there was something curious about it. Then, as Crash was about to return to the duties of barkeep, he paused and said:

"You fellows enjoy the beer, and be careful, don't cut your lips on the cans."

Immediately after Crash left, as Blackjack and Gustav swilled unabashedly, most of all perhaps, Dad very carefully examined the rim of his power steering fluid can in an effort to assay the disposition of tissue samples bequeathed by previous customers. Being satisfied that no concentrations larger than a few cellular clumps were present, he proceeded to ardently, yet cautiously, imbibe the robust leachate therein impounded. He always professed it was the best beer he ever drank, before or after. Within seconds all stood ready for a refill.

"Barkeep, bring another round – please." yelled Blackjack.

This time when Crash came to the table he brought what appeared to be a galvanized water can. But instead of water it was filled with about three gallons of home made beer. Crash then decanted the brew into their oil cans until foam floated popcorn hulls off the table. Before he could get away, Blackjack spoke:

"Crash, I'd like to introduce you to a good friend of mine: Adam McCasoway. Adam, this is Crash Burns."

"Pleased to meet you Mr. Burns."

"Back at you there friend."

Crash took cursory note of Dad's well-attended facial injury. The dim light made it less conspicuous, but it was obvious that there either was currently, or had been a problem. But Crash was certainly not someone to call attention to another man's disfigurement.

"Adam here is a world renowned gun expert. On the way over I was telling him about your special one-of-a-kind L.C. Smith shotgun, the *eleven-gauge double-barrel*, but I don't think I did a very good job explaining its background." commented Blackjack.

"Gun expert huh? You know much about L.C. Smiths?"

"Enough to know they never made an eleven-gauge anything."

"Well I've got news for you mister: They did, they made only one, and I own it. In 1879 L.C. Smith himself commissioned it as a special gift to Prince Eugene XI of Prussia. But the bastard died of typhus in a

Turkish brothel two weeks before it was to be presented at the World's Fair in Brussels, so L.C. kept it for his own collection. But he never fired it. My great grandfather, Bill Dalton, bought it at an estate auction in Tishomingo, Oklahoma Territory, in 1883 for five bucks. The serial number is '1.' Bill Dalton is said to have used it in several train robberies and at least one bank job."

Dad had a skeptical look on the uninjured part of his face. Sensing a forensic impasse perhaps, Blackjack jumped into the discussion at this point:

"Adam, would you like to see the gun? Would you believe him then?"

"I'll look at it, but I'll call it like I see it. If it's a forgery I'll know right off."

"Do you have it here Crash?"

"Yeah, it's in my office. I'll go fetch it."

By this time some customers at adjacent tables had taken an interest in the energetic conversation and a few propositions of wagering were overheard among the wider field. Blackjack, Gustav, and Dad all looked at each other and nodded. Presently Crash returned with the shotgun. The crowd parted to let him by but closed behind him as he passed. To get through, Crash finally had to hold the weapon over his head with both arms. But he finally made it to their table and rather exhaustedly said:

"Here it is cowboy, you look at it and tell me what you think. It ain't loaded, I checked it."

Dad reached out and grasped the weapon smartly but respectfully. He then pulled it close to his chest and hefted it three or four times as though assaying its weight distribution. As he did this he also turned his injured side more away from the light. He then grasped the weapon near the end of its barrels with one hand and the by the end of the stock with the other, and rotated it about its linear axis examining the overall form. He then zeroed-in on the receiver area of the gun, examining any lettering or numbers embossed thereupon. As he did this the crowd watched in absolute awe. The brutal, cut-to-the-chase finality in his movements fully conveyed the appearance of a seasoned gun expert engaged in his craft.

Except for an occasional snort or wheeze, the crowd was totally silent. They hung on his every movement. No mannerism, sigh, nor blink went unregistered. Taking care not to point it toward anyone, he then opened the weapon and judiciously searched for patent numbers or other insignia inside the receiver. After another ninety seconds of intense observation, and apparent profound contemplation Dad finally spoke:

"Okay, it could be an L.C. Smith, I freely admit that. All of the features seem right. And if it is an L.C. Smith, then it truly is a one-of-a-kind. Even if it's a forgery, it's a damned good one. It's good enough that you may as well call it an L.C. Smith. But the only way to truly know for sure is to give it the so-called, *chamber test.*"

"What's that?" queried Crash.

"On all first-run shotguns in a series, L.C. Smith had his wife's name engraved inside the chamber of the right barrel. It's a little-known fact shared among your finer gunsmiths and curators; and only the most dedicated collectors. If what you say is true, then this is obviously, by definition, the first model of its series.

Admittedly, your claim is strengthened, but not proven by the fact that the number "1" is clearly marked on the receiver. But if it is an L.C. Smith, it will also have the engraving in the chamber. If it does not have the engraving, then it's a forgery. You asked me for my opinion, and that's my call on it."

Every mouth in the crowd seemed agape in absolute, rapt intrigue. Their attention now became fixed on Crash, waiting to see what his response would be.

"Well where can I get this chamber test done then?" asked Crash.

"I can give it the test. But be absolutely sure that you want me to because if I do, I may not be able to tell you what you want to hear. I'm sorry, but you must understand and accept that completely or I simply will not do it."

"No, no, I want you to. I want to find out for sure. Go ahead, give it the test."

"Are you absolutely positive?" Dad asked one last time.

"Shoot yes man!"

"Well...okay..."

Dad held the breach of the gun up near his face, turned directly toward the crowd, and then abruptly popped his eye out and let it dangle down into the chamber of the right barrel. When he did this a very brisk, sharp convulsion spread through the crowd. It was like everybody took a breath at the same time.

The people closest by took a step backwards, almost like they thought the eye was somehow going to get them.

There also instantly erupted from the field an initial flurry of no fewer than twenty instinctive utterances, all occurring within a few milliseconds of each other. Some were coarse, some rude, some quasi-religious, but all were sincere in earnest. These included:

1. *"Yee-ow!"*
2. *"Shee-it!"*
3. *"Holy Jeezus!"*
4. *"Lord have mercy!"*
5. *"Land-a-Goshen!"*
6. *"Sumbitch!"*
7. *"Whaaaa!"*
8. *"Hey!"*
9. *"Woo-hoo!"*

A general disorderly commotion drifted through the room. A couple of people ran out the door. In the background, amid the din of the crowd's jittery shuffle, one could pick out the distinct sound of someone apparently gagging into a bucket, or spittoon, with mixed success. A woman near the front of the crowd fainted and was caught by adjacent customers. Her Marathon SAE-30 can of beer hit the floor like a keg of slaw. But Crash just stood there, silent, in total amazement. Finally, after the crowd had settled down, he simply said:

10. *"Angels and ministers of grace defend us!"*

Then Dad suddenly spoke up:

"Hold on! Hold everything, I see something...yes...there are definitely letters of some kind engraved in here. I can almost make out an 'N,' no, no, it's an 'M' and an 'R.' What is that? Just a minute, just a minute... there's an 'S.' No...no...make that two esses...'M'..."

The crowd started to ease closer, hanging on every letter, trying to decipher the code. Finally he blurted out:

"MRS. SMITH!"

There was a collective gasp in the room. In the back there were a couple of "yee-haws" presumably by winners of sundry gambles. Crash got a look of total bewilderment on his quasi-mutilated face. Dad extracted his eye from the barrel and faced the crowd, letting the organ remain pendulous as he spoke.

"I believe you've got a genuine article here. It is very rare and very valuable. You should clean the barrels though, looks like there's a wasp nest in this one. Do you want me to check the other barrel?"

"No...no, that's okay son. I tell you what, I sure appreciate you helping me out and all, but maybe you ought to reel that bad boy back up...I mean, you know, you're scaring the customers."

"What do you mean?" Dad asked, very seriously.

The inordinately inquisitive crowd lingered close by, stretching their necks obnoxiously to catch every detail of the continuing conversation.

Curiously, Crash's eyebrows were drenched with perspiration. He wiped them with a handkerchief and responded to Dad's interrogative.

"Your eye, can you put it back into your face?"

"What for?"

"Because it's frightening the customers."

"I ain't skeered. How 'bout you Junior, you skeered?" said an unidentified voice nearby.

"Skeered? Shoot no, I ain't skeered of no dang eyeball!" replied someone, Junior presumably.

Unexpectedly, inexplicably, another episode of gagging sounds was heard coming from somewhere in the crowd, but considerably closer and louder this time. Still maintaining, ahem, eye-contact with Crash, Dad resumed his line of questioning after the brief distraction.

"So are you telling me that a man with a little sty in his eye is not welcome in this business establishment?" Dad asked.

"Oh no sir Mr. McCasoway, I never meant anything like that. I meant, as a gentleman, maybe it would be better for the womenfolk and all if you...adjusted it a little...that's all I meant."

Dad silently conducted what appeared to be a very rigorous logical analysis of the proposition. After some interim he finally rendered his assessment.

"Well okay, since you put it that way, I guess you're right."

He subsequently re-calibrated the freethinking light sensor to its recommended default specifications and sat down in his chair. A collective sigh seemed to emanate from the crowd when he did this, almost as though an immense weight had just been removed from everyone in the room. Some of the onlookers even started returning to their tables. Dad was preparing to take a sip from his Sinclair can when Gustav unexpectedly reached over and patted him on the shoulder and said:

"Well done!"

But when he did this it caught Dad off guard and the force of the manly pat made his eye fall out again, landing in his beer. The crowd went wild. Dad recovered the jaunty peeper and re-installed as quickly as he could, but it was too late. True chaos had erupted and there was no turning back now. Again, Crash was sincerely perplexed. Perspiration flowing from his eyebrows formed small rivulets as it ran down his partially-cloned jowls. The look on his face finally became too much for Blackjack and Gustav to endure and they started laughing. This got Dad to give over his composure as well. He laughed so hard tears began to flow. This of course made the eyeball pop out again. Each time it popped out there would be another roar from the crowd and the whole cycle would repeat itself. It was one big cheese party and Dad had the knife.

After about three or four minutes of this intense weirdness, some old cowboy worked his way to the front of the crowd and hobbled up to Dad's table. Inexplicably, he was carrying what appeared to be a spittoon. Then for reasons known only to himself, after carefully placing the spittoon onto the floor, he reached over and grabbed his own leg between the knee and ankle, twisted it, and extracted a prosthetic lower leg. He then took the artificial appendage, with the boot still affixed thereto, and placed it upright on the table. After securing his weight on a nearby chair, he reached down into the leg and extracted a fifth of expensive gin. It was a scene somewhat similar to a magician pulling a rabbit out of a hat. Again, the crowd roared. The old cowboy never said a word. He used his teeth to uncork the bottle. He then decanted the gin into Dad's Sinclair can until it was full.

"Thanks partner." Dad said with copious hope and enthusiasm.

"I walked all the way from Amarillo on that bottle. I want to share it with you." the old cowboy replied.

"I am deeply honored sir." declared Dad.

Wanting to be sociable, Dad quaffed an inordinately massive slug of the pale concoction, taking extra care not to cut his lips on the jagged metal of the oil can while at the same time trying to keep his injured eyeball under control. But it got tough quick. The gin was still at or near 98.6 degrees from its cross-country stint in the peg leg. And to top it off, it was at least 180 proof. It had a bite so powerful, my father later explained, that it just about popped out his good eye too. Because it was more or less like drinking pure battery acid, his body's involuntary reflexes wasted no time expelling the toxic liquid. The external manifestation of this phenomenon involved Dad abruptly hurling into the cowboy's conveniently located spittoon. The old cowboy then spoke up:

"Don't worry son, it does the same thing to me."

In the interim between the coarse choreography of Dad gagging up gin-impregnated bile and attempting to induce some semblance of jurisdiction over his by now out-of-control eyeball, another stranger approached the theater. He appeared to be a fairly average looking individual, not so much a cowboy as an aluminum siding salesman, or a successful chicken farmer perhaps. He was decked-out in a fashionable sand colored Nehru jacket, a peach turtleneck sweater, burgundy slacks, and a pair of white patent-leather loafers.

But this average looking, would-be poultry magnate had a dark secret concealed beneath his stylish attire. That is, he was gracious and thoughtful enough to open his jacket and display for everyone what would most tactfully be described as an inordinately substantial gall-bladder scar, extending from a specially modified portal in his sweater. What's so bad about that? Well nothing perhaps, except that this particular gall bladder scar was prehensile. The surgeon who performed the operation must have gotten some abdominal muscle nerves crossed in an extraordinary way when closing the incision. The result was an organized concentration of animate scar tissue that exhibited the unanticipated emergent property of bilateral opposition, just like a human hand – a human hand with about 19 fingers and 11 thumbs that is.

So the first thing the chicken farmer-looking guy did was pick up the cowboy's bottle with his gall bladder scar and pour the rest of the gin into Dad's Sinclair can. Dad didn't know if he should thank the guy or punch him. Meanwhile, Blackjack and Gustav, like everyone else within sight, seemed to be strangely entranced by the scar phenomenon and remained silent.

The guy then produced from his coat pocket a deck of playing cards and asked if anybody would like to see some tricks. There wasn't a citizen present who seemed to have the heart to say no to the guy. So the well-dressed stranger reached down and passed the deck to the scar. The scar went absolutely nuts with those cards. It was like nothing they had ever seen. The scar shuffled, cut, and dealt the cards faster that any pair of hands could ever do. The crowd loved it. During this display Crash finally reached a critical threshold in his overall bearing. He looked around and saw his tavern full of happy people spending money.

He then considered the truly fortuitous fact that he was getting to enjoy the splendid wit and company of two great Americana quasi-celebrities of the back-country pub and roadhouse circuit: *Texas "Gin-Leg" Hodges* and *Benny "The Gripper" Fuquay,* not to mention good friends, both old and new, like Blackjack Higgins, Gustav Blount, and Adam *"Chamber Test"* McCasoway. It was a night he would never forget. So, presumably, with the collective mood thus appropriately vibrant, Crash could no longer resist the impulse to let down his guard and unwind a little. Within five minutes he had climbed up onto the bar and was doing vigorous calisthenics to the primal beat of Western music played by Blackjack and Gustav with vocals by Dad. They opened with *Cool Water.*

To an accompaniment of rowdy cheers, he danced around doing a difficult-to-describe version of a drunken strip tease, mostly tease, until eventually, to the tune of *Rawhide,* he removed his work shirt and tossed it into the yelping crowd. Much to everyone's amazement, it was thereby revealed that where other reconstructive surgery patients presumably exhibit reconstituted tissue, Crash instead displayed what appeared to be a dense layer of short, stiff, black hair, with a single stripe of white hair running across his back at about shoulder level, not entirely unlike the color scheme of a breed of pig called *Hampshire.*

Prior to the operation the doctors had repeatedly warned him that interspecies skin grafting was a whole new territory in medicine. They informed him straight out that there might be some unforeseeable residual effects, but nothing serious or life threatening was expected. This he generally found to be the case. However, there was one exception he could think of. It was the time he supposedly made the grievous error of engaging in a little sun bathing and light swimming at of one of the canals next to the bacon mill over in East Dunlapburg.

Before it ended they had eight security guys down there trying to herd him back into the stockyard. One of them actually jabbed him with a fully charged cattle prod. Crash never went swimming again. And understandably, he became real choosy about when and where he removed his shirt. But this night all inhibitions were released, the safeties were removed.

After Crash's big show, things mellowed out a little and the crowd spread out for the most part. Crash left the serving up to a couple of his helpers so he could hang out for a little while. They all returned to the table they had been sitting at before the impromptu concert and started shooting the bull. They were telling war stories and having a real good time. As the old timers like to put it: they were *cutting a hog in the ass with a big knife.* The stunning conversation progressed:

"So Benny, what do you do when you're not dealing cards with your abdominal muscles?" inquired Crash.

"I sell ink products."

"Ink products?"

"Yes sir, I sell ink to twenty-two newspapers and about fifty print shops in three states."

"How many colors?"

"About thirty-five."

"What's the biggest mover?"

"India."

"Splendid! How about you cowboy?" Crash said, looking toward Gin Leg Hodges.

"I work for the Acme Cement Company out of Lubbock."

"You work in a limestone quarry?"

"No sir, I just sell the stuff."

"Sell what?"

"Mostly cement, agricultural lime, and limestone block – like for making rock walls and buildings. I went straight from roping doggies to hawking boulders in the fall of 1933. Been doin' it ever since."

"Yeah, but are you making any money?" quipped Gustav.

"Well, they call me the *Limestone Cowboy...*"

"What ever made you give up being a cowboy to sell the fossilized remains of dead sea animals?" asked Dad.

"Oh I don't know, the forty-below winters, the 110-summers, the parasitic flies, the stinking cows, getting my leg gnawed off by a grizzly bear...I think it was a combination of things."

"I heard they are extremely powerful animals. What did he do, just nip it off in one clean bite?" asked Blackjack.

"No, it was an old bear. Most of his teeth were missing. It took him an hour and a half of gumming around on it to get it gnawed all the way off."

There was a collective pause as everyone seemed to be both visualizing the spectacle of this circumstantial presentation and cogitating its situational ethics. Then Gustav spoke up:

"Crash, I've always been curious, why do you have a piece of burnt bologna glued to the cash register?"

"That ain't bologna son, that's my wallet, or what's left of it. It was in my pocket when I had the wreck. My little brother had it coated with Plexiglas for me. There's 275 dollars in there somewhere, believe it or not."

"How long were you in the hospital?" queried Gustav.

"I was in the intensive care unit for thirty-seven days and then in the burn center for another 212. I got to be pretty popular with the nurses."

"Are they the one's who got the 'Crash Burns' thing going?" inquired Gripper Fuquay.

"No sir, some orderlies down at the V.A. hospital in Memphis got that started. Those guys had funny names for everyone."

"Like what?" requested Gin Leg Hodges.

"Well..."

Just then Crash noticed a group of customers entering the tavern. He elbowed Dad and said:

"See that gal coming through the door over there?"

"Which one?"

"That one right there – the big gal, the one who stands out like a diamond in a goat's ass."

"Yes sir." Dad replied.

"Well, she's got quite a reputation around these parts for being an uppity, snobbish type."

"What do you mean?" asked Gripper Fuquay.

"Let's put it this way, at one time or another she's smacked just about every man in this bar."

"Even you?" asked Gustav.

"Yes sir. She nailed me a good one last March."

"What did you do to her?"

"Nothing."

"Right, I'm sure she smacked you for nothing." said Blackjack.

"All I did was make a little joke about her name. People kid about my name all the time. It doesn't bother me. It's one of the things we all do around here to keep things entertaining. I never dreamed she was going to take a whack at me."

"What is her name?" asked Dad.

"Helen Dalmatian."

"Hell and Damnation?" commented Blackjack Higgins.

"That's what I said, and the bag slapped me!"

"She hit you in the face?" asked Dad.

"Yes sir, she did. And it hurt too. She blind-sided me on the left temple. It caught me completely cold. I had a bruise for three months. I almost called the sheriff on her. But the more I thought about it the more I figured it would just be bad publicity. She still comes in here just to spite me. She doesn't even pay her tab half the time."

"You're making this up!" said Blackjack.

"No sir, I am not."

"Why do you even let her in then?" asked Gustav.

"I don't know. I guess I'm just waiting for the right time to throw her out."

"Hey Adam, why don't you ask her for a date? She sounds like your type." commented Blackjack.

"I don't think I could play that kind of guitar."

"Why not?"

"It's got too many strings." replied Dad.

"Can you get her to come over here?" asked Blackjack.

"Lord have mercy! Why would I want to do that?" Crash replied. Blackjack looked at Dad:

"You think we ought to fix her up?"

"Maybe." Dad replied

"Can you get her to smack you again Crash?" asked Blackjack.

"Are you kidding? The question is: how can I make her not smack me?"

"No, if you can just get her to smack at you, Gustav here will see to that she doesn't actually ever hit you. Right Gustav?"

"Affirmative."

"Now just a damn minute fellows, I don't want anybody roughing her up, I don't run that kind of place..."

"Nobody's going to touch her. We're all gentlemen here, right boys?" Dad said.

"Always."

It took about ten minutes to get everything in place. A trip to the kitchen was required for supplies. In the interim a few onlookers sensed that something was about to happen and began to assemble. My guess is that the strong rope lashed around Crash's chest was the actual signal that alerted them of imminent action. As Crash took his final position the rope was concealed beneath a heavy wool jacket. When everyone was in place, Crash finally called out:

"Miss Dalmatian. Miss Dalmatian, there's someone here who'd like to meet you!"

From across the room she examined the scene as if sensing a trap, but she came anyway. The onlookers parted to create a path for her as she approached.

"What do you sumbitches want?" she queried.

"A member of the band would like to meet you."

"What band? I never seen no damn band. Why are you wearing a coat?"

"They played earlier tonight, before you arrived. I'm cold."

"Which one of the no-count bastards is he then?"

"This feller right here, the leader of the band: Adam McCasoway. Adam, I'd like to introduce you to...*Hell & Damnation...*"

Crash had not much more than gotten the last syllable out before she had her right arm airborne in a vicious forehand swing. It was coming in low and at a slight upward angle. It had some power behind it. In Crash's position he would clearly be subject to the peak of its kinetic energy upon impact. However, at the last instant Gustav yanked the rope in one enormous Herculean tug, jerking Crash out of the way like he was a tattered old rag.

But Dad was in just the right position next to Crash to take what was left of the smack on his left jaw, at a much reduced force. At the instant of impact, Dad flexed his wink muscles and the eyeball came rolling out. Helen Dalmatian got a look of 100% pure mortal terror on her face. Meanwhile, in one smooth motion after the initial impact, Dad then fell against Gripper Fuquay and Gin Leg Hodges at the same time, knocking the latter off of his prosthetic leg, and bending it backwards in a classic Joe Theisman style apparent break, with Gin Leg issuing a deafening scream of mortal agony.

Meanwhile Gripper hit the floor face down to the sound of shattering glass (provided by Gustav stomping a wine glass under the table). Gripper then screamed and rolled over holding his scar. Someone pulled Gripper's shirt open to reveal the scar with a broken gin bottle embedded in it. Gripper started shouting:

"Ahhhh...get it out...somebody get it out...please...ahhhhhh!"

Crash reached down and quickly pulled the broken bottle out of the scar. The scar then began to spew forth tomato paste and day-old oatmeal, followed by a sporadic series of raw chicken livers, two and three at a time, just like dealing cards. One of these gamy morsels grazed Helen on the jowl and then sloughed down her neck, coming to rest on the lapel of her stylish frock. Everybody in the room suddenly took a step backwards. She turned white as a sheet, dropped her Sunoco 10W-40 beer can, let out an odd, loud, melodious primal scream of some protracted duration, and then without further ceremony hit the door like a flash. To this day she has never been seen or heard from again in the greater Dunlapburg area or the surrounding tri-county region.

There was a rumor that she ran off to a convent and became a nun. Another theory purported that they had to send her to *the Home* somewhere in Alabama. Dad always claimed he intuitively sensed that he would end up being married to her in another life as some kind of karmic quid pro quo. After a final jam session of *Blue Moon of Kentucky,* Dad and the boys cordially departed to a standing ovation. As they left, the mean adrenaline level in the tavern was significantly greater than when they arrived.

They hadn't been on the road too long when it became clear that my father was in serious need of real medical attention. The swelling had doubled and he was running a fever. The closest real hospital was in Louisville, over a hundred miles distant. But there was a small country hospital in the town of Gomorrah, Kentucky, less than ten miles away. So they decided to go to the closer facility first where they figured Dad would at least be able to get a penicillin shot to hold him over until they could make it to a more metropolitan hospital.

On the way they had a few minutes to logically analyze their situation. Via this rigorous cogitation, they decided that since they had been drinking alcoholic beverages it might be a good idea to not discuss details of the accident with the attending physician. Even though the mishap occurred before they consumed the booze, they considered the appearance of impropriety to be too overwhelming. Plus the circumstances of the affair were sufficiently extraordinary that their complete appreciation would be unlikely by anyone other than those who actually observed them. With the exception of Dad, Gustav, Blackjack, and a few customers in an obscure mountain tavern, that pretty much encompassed the balance of the population of the planet. They understood this. So with better ideas in short supply, the sty angle referenced earlier by Dad, would have to suffice.

Gomorrah Mercy Hospital - 1:39 a.m.

It appeared to be a slow night at Gomorrah Mercy. The only employee present was a cantankerous old nurse. She wore a name tag inscribed as follows:

A. LOVELESS
R.N.

She must have smelled the beer on them as soon as they walked through the door. She automatically refused to accept the medical validity of the sty story and she let them know it straight out.

"What, did you smart-off to the wrong customer and get your bell rang?" she asked snottily.

"No ma'am, me and the boys here work at the uranium enrichment plant over in Phlegmingsburg. One of the pumps blew a seal and Adam got hit in the eye with some of the back-flush. We think it might be infected, you know, like a sty. All we want you to do is give him a shot of penicillin and we will get out of here and let you go back to what you were doing." said Blackjack.

"Back-flush, huh?"

"Yes ma'am, the worse kind of flush, not like fore-flush at all, right Gustav?"

Gustav was a little slow, but he eventually picked up on it.

"Yeah. The fore-flush ain't that bad. Hell, I've drank the stuff before. But man-o-man, that damn back-flush, whew, I'm telling you what! Shoot lady, when we was kids we used to..."

Blackjack nudged Gustav before he got too carried away. The nurse looked at them blankly.

"My great grandson is a supervisor at the Phlegmingsburg plant. Maybe you know him, Shep Magnard?"

"Sorry ma'am, we are strictly prohibited from discussing the names or addresses of our fellow employees. It's a government regulation under 10CFR-30. Actually we're breaking the law just talking about it." quipped Blackjack.

"Right. Well anyway, he told me they have special suits for jobs like that." replied the nurse.

"Ordinarily that's true, but we were installing new equipment in a space that is too small for a protective suit. They use ethanol as a coolant. When the valve blew it got all over us." Gustav said.

"Ethanol huh? Smells like ethanol that has been contaminated with juniper berries!" replied the nurse.

"All he wants is a shot. Can you help him or do we move on?" asked Blackjack.

"I can't give him any penicillin until I get a look at that eye."

The nurse started poking around on Dad's eye with a tongue depressor and a chrome shoe horn-like object.

"Ouch!"

"Calm down, this won't hurt."

"Well I'm sorry, but it does."

"I'm going to spread the eyelids apart, so be still."

"No, please, I wish you wouldn't do that, it hurts too bad."

"Shut up you damn punk. I know what I'm doing. I've only been a nurse for sixty-seven years. You think I haven't poked around on a few pinkeyes before?"

"Sixty-seven years! Let's see, that means you've been a nurse since 1892. That must be some kind of a record. Did you ever work on anybody famous, like *Abraham Lincoln?*" inquired Blackjack.

"I'm not that old you smart-mouthed punk. But since you brought it up, I once gave a bladder massage to Roosevelt."

"Franklin?"

"Theodore!"

Meanwhile Dad continued protesting:

"...I don't care, I think it would be better if you left it alone and just gave me the shot instead."

"Don't move, I'm going the squeeze on it a little."

"No, please..."

"SHUT UP AND HOLD STILL!"

The nurse reached up and very roughly spread Dad's eyelid apart, rudely wedging in the shoe horn. This caused the eye to abruptly shoot out, almost hitting her cheek in the process. She immediately flinched like a snake had struck. At the same time Dad began to moan like he was dying.

"Ahhhhh...oooooo...help me...it hurts...please..."

"Oh hell!" the nurse exclaimed. She was visibly shaken.

"Now see what you've done? He asked you not the mess with it. All he wanted was a shot. Adam, Adam, are you okay Adam?" asked Blackjack.

"It hurts pretty bad. Somebody get me to a hospital."

"This is a hospital!" the nurse sharply reminded them.

"Hospital! Hospital? This ain't no damn hospital! This is a torture chamber!" Gustav yelled at the nurse.

"Will you fellows get me out of here before she kills me!" Dad said.

"Adam, you need that shot of penicillin before we leave or you're not going to make it." emphasized Gustav. Blackjack then followed up:

"He's right. Nurse, are you going to give this man a shot or are you going to let him lose the eye, or worse?"

"That's it. I'm calling Dr. Butcher right now!"

"Dr. who?"

"Dr. Yuri Butcher. He'll straighten you damn punks out."

"Okay, I'm out of here." Dad said as he leaned toward the door.

"Whoa there Adam, take it easy." said Blackjack.

"I'm not letting any damn Butcher doctor touch me!"

Dad started to get up but Gustav and Blackjack wouldn't let him.

"Now Adam, you know that eye needs to be looked at by a professional."

"Good point Gustav, but I don't need some damn Butcher poking around on it. Let's go someplace where they have real doctors."

"Dr. Butcher is a licensed surgeon!" emphasized the nurse.

"Is that so, where did he go to medical school?" Blackjack asked.

"He was born in French Guyana but he got his medical degree through a special U.N. exchange program at Stalingrad Polytechnic." the nurse answered.

"Stalingrad Polytechnic!"

The three of them just looked at each other.

"Okay, that is it. We're outta here." said Blackjack.

"What for?" asked the nurse.

"We ain't letting no damn communist Butcher latch his mitts onto our friend."

"Yeah, that would be remiss of us." added Gustav.

"Well what do you worthless bastards intend to do then?"

"Are you going to give him the penicillin shot or not?" replied Blackjack.

"Not a chance in hell!"

Dad looked around the room. He spotted a bottle of alcohol and some bandages on a table. Dad gestured toward the bottle with his hand and then nodded. Blackjack reached over and grabbed the bottle, opened it and handed it to Gustav. Dad then laid down on the examination table and Gustav poured the alcohol directly into Dad's eye socket.

Dad immediately generated a subtle groan but otherwise remained composed. Gustav patted the area dry with his handkerchief and restored the eyeball to its rightful location. He then put a band aid across the eye to hold it in.

"There, good as new." said Gustav.

"Now, let's get the Stalingrad out of here!" Dad said.

"Hold on, I'm going to have to charge you for the alcohol and the band aid."

"Put it on my bill!" said Blackjack.

They headed for the door. The nurse followed, berating them harshly.

"If you leave here without paying I'll call the State Police."

"Lady, if you do that, there's going be a lot of questions asked. You know, questions about the little details: like how an incompetent nurse used a shoe horn to gouge a poor man's eyeball right out of his head." said Blackjack.

"That was not my fault! I did not gouge that hard."

"Okay, okay, how much?" queried Dad.

"Twenty-five dollars."

The year was 1959. Twenty-five U.S. dollars would have made a substantial down payment on a two-bedroom ranch-style bungalow on a nice lot in the suburbs. It was such a ridiculously excessive amount for the items in question that they were literally stymied. Not only that, they each knew that it was doubtful that they even possessed such a sum between the three of them. They started laughing.

"Shoot lady, I could get a leg chopped off, two appendectomies, and a gall bladder job back home for that much." stated Blackjack.

"Dr. Butcher specializes in gall bladder operations."

"Oh yeah, ever do any work for a man named Benny Fuquay?" asked Gustav.

"That was not entirely Dr. Butcher's fault. The power went off in the middle of the operation. He had to finish by candle light. And besides, Mr. Fuquay has still not paid his bill."

"At these rates I can see why!" said Blackjack.

With arms akimbo, she retorted:

"Cash or check?"

"Check." said Dad.

"On what bank?"

"SFF & MMCFCTOI."

"What?"

"Seventh-Fifth Farmer's & Merchant's Mutual Chemical Fidelity Commercial Trust of Indianapolis."

"Sorry, no out of state checks."

They each rummaged through their pockets and amassed their currency into a pile on the counter. Their combined cash assets totaled $17.44.

"You're $7.56 short." emphasized the nurse.

"How about an I.O.U.?" Dad asked.

"Nope."

"I've got a nice set of cuff links in the truck." Dad said.

"No can do."

"What would it take then?" asked Gustav.

"Twenty-five dollars, U.S."

"Besides that." said Blackjack.

"Nothing. Either pay in full or I'm calling the State Police."

"We don't have it."

"Is there anyone who can bring the money to you?"

"Yes, I could call my secretary." Dad said.

"What city?"

"Red Boiling Springs, Tennessee."

"No long-distance calls allowed."

"I can call collect, there will be no charges to the hospital." emphasized Dad.

"I don't care, you're not making a long-distance call on my shift."

"Well, what are we supposed to do then?" yelled Blackjack.

"Pay your bill."

"But we don't have enough cash to do that!" reiterated Blackjack.

"You should have thought of that before you came barging in here in the middle of the night demanding emergency medical care."

"But this is a hospital!" Yelled Gustav.

"Don't talk to me like that!"

"Look lady, we've given you all the money we have. Let's be reasonable, it's late, we want to leave." Blackjack pleaded.

"I don't want to hear it!"

"Since we don't have any more money to give you, we're going to walk out that door over there and you won't see us again, that much I promise." said Blackjack.

"Well, if you're not going to pay in full, I'm taking the band-aid back then."

Before he could react she reached up and aggressively yanked the adhesive bandage from Dad's eye. The eyeball instantly came shooting out. Dad screamed and hit the floor, and commenced to thrash around like a carp on the hood of a LaSalle.

"Oh no, not again!" said Gustav.

"Shut up you freak! He'll be okay once the pain stops." screamed the nurse.

"Can I ask a question?" said Gustav.

"Oh what the hell, go ahead."

"I just want to know one thing: Did you study medicine in the Soviet Union too?"

By the time it was all over, they got their $17.44 refunded and Dad received his penicillin shot for no charge. However, this was accomplished only through repeated threats of litigation with special emphasis on the negative publicity that would understandably be associated therewith. It was a bitter pill but the nurse finally swallowed it.

Supposedly, the next morning Dad did the eye-popping-out-thing in the emergency room at a major hospital in Louisville and the attending physician almost had a heart attack. An entire team of advanced trauma surgeons subsequently descended upon my father and stitched up the wound thereby permanently terminating the pedestrian antics of the wayward eye.

After receiving an anonymous tip, the Kentucky State Police arrested nurse Loveless for shaking down patients, ending a criminal enterprise that had lasted for over half a century. Dr. Butcher was also taken into custody for practicing medicine without a valid U.S. license. After further investigation it was discovered that he was the infamous "Butcher of Stalingrad." He was subsequently remanded to officials of the U.N. War Crimes Commission and returned to Geneva to spend the rest of his life in prison. It took Dad several weeks to fully recover from the eye injury. During this period he, Blackjack, and Gustav drilled the well at the location they had set up on the night of the accident. It still produces oil to this day.

Chapter 19

The Hockertown Gang of Four

Somewhere in the hills southwest of Hockertown, lived a family of exiled continental Western Europeans known locally as the Kochsacheurs. There were three brothers: Pablo the oldest, followed by the twins Jacques and Jean Claude, and their little sister Pandora. They more or less raised themselves after their unregistered arrival in America as children back in 1954. This compulsory autonomy was primarily the result of their uncle Sartre Kochsacheur abandoning them less than a year after they all came over together from their homeland.

What little social aptitude they did possess was learned from Sartre's example. And he honestly did for a while try to instill in them the most redeeming points of his vast knowledge and skills. Unfortunately, power-funneling vodka, grave-robbing, and operating bootleg tattoo parlors were not as lucrative, or appreciated in the New World as they presumably were in their home country. Consequently, with no formal education or marketable skills, their economic options were severely restricted.

Also, because of their unorthodox upbringing, the Kochsacheur children never really fit in socially in the tri-county region. That is, their general oddness and self-imposed isolation, not to mention the language barrier, meant that by definition, they lived between the cracks of society. Despite these handicaps however, or perhaps because of them, they eventually learned to survive by scavenging resources others either left behind or neglected to guard adequately.

They never had jobs. They never possessed property. They never owned a house, paid rent, or sent a check to the IRS. They were perpetual squatters. They naturally evolved a very effective technique of digging in like chiggers on a secluded parcel of land and remaining there until the rightful owner was able to bring to bear persuasive pressure of sufficient robustness to permanently dislodge them.

By process of elimination therefore, the Kochsacheurs ended up settling on some isolated coal reserve property owned by a major mining corporation headquartered in Chicago. The company in question was very successful. One of the factors contributing to this success was their practice of maintaining extremely detailed records of their outlying assets. These records were continually reviewed and updated by an aggressive information management infrastructure.

As a result, the company knew the precise location and size of every tract of land they owned. They knew the developmental status of each site. And they also had a realistic picture of the fair market value of each reserve, and all equipment thereupon affixed. Unfortunately however, they did not have an apparatus in place capable of detecting encroachment by clans of derelict Europeans. Because of this intelligence deficiency, the Kochsacheurs enjoyed the closest thing to a permanent residence they had known since they departed Ste. Mere Eglise.

In the subsequent months they created an elaborate living space within the network of abandoned underground mining tunnels beneath the property. During these introductory days the family continued to roam about the countryside like always, foraging for whatever they could find. But now they could return to their subterranean encampment at night and fatten upon the loot in relative security. The mine provided them with protection from the rigors of foul weather and a place to establish a base of operations. By the standards of their previous lifestyle, this new mode was a veritable windfall of near-Utopian proportions.

And so they prospered and the daily affairs of comfortable living thus prevailed for them over an appreciable span of time. They enjoyed this rich life largely unmolested, and entirely detached from the civilized world, unscathed by its prying, meddling eye, and unburdened by its chains. Such an arrangement they most likely could have maintained practically forever. Unfortunately, but not surprisingly, the darkest elements of human nature inevitably unmasked their unsightly countenances. It began innocently at first, then worsened at a frightening pace. Apparently, in their haughty, new-found prosperity, they began to grow irreverent and brazen.

That is, as they carried out their routine foraging in the countryside, they slowly began to wander closer to town each day. Then one lazy afternoon in August, after much observation and forethought, coyly at first, they briefly ventured into the outer suburbs of Hockertown, promptly impounded some sirloin steaks from an unattended barbecue grill, and skedaddled. This paranoid, go-for-broke maneuver took less than a minute from start to finish. However, apparently based on this initial success, their shyness abated exponentially. Within two days they were in the heart of the city, unabashedly using stolen golf clubs to brutalize chipmunks on the courthouse lawn. They had finally discovered the proverbial Promised Land of Scavenging.

They were completely overwhelmed by the broad and encompassing scope of modern civilization and all of its strange fixtures, complexions, and commotion. Everything was new to them. And they found it entirely irresistible. So they immediately sought to experience all that society had to offer. But with no moral compass to blunt the point of their wanton urges, their scavenging was prosecuted with little just consideration, coordination, form, or purpose, and seemingly without regard to the potential consequences, harmful or otherwise. They were like unsupervised children running loose in a gigantic candy shop (three-hundred pound, wild, mutant, heathen children that is).

Shortly thereafter, it became commonplace to observe the Kochsacheurs arrayed as a rude gang, sitting in some poor citizen's vegetable garden, grooming one another between bites of rhubarb; or pawing through garbage cans behind the American Legion in search of pie crusts, or using a windshield wiper from someone's new Electra to root the grubs out of a landscaping timber. They prosecuted these transgressions somewhat freely, even leisurely, because common citizens were simply afraid to confront them.

On those occasions when the authorities were summoned, they always seemed to arrive after the Kochsacheurs had scurried off to a different part of the city in pursuit of another of their varied and exciting pastimes. These included their seemingly incessant raiding of pigeon nests on the roofs of old buildings downtown, or their inconsiderate harvesting of ducks and goldfish in the fountain at the city park.

Ironically, authorities theorize that it was at this latter venue where they quite serendipitously discovered another facet of civilization that was hitherto unknown to them. That is, while wading in the fountain pool they had their first encounter with the mysterious shiny disks. Curiously attracted to these strange objects, they gathered all that the fountain would easily yield and sped away to their den in the hills. It was there that they carefully assayed every artifact. Taking note of the elaborate carvings on each.

After some coordinated contemplation they recognized a curious, almost deliberate or intended pattern among the field of objects. With the investment of another full day, they finally were able to sort the strange articles into approximately five or six basic classes based on size, color, taste, and odor. Jacques theorized that they were nothing more than fancy washers without holes. This proposition being based on his knowledge of washers in general. His understanding of washers was related to the fact that the Kochsacheurs had by necessity grasped downward, deeply into the dark well of primal human potential and revived the very ancient art of throwing projectiles in order to dispatch prey animals.

When re-learning the art of projectile hurling, there is an understandable progression from the primitive to the more sophisticated as the practitioner refines his or her methods by trial and error, and rote repetition. Stones are used at first. Tennis ball- thru grapefruit-sized stones are most effective against mesofauna within a fifty-foot radius. For greater distances, smaller stones are progressively employed. Stone throwing is a very effective method for applying lethal force at a distance. Curiously, the human hand seems almost as if it evolved specifically for throwing stones about the size of a baseball. Consider a major league pitcher for example. The talent for delivering a projectile like a baseball at regulation distances, with such force and accuracy is no coincidence. The pitcher does not do anything the rest of us cannot. He just does it to the fullest potential of the human algorithm.

It is likely that if a really good major league pitcher could go back to prehistoric times, he would excel as a hunter. The rest of us would probably lose a few pounds before we got the knack of it. But eventually, we'd catch on too. The human being is a natural throwing machine. Baseball pitching, like practically any other modern human faculty, clearly has a foundation in survival instincts left over from the cave man days.

However, as robust as they are, stones do exhibit certain limitations. For example, luck would have it that in those places in the environment where stones are usually abundant, there are very few suitable animals to throw them at. And not unexpectedly, in areas with a high proportion of animals, there are usually a minimal number of stones. So stones must be laboriously transported in order to hunt effectively with them. This of course emphasizes perhaps the most significant shortcoming of stones: their excessive weight. Once these fundamental limitations are appreciated, the primitive hunter begins to experiment with alternate methods and technologies.

It is possible that in developing human cultures, the next logical stage after the natural stone projectile is the sharp stick. This progression was generally true for the Kochsacheurs as well. However, it is believed that they also experimented with a variety of alternative projectile concepts before changing to the stick paradigm entirely.

One of these alternate projectile methods involved the throwing of standard-grade flat washers. Although this may sound relatively harmless to the casual observer, the killing power of a washer is actually quite formidable when in the hands of an expert. Also, the force delivered can be significantly multiplied by the employment of refined throwing techniques. The Kochsacheur method was to whip the washer off the end of the index finger, in a leveraged concentration of power emanating from the entire upper torso and telescoped down the arm. Flinging the washer in this manner both considerably compounded the kinetic energy and added a gyroscopic spin element. This resulted in a flatter trajectory, greater range, higher accuracy, and cleaner kills.

The Kochsacheurs discovered these techniques purely by random trial and error. They eventually became quite adept at dispatching small mammals, reptiles, amphibians, and various fowl with manually launched washers. Jacques it is rumored, had the ability to propel a standard 9/16" flat washer with sufficient force to fully penetrate a seasoned oak plank two-inches thick. In other words, he could throw a washer completely through a dog. The only limiting factor was that washers were difficult for them to obtain. When they were able to scavenge a box or two, a period of feasting would usually soon follow. So when they stumbled onto what was arguably a limitless supply of fancy washers without holes, it was considered a stroke of good fortune of the highest order.

In the immediate weeks after their serendipitous fountain discovery, the Kochsacheurs were able to harvest virtually any animal species they chose, in any quantity desired, using coins in lieu of washers. As a result, their protein and calorie intake went up approximately five-fold. The increased efficiency of their hunting also had an accompanying trickle-down effect in other parts of their lives. For example, they suddenly found that they had more free time. This allowed them to engage in many new creative pursuits, whimsical antics of sport, and a variety of other fairly harmless activities.

However, in their new-found luxury lifestyle, they also apparently discovered how to ruminate and brood. Subsequently, in the midst of this period of unprecedented plenty, they somehow managed to convince themselves that they were entitled to a great deal more. Apparently, they were not satisfied with just a mere surplus of food and all the free time they wanted. But unsure as to how to obtain their due entitlement, or even who exactly owed it to them, they became deeply frustrated. And they relieved their frustrations in a variety of ways. Among these antic pastimes was their habit of hunting purely for mischief, openly killing and mutilating animals they had no intention of eating.

In the subsequent investigation, the authorities were able to assemble evidence strongly indicating that between October of 1960 and July of 1964, the Kochsacheurs used ballistically hurled U.S. and Canadian coins of various denominations to seriously maim, or cause lethal injuries to at least 12,596 known registered dogs and cats in the Greater Hockertown area. Dead dogs were everywhere. There were mutilated mutts in median of the Metro. There were passed-away pooches in parking lots, heaped up on school playgrounds, and melded to the roofs of barns. There were terminated tabby cats lodged in all fourteen of the gutter downspouts at a major downtown drug store. A room-temperature Rotweiler even washed up on the intake grate of the water works at 51st Street and Mission Avenue.

In addition to this holocaust of domesticated animals, there was also a remarkable attrition visited upon the population of feral species as well. For example, there were dead muskrats, raccoons, woodchucks, and opossums scattered in arbitrarily clustered pockets throughout the region as a whole. Supposedly, the Kochsacheurs killed every single opossum in the Townships of Lockhart, Cass, and Lower Bainbridge. Things were getting out of control. Finally, a smart-alec game warden passing through the area noticed the large number of dead animals and began asking questions.

Mostly because of his general unpopularity however, local informants were reluctant come forward. But he still saw enough to convince him that a sinister force was at work. He immediately notified his superiors at the Department of Natural Resources and increased his patrols of the area. In the meantime, despite his best efforts, the atrocities continued unabated.

No one is 100% certain of precisely when the park fountain ran completely out of coins. Once it happened however, the pressure became enormous to find a replacement source. Apparently after much observation and brainstorming, the Kochsacheurs concluded that standard parking meters represented the most feasible and accessible option. So, over a period of nine days they executed a series of stunning pre-dawn raids that netted them literally thousands of coins, and instantly cast the city into a dismal period of parking chaos.

It was in the midst of this epidemic of municipal vandalism and general faunal carnage that my father arrived upon the scene. He was in the area to evaluate several non-operational mine properties owned by the previously referenced company from Chicago, with the ultimate intent of making a cash offer on one or more of them, if the remaining reserves and existing facilities appeared suitable. The only problem was that my poor father had no idea that he was entering a region of unmitigated mutant warfare. It never occurred to him to be prepared for wild humans lawlessly roaming about and inciting general civil unrest. To him there was no reason to expect anything other than business as usual.

He decided to drive on through the city and report directly to the project site to commence his pedestrian survey of the subject real estate, the Hocker Creek Mine. His trip through town was relatively uneventful. However, about four miles on the other side of Hockertown he encountered a stalled and apparently abandoned late model sedan parked beside the road. He stopped parallel to the car and looked over the situation. Since no one was around, there was little else for him to do other than to move on. However, just as he was pulling away, he detected an odd noise. He shut off the engine. That's when he heard the apparent sounds of a crying woman coming from inside the stalled vehicle. He immediately got out of his car and went to investigate.

He discovered a young woman lying across the front seat of the car. She appeared to be pregnant. The problem was that she was not merely pregnant, she gave all the outward signs of being in the throes of advanced labor. She was nearly hysterical with pain. Dad quickly determined that her level of suffering seemed considerably greater than what would be expected with typical labor contractions. Dad interrogated her in an effort to determine how to best proceed. His astute questioning and observations eventually compelled him to conclude that the baby was breached in the birth canal. He had seen this sort of thing in livestock many times before. It was clear that the lives of both the mother and the infant were in grave jeopardy. If something were not done immediately, the consequences could be dreadful. He saw little other recourse but perform an emergency righting of the obtuse infant.

After obtaining the woman's categorical and unequivocal verbal consent, he proceeded to manually re-align the child, using techniques not entirely unlike those he perfected by working with farm animals. The woman's suffering was immediately mitigated and within only a few seconds she gave birth to a beautiful, healthy, seven-pound, ten-ounce baby girl. He used his pocket knife to carefully truncate the umbilical cord and then cinched it off with a shoelace obtained from his kit bag. He cleaned and wrapped the newborn infant in a towel that he took from his suitcase. When all of this was done, he proudly presented the woman with her baby and it everything was okay. The happy mother received the baby with utmost élan and enthusiasm, thanking Dad profoundly. As she cuddled with her new child, Dad leaned against the door of the car, wiped his brow and tried to catch his breath.

It was about this time that an approaching wrecker pulled over and stopped. Two men were in the cab of the vehicle. The driver was a large, brawny mechanic, appearing to be perhaps in his late forties, and was still greasy from working on cars. He wore a green uniform shirt with a name patch sewn over the left pocket that said:

MOODY

The passenger in the wrecker appeared to be the woman's husband. He had evidently walked or hitched a ride to the nearest service station after their car stalled. While he was away, without warning and completely unbeknownst to him, his expectant wife had abruptly gone into labor. If Dad had not stopped, chances are that the man would have returned to a very tragic situation.

The husband was inordinately inquisitive and suspicious at first but his wife quickly explained the circumstances to him in no uncertain terms. She made it especially clear that had Dad not stopped when he did and taken the steps that he did, in the order that he took them, she and the child would have died. Upon receiving the baby into his arms the husband immediately saw the self evident validity of all that had been said, and became overwhelmed with joy. Through streaming tears, he thanked Dad repeatedly. The man then got into the car and embraced his wife, who also became quite emotional. It was a very moving scene. Dad suddenly detected a curious noise coming from behind him. He turned around to discover that the wrecker driver was also crying.

Dad knew his work was done and that it was time to move on. He commenced his goodbyes and began to move toward his vehicle. The new father and mother sincerely thanked him several more times. As Dad tried to turn and leave however, the wrecker driver, still sobbing, spontaneously reached out and gave my father an enormous, burly hug. As Dad held the highly emotional mechanic in his embrace, consoling him and patting him on the shoulder, he noticed some kind of large, ambiguous thing moving across the highway, far off in the distant haze. He could not identify the object but his instincts somehow sensed that it was not normal. There seemed to be a sinister quality to it. The hair stood up on his neck. Finally, he asked the mechanic:

"What is that?"

"Huh?"

"Do you see that? Down there in the road...about half a mile. Can you tell what it is?"

The mechanic released Dad from the hug and turned around and looked in the direction that he was pointing. His demeanor of teary happiness suddenly was cast aside for one of deep concern and fear.

"We've got to get out of here!"

"What?"

"Come on folks, I'll take you to the hospital right now and then come back later and tow the car...no extra charge."

"What's going on?" Dad queried.

"Look mister, if I told you, you wouldn't believe me. Just get in your truck and keep heading west. And what ever you do, don't stop till you cross the county line! Now I've got to get these folks over to the Women's Reproductive Health Wing of Hockertown Mercy General. Best of luck to you sir. And remember, don't stop!"

Dad got into his vehicle and drove away. He could not help being concerned about the wrecker driver's comments. He wondered why he had been so emphatic about not stopping until he crossed the county line. He slowed the vehicle in the area where he had seen the strange moving object. There was no indication of anything remarkable. But curiously, the hair on his neck stood up again.

Upon reaching his destination, Dad parked his truck in the service lane the on the left side of the entrance to an old iron bridge, just like the instructions indicated. The bridge had two signs attached to its superstructure. One was a large sign. It was dark blue with white letters. This sign read:

HOCKER CREEK

The other sign was smaller. It was white with black lettering:

ENTERING
JOHNSON COUNTY
LEAVING
CLAY COUNTY

Dad now realized what he had apparently overlooked on the mine maps: the Hocker Creek Mine was located in Clay County. Of course it had not really been an issue until now. He decided to ignore the warnings of the wrecker driver and proceed with his original plan. He did however, take along his pistol just in case. So he got out of the truck and followed the narrow footpath along the creek to the left, just like the detailed directions said. This led to a clearing at the base of a steep hill. The mine entrance and accompanying facilities could be seen about half way up the side of the mountain, approximately 400 yards away.

The trail leading up the mountain was severely gullied, clearly making it impassible to traffic. It had been a good road back when the mine was operational, but years of neglect and erosion had rendered it unsuitable for use by conventional motor vehicles. Dad understood this to be the only of access road to the site. This was not an insignificant point. He had good reason to notice because the restoration and maintenance of this road represented a substantial monetary consideration in the overall feasibility of the project. As he climbed the hill he was silently calculating the cost to restore the road.

Even with his mind racing in logistical contemplation, when he finally reached the mine level, he was instantly taken aback by the overwhelming organic presence of the site. A significant untidiness characterized the area. This was primarily manifested in the form of a coarse midden heaped up in sporadic lobes and windrows around the wider field. This material consisted mostly of general rubbish such as empty food containers, assorted discarded household items, and rotting paper products. However, the debris also seemed curiously predominated by opossum bones, pigeon feathers, turtle shells, chewed popsicle sticks, and broken mayonnaise jars. Seeing all of this, Dad immediately concluded that there must have been another access road because obviously whoever had dumped the garbage did not use the route he had just laboriously ascended.

Surveying the greater scene, Dad quickly noticed that the mine office and the maintenance shop had been completely ransacked. Both structures were literally stripped and gutted. Piles of demolished construction materials were scattered around the teetering frames of the former buildings. It was his understanding that these facilities were in useable condition. The photographs he had been given clearly showed two buildings where there now remained only debris. He maneuvered his way through this impolite theater until he finally located the actual mine entrance. And it was there, again much to his surprise, that he discovered a pathway of some substantial breadth, forged through a thicket of locust saplings growing directly in front of the mine portal. The clay along the path was freshly packed, and there was a great deal of trash and opossum skeletal remains along either side of this rowdy way.

A cursory summing up of the situation compelled my father, as it arguably would have anyone, to reach two significant initial conclusions: 1, that the path was being traversed on a daily basis by an organism of substantial mass, and 2, this creature, whatever it was, apparently had a remarkable keenness for both opossums and garbage. Dad hypothesized that perhaps bears were utilizing the tunnel as a den, a concept not unheard of in the local folklore.

However, rather than any obscure regional idioms of the oral tradition, his initial hypothesis was based mostly on the unique odor gushing from the mine. The bear theory also seemed to fit nicely with the fact that the entire site was little more than an enormous apparent illegal trash dump. So it was not unreasonable to suppose that bears could be exploiting the garbage as a food source and concurrently taking advantage of a conveniently located shelter. But as Dad journeyed onward past the thicket of saplings and into the darkness of the mine tunnel, his flashlight soon began to illuminate items and features causing him to abruptly realize that the creatures inhabiting this Dantesque labyrinth were probably not members of the genus *Ursus*.

He suspected that bears probably could not have weaved dried opossum tails into disgusting-looking hammocks and baskets. Bears probably do not coat the walls of their dens with cardboard. Nor do bears typically possess office furniture, build fires, or produce mud art. And most importantly perhaps, as far as Dad was concerned at least, bears never deliberately use the ceiling of their abode as a place to hang thousands of plastic bags filled with piss. Just as Dad's logic circuits were beginning to meaningfully iterate some of the fearsome ramifications of this final deeply disturbing overhead spectacle, he noticed a sparkling effect when the beam of his flashlight shone toward the floor. Upon closer investigation he discovered that the underlament of the cavern was strewn with coins. He reached down and picked up one of these instruments of legal tender. It was a brand new 1964 quarter, the current year.

A growing suspicion he had was now confirmed: the forces and circumstances responsible for the transportation and deposition of such a coin, and all of the other artifacts as well, in such a location and manner were not only extraordinary, they were also ongoing right that very moment, or *real-time* as it would be called in the modern vernacular. He understood perfectly therefore, that the cruel inhabitants of the mine were probably either lurking dangerously nearby in the darkness at that very moment, or were likely to soon return. A cold chill ran up his neck. It was the same feeling he had gotten back on the road when he saw the unidentified moving object. This realization acted as a catalyst, compelling Dad to conclude, based on what he'd seen so far, that the agents perpetrating these exceptional phenomena were of an order and disposition such that special measures were called for.

That is, my father just seemed to instinctively know that reasonable men, or those of good conscience, even to this very day and for all of time, naturally strive to protect women, children, and the faint of heart from ever knowing that aberrant beasts like these could exist. Because such knowledge would so harrow up their souls that they would surely forever lose hope. And all good men cultivate hope, not destroy it. It was morally incumbent upon him therefore to proceed accordingly. Evil must be rooted out wherever it is found, and as discretely as possibly.

As my father contemplated these things, weighing also the facts that the buildings were not useable as promised, the extremely poor condition of the access road, the enormous amount of trash that would have to be cleaned up, and other factors, he was more or less convinced that this particular project site was entirely unsuitable for his needs. He consequently decided to terminate his exploration of the underground mine and return to the surface. As he ceased his advance and maneuvered around however, he inadvertently stood fully upright for a moment, bumping into one of the bags hanging from the roof of the tunnel, nearly rupturing it. That is when it finally occurred to him just how many of these pendulous objects there really were. He also reasoned that even though it was a profoundly ghastly expression of human subversion, still from an engineering standpoint, it represented a truly remarkable and unique phenomenon.

When he directed the light down the smoky, hot, dank tunnel, the bags seemed to continue into infinity. They were spaced about a foot apart, extending from wall to wall across the ceiling of the tunnel and as far as the eye could see along the length of the mine. Each bag was about two feet long, and contained approximately four gallons of liquid. They were constructed from what appeared to be dry-cleaner's bags which are made from a very thin and fragile type of plastic. When deployed in this manner, they took on the appearance of large yellow pears (large yellow pears in the very pit of hell, that is). It was like a scene from the movie *Alien,* inside the nursery on the mother ship perhaps. Dad's thoughts raced now, as he beheld the gleaming pods arrayed before him. *"What kind of mind could create such an abomination?"* He quickly cogitated the available data and reduced an answer to his own internalized rhetorical question. The result was unexpected. That is, despite the context the conundrum was examined in, the conclusion always came out the same: *only the worst kind of mind* would be capable of generating such a potent manifestation of pure, unequivocal unwholesomeness.

While Dad was on the way out of the mine he directed the flashlight beam into a room on the left side of the tunnel that he had overlooked when coming in. In this chamber he discovered four large opossum-tail baskets filled with approximately 250,000 coins. Lying adjacent to these baskets were hundreds of broken parking meters each bearing a tag that read as follows:

PROPERTY OF
THE CITY OF HOCKERTOWN

Dad was now convinced that he had stumbled into a nest of malfeasance and criminal depravity far beyond the common fears of reasonable men. That's when he reached into his pocket and pulled out the semiautomatic pistol. The mining project was now of secondary interest. The main issue was to relay this newly obtained intelligence to the rightful owners. Therefore, as far as he was concerned, the paramount impetus now was that he expedite his departure with post haste dispatch. Taking great care to remain stooped over enough to safely pass beneath the layer of plastic bags, he prosecuted his exit without further incident.

He returned to Hockertown and made a phone call to the company in Chicago, informing them of his findings. Upon hearing the news they displayed much astonishment, dismay, and concern. They graciously apologized to Dad for any inconvenience he had experienced and then formally requested that he escort the local authorities to the site. They advised him to keep an accounting of his time and expenses and that he would be handsomely compensated for both bringing this heinous situation to light and for following up on any applicable due recourse. Dad cordially agreed to perform these duties.

.

Dad paid a visit to the county sheriff headquarters at the behest of the company from Chicago, in effect serving in the capacity of their defacto field representative. He approached the receptionist's desk. She was a beautiful young lady wearing a very smartly tailored police uniform and a name tag inscribed as follows:

P.H. COX

The receptionist escorted my father into the sheriff's office and introduced him.
"Sheriff Hale, this gentleman would like to speak with you."
"Thanks Putnam."
Dad extended his hand.
"Hello, my name is Adam McCasoway."
The sheriff firmly clasped Dad's hand. He was a large man, with broad shoulders and a disarming smile. He wore a name tag that read:

W. HALE

"Pleased to meet you. I'm sheriff Hale."
The sheriff paused for a moment and silently observed the receptionist as she exited his office.
"Those pants are so tight she must be chaffed raw. I bet she's red as a beet under there. Boy, she's something isn't she?"
"Excuse me?"
"Putnam, my receptionist, didn't you notice her?"
"Yes I did notice her sheriff Hale. She is a very lovely lady."
"That's an understatement!"

"*Putnam* seems like an odd name for a girl."

"Odd? In what way? Her parents were good friends of mine. I'm not sure why they named her Putnam. But I do know that they were obsessively protective of her. Now that they have passed away, their estate attorney, Mr. Hyman, has been watching after her. Her parents insisted on writing it in the will that way. He's pretty strict too. As a matter of fact, he's the person who got her this job. I mean how much safer can it be than in a police station?"

Dad realized that the services of an attorney might be needed before the conclusion of this affair. He opened his notepad and prepared to jot down the name.

"What did you say the attorney's name was?"

"Mr. Hyman."

"Yes, but his first name?"

"*Gardner.*"

"I see. And he is the legal administrator of record for the estate of Miss Cox?"

"Yes, but everybody call hers '*P.H.*'"

"What does the 'H' stand for sheriff Hale?"

"*Hanover.*"

"I see."

"And you don't have to call me sheriff Hale. Just call me by my first name."

"I'm sorry, I guess I didn't catch that."

"*Warez.*"

"Excuse me?"

"Warez. My first name is Warez. Just like the town."

"I see. Well, Warez, sir, she is very pretty. You must be proud."

"Yeah. She reminds me of my wife when she was that age. I met her in Algiers after the blockade. Golda is still as beautiful as she was the day I married her."

"That's extraordinary."

The sheriff stared blankly out the window for a moment. He then looked toward my father and commented:

"I see you've met Moody. What, did you have car trouble?"

"Excuse me?" Dad replied.

"You have axle grease across your shirt. Looks like you got a hug from Moody."

Dad made a token attempt to brush off the stains, but they were ground in.

"Don't worry about it. Moody hugs everybody. Just soak it in gasoline overnight."

"I wondered about that!"

"Now, Mr. McCasoway, how may I help you?"

"I'm here to report a case of criminal trespassing."

"That is a very serious charge. What evidence do you have?"

"Damaged buildings, stolen goods, hides of poached animals, goat heads nailed to trees, baskets filled with coins, piles of uprooted parking meters bearing tags saying *'Property of the City of Hockertown.'* Is that sufficient, or should I continue?"

"Yes sir, that ought to do it. Where did this alleged trespassing occur?"

"About eight miles from here, at the old Hocker Creek mine."

"Is that in Clay County?"

"It's east of the bridge on Route 184."

"Well, it's in Clay County then. Are you the owner of the Hocker Creek mine?"

"No sir, the stockholders of *Chicago Ore & Coke Company* own it. I represent them in this matter. If you would like to verify my credentials I have a phone number that you may call."

"Are you an attorney?"

"No sir, I am a geologist."

"What, you work down at the Women's Reproductive Health Wing of Hockertown Mercy General? *Do you know McCracken Hertz?*"

Dad paused for a moment, logically dissecting and then carefully cogitating the subtle idioms being bandied about.

"No, I'm a *geologist*, not a *gynecologist*."

"Oh, sorry. I'll bet you get that all the time!"

"Actually, you'd probably be surprised at the amount of overlap between the two fields."

After some subsequent chit chat, the sheriff expressed his sincere gratitude to Dad for finding and reporting the location of the camp. Dad asked the sheriff point blank if he had any information on the identities of the alleged perpetrators.

"Do you know who these people are?"

"Well, yes...we think we have a pretty good idea."

"Who are they?"

"They're a bunch of *Kochsacheurs!*" the sheriff calmly declared, as he dipped a doughnut in his coffee.

Dad was very surprised by the somewhat imprudent frankness of the officer.

"Well, *naturally*, but I mean do you know their names?" Dad replied.

"That is their name – *'Koch-sach-eur.'* We have good reason to believe that they may be from the nation of…(taking a bite)…*France.*"

"Oh, I see." Dad replied.

The sheriff paused as he refilled his coffee cup.

"They're in the United States illegally. A lot of people certainly want to find them. The Immigration & Naturalization boys would like to get their hands on them. The damn game warden has been trying to track them down for nearly a year. The Hockertown Retailers Association has lodged a formal complaint with the State Attorney General. The park board has been raising hell for six months. And the guys down at the street department have gotten to where they won't even speak to me anymore."

"That bad huh?"

"Pretty hairy."

"How many of them are there?"

"We think there are around six or eight. Nobody's certain though, we just don't know. Information is hard to come by. I've had men out combing the hills for weeks. Sure we find a set of possum bones here, a mayonnaise jar or two there, but never anything solid - until just now when you came in, that is."

"I'm glad to be able to help sir."

"Hockertown hasn't seen this kind of trouble since that damn arsonist episode a few years ago."

"What do you mean?"

"Back in '57, some guy got hopped-up on gin and flew over town in an airplane dropping Molotov cocktails. He didn't hurt anyone thank God, but he managed to burn the baby milk factory and a couple of rice fields before he ran out of gas. Needless to say, it was a pretty bad deal for a while."

"That's incredible. Was he from around here?"

"Yeah, he was a local crop duster named *Nate Palmer.*"

"I see."

The sheriff nervously lit a cigarette, leaned back in his swivel chair and proceeded to inform Dad that he had not been looking forward to actually finding the Kochsacheurs. It had been his deepest hope that they would turn up in some other sheriff's jurisdiction. He went on to explain how everyone feared the Kochsacheurs, including him, and how anyone in their right mind ought to. Further, he declared that he categorically refused to attempt to serve an arrest warrant on the Kochsacheurs without adequate backup. The sheriff explained how no one knew what to expect from them. Caution was the professed order of the day for this seasoned lawman and he did not mind admitting it. With such a grave and sober outlook, truly the mark of an experienced skirmisher, Dad reckoned that this lawman should be able to get the job done, with a little luck. The sheriff pushed a button on the intercom.

"Putnam, I need the phone numbers of U.S. Immigration and that damn game warden...Clyde what's-his-name."

"Yes sheriff Hale."

Presently the receptionist brought a piece of paper and handed it to the sheriff. As the sheriff dialed the phone, she remained by his desk for a moment, looking at Dad and smiling charmingly. Dad gracefully returned the gesture. As the sheriff waited for the phone connection to go through, he turned and spoke.

"Putnam, this is Adam McCasoway. He's a *geologist!*"

"Pleased to meet you ma'am. The sheriff has told me a great many things about you."

"Hello. Geologist huh? *Do you know McCracken Hertz?*"

"*Ahem*...yes, sheriff Hale did mention something about that. Here's my card. *Please call me any time for a free consultation.*"

After the sheriff phoned the local game warden and the U.S. Immigration authorities, he commenced the process of tracking down and swearing in deputies. He invited my father to ride with him in the police cruiser as this critical phase of the operation was carried out. Dad agreed. The game was afoot.

Not far into the impromptu SWAT-team building process however, Dad started to become seriously concerned about the chances for a successful prosecution of the law. That is, after exhausting all of the normal avenues of deputy acquisition, each to no avail, the sheriff finally had to resort to entering a local bootleg joint and soliciting the assistance of twenty concerned citizens. The plan for attacking the Kochsacheur compound was subsequently formulated by the sheriff and several of these customers in approximately four minutes, while standing in the parking lot of said establishment. Based on what Dad heard during this planning session, he decided to remain an impartial observer. Additionally, the sheriff actually ordered my father to stay back and let them handle it. Dad agreed, but decided to observe from a safe distance using binoculars.

Dad then led the sheriff and his newly conscripted deputies to the trail at the base of the mountain. He unrolled the site plan on the ground and pointed out the key features of the facility for them. He indicated where they would find the demolished buildings and the piles of bones. He told them about the path through the locust thicket and about the coins in the little room on the left. He harshly warned them about the appalling nature of what he had observed in the tunnels. And he emphatically enlightened them about the thousands of bags of piss suspended from the ceiling of the tunnel. With this last bit of intelligence they all looked at him like he was insane, and then assured him that they would indeed be careful.

The sheriff and his deputies gathered at the base of the mountain and began the strenuous climb to the Kochsacheur fortress. After two or three rest stops along the way, they finally made it to the mine level. In the meantime, Dad moved to a superior forward observation position approximately one hundred yards from the mine portal. From this location he commanded an unobstructed view of the entire theater. He watched intently as the duly sworn assault team made their way through the debris field. He observed them locate and cautiously enter the mine tunnel. One by one they disappeared into the dim, black colliery. The last man in looked back a few times before he too vanished. So far, the operation appeared to be unremarkable.

A few minutes passed. Nothing happened. Some more minutes went by, still nothing. Then the shadow of a hawk unexpectedly scanned across the scene. Dad instinctively looked up to locate the source. He watched the graceful creature balance and weave on the invisible legs that we humans call thermals. The hawk's featureless silhouette pasted against the brilliant blue firmament resembled its shadow on the ground he thought. He pondered the metaphysical ramifications of two shadows incessantly racing against one another. My father's mind had wandered considerably into this dreamlike state when he was suddenly pulled back by what sounded like a muffled scream, as if a great distance away, but with its location being obscured by random breezes and sundry birdsong. Then he detected another. A few seconds passed. Then he heard a succession of screams, somewhat closer, followed by many undecipherable urgent shouts and other indistinct, attenuated expressions of lament or dark misery. This latter flurry stirred an element of mortal pity in Dad because he sensed that the poor fellows were enduring an ordeal that he perhaps could have prepared them for more adequately. But it was too late.

Then the men started emerging from the tunnel at a dead run, one and two at a time. For some reason their eyes were closed and their faces locked in an appalling grimace of indescribable horror. They immediately collided with the wall of wiry saplings. However, these minor obstacles did not impede their flight in the least. Those who were knocked down by the impact simply got up and tried again, some crawling if necessary, but within a few seconds all of the deputies were able to negotiate the initial obstructions and reach the open ground beyond. They appeared to be dripping wet. Most had dozens of shredded plastic bags stuck to their heads, upper torso, or around their necks. All were gagging, hacking, moaning, and convulsing deeply in the throes of indescribable suffering. Once they made it to an open area about 50 feet from the mine portal, they more or less collapsed out of exhaustion and/or shock. Some squatted on one knee, some sat weakly upright, while others prostrated themselves upon the sun-ripened trash and wallowed in cathartic agony.

Apparently they saw and/or heard something that compelled them to exit quickly. What they saw was unclear. One thing was certain however, they had not fully heeded Dad's warning about the overhanging plastic bags. Looking through binoculars, Dad was so stricken with the spectacle, even at such a great distance, that he too was compelled to summarily emancipate his most recent repast. But while prosecuting this unpleasant protocol, he nearly laughed himself into unconsciousness. He cackled with such ferocious vigor that he seriously sprained his neck and fractured three ribs.

The sheriff and his deputies had for the most part stopped vomiting when Dad finally gathered enough strength to hold his binoculars again. Some of them were even starting to open their eyes. Whenever Dad would recount this story he always asked the listener to try to imagine what the deputies were thinking at this point. "Perhaps they were thinking, that even though things were admittedly bad, now that they had made it out of the mine, the worst was finally over." But the fact was that they had no clue as to the degree of misconception with which they had allowed themselves to become encumbered. Because just when they had started to relax, it was at that precise moment when the Kochsacheurs suddenly came charging out of the mine screaming like wild animals and hurling projectiles with unimaginable fury. The poor deputies were caught completely cold. They were instantly overwhelmed by a punishing hail of high-velocity coinage.

The robustness of the human survival instinct cannot be exaggerated. It is pure art to behold. Just when these sluggish men thought they were spent, they straight away drew from the mysterious inner abyss, sufficient strength to once again undertake an extraordinary mortal flight of great adroitness. They sped headlong over the precipice, hurdling toward lower vistas and perceived ultimate safety.

The Kochsacheurs pursued the deputies at least half-way down the side of the mountain and then continued to harass them until they had retreated out of range. In addition to this devastating frontal assault, the Kochsacheurs were also able to taunt and demean the poor fleeing officers with a liberal assortment of crude vocalizations and coarse gestures wholly untranslatable in a verbal sense, but nevertheless shockingly clear in their general meaning.

Dad came around and met the officers at the vehicles by the bridge. They were just arriving when he got there. They looked pretty bad. Most were limping. Some were being helped by others. At least one man was being carried on a makeshift gurney. It was about this time when the game warden drove up in his official station wagon.

"Oh no, not that damn game warden!" the sheriff commented.

The look on the game warden's face cannot be honestly described as he observed the wounded deputies hobbling toward him. Their injuries were frightful. They had been showered with a deadly onslaught of coins, stones, and spears. Every man sustained at least some coin-inflicted injuries, many of which were very serious.

"Why are you people bleeding? Why are you wet? What is that smell?" obnoxiously queried the game warden.

While the sheriff and his deputies slowly tended each other's wounds, Dad took a few minutes to brief the game warden about the series of unfortunate events that had brought them to this juncture. He then went on to explain the high points of what he had observed through his binoculars.

The final, official medical report submitted to the State Police by Hockertown Mercy General indicated that the per-capita cash equivalency surgically removed from the officers ranged from approximately 49 cents to $15.27, with a mean of $5.58. The grand total was $117.08. The sheriff had $8.75 worth of quarters and half-dollars removed from his buttocks alone, plus an additional $6.40 worth of nickels and dimes from other parts of his body. Moreover, the sensitive disposition of some of the coin injuries resulted in several of the men being transferred to *the Women's Reproductive Health Wing of Hockertown Mercy General* for treatment.

Other injuries of note included a dime that grazed sheriff Hale's skull and was deflected through the side of his scalp, coming to rest in his ear canal. Also, a Canadian nickel had hit him in the forehead causing a bruise in the near-perfect likeness of Her Majesty Queen Elizabeth II. One deputy was struck so harshly with a cobblestone that part of his intestines were literally protruding from his armpits. Everybody thought it was funny at first, but the guy almost died. He was messed up for quite a while and had to spend some time in *the Home*. But he supposedly eventually made a full recovery and became a successful motivational speaker.

Luckily, no fatalities or permanent disabilities resulted from the attack. However, some of the men complained of unpleasant dreams in the immediate weeks afterwards. Several of them received pharmaceutical therapy in an effort to mitigate the symptoms. Curiously, in later interrogation, these men all agreed that the nightmares were not so much related to the events that occurred at the mine as they were to what happened after they were transferred to the Women's Reproductive Health Wing of Hockertown Mercy General and placed in the care of a doctor there by the name of *McCracken Hertz.*

As Dad recounted the history of the day's events, the game warden clearly became more disconcerted. Meanwhile the Kochsacheurs could plainly be seen grouped on the side of the mountain, still shouting and gesturing boastfully. Finally the game warden had endured his limit. He drew his weapon and started down the trail. The sheriff quickly called out to him:

"Don't go up there Clyde! They'll kill you." the sheriff proclaimed.

The game warden thought about it for a moment and then wisely returned his weapon to its holster and relaxed his offensive posture.

"What are we going to do then?" the game warden asked emphatically.

"Well, the first thing we have to do is get these men to a hospital. Jimmy, call dispatch and get an ambulance out here."

"I already tried Warez. There's no signal. It must be all these trees and the hills."

"I can't reach base when I'm out here either." said the game warden.

"Did you try the state police frequency?"

"Yes sir, nothing there either."

"Damn it! Okay, there's a little grocery store about two miles back up the road. They have a pay phone out in front. Somebody needs to drive up there and call headquarters."

"I'll go, I'm the only one here not injured." said the game warden.

"Alright then." replied the sheriff.

"I just have one question."

"What then?"

"Which one of you pathetic sumbitches is going to shit out a dime for the pay phone?"

"Go to hell Clyde!"

The National Guard finally had to go in and expel the Kochsacheurs from the mine. But it was not easy. It turned out that the bag phenomenon was an old trick from the first world war. Back before the invention of the gas mask, the French army was desperately searching for countermeasures against the tons of poison gas being continuously dumped on them by the Germans.

During this dark period of the human saga, some poor soul discovered that urine neutralizes poison gas (to a very, very limited extent). There are many theories on how the discovery was made. But no one can precisely say with absolute certainty how it occurred since the project was classified *Most Secret* and also because only fragments of information on the subject survived the war.

Investigators point to a reference in an obscure Belgian plumbing journal of the period that states: *"...a young, conscripted French sewage worker played a key role in the discovery."* Because the records were totally destroyed, this man's name was never officially known. However, local folklore maintains that the discoverer was actually *Rene Kochsacheur,* grandfather to Pablo, Jacques, Jean Claude, and Pandora. This theory is supported by two significant facts: 1, Rene Kochsacheur was believed to be a Paris sewage worker who retired with full benefits in 1930, and 2, the initials R.K. appear on several government military construction contracts dated after 1931. The contracts indicate that this mysterious "R.K." was installing ceiling-mounted gas countermeasures deep inside the tunnels of the Maginot Line, France's vast underground, defensive system along the German border, when the Nazis took Paris on June 14, 1940.

June 23, 1940, Hitler touring Paris. *(Photo courtesy of U.S. National Archives.)*

The Maginot Line however, had two serious flaws: 1, it was a fixed fortification. That is, forces committed to it, by definition, sacrificed their mobility, and 2, it was not infinitely long. It extended primarily along the border between France and Germany. The Nazis simply went around it and captured the country with scarcely a shot fired. France's faith in the

Maginot Line is considered to be one of the greatest strategic military blunders of the twentieth century. And in an ultimate irony, those brave individuals who remained on the surface and actually fought the enemy were called the *French Underground.*

The evidence indicates that their uncle Sartre Kochsacheur had apparently been fairly successful in teaching them at least one family tradition that also happened to be a useful skill. Presumably, any time the Kochsacheurs found themselves employed, residing, and/or cowering within underground tunnels, they traditionally took the added precaution of installing poison gas countermeasures.

After the National Guard shot hundreds of pounds of tear gas into the mine tunnel, countermeasures notwithstanding, the Kochsacheurs finally came scurrying out. Once they were in custody, the U.S. State Department made arrangements with the government of France to have them repatriated. The Kochsacheurs officially left U.S. soil in a specially modified B-52 bomber at 03:53 a.m. Eastern Standard Time, on August 13, 1965. However, the plane was ultimately denied permission to use French airspace, so it landed in Iraq instead.

Once back in their home country, the Kochsacheurs supposedly re-assimilated into society with surprising ease. Many of them reportedly changed their surnames to circumvent any potential anti-American perceptions by the French public. To this very day however, their legend still remains very deeply imprinted in the oral tradition of the Hockertown area and surrounding tri-county region as a whole. The reader does not have to take my word for it. Just ask any of the citizens on the street there and they will all say the same thing:

Interviewer: "Excuse me ma'am. What can you tell me about the nation of France?"

Citizen: "Not too much really - the Eiffel Tower is there. We ran out the Germans twice for them. *Kochsacheurs have apparently taken over the country.*"

Chapter 20

The Nerd Days

Adam D. McCasoway was widely known as a skilled hunter of squirrels, a visionary geoscientist, an honest businessman, an accomplished guitarist, and a formidable forensic pugilist. What few people may realize however, is that he eventually acquired something of a reputation as a prodigal computer programmer as well. Dad started dabbling with personal computers around 1975. He assembled his first general purpose computer using parts obtained from a variety of TV repair shops, hardware stores, and electronics catalogs.

Obviously, graphical user interface operating systems for personal computers did not exist back in those days. Software supporting features like error windows and tool bars, either was not available to the average information technology hobbyist, or did not exist at all. Even if such programming had been available, the personal computers of the era could not have used it because of their extremely low memory capacity.

It was a time when the concept of "clicking on something" had not been imprinted within the collective consciousness of the human race, a "compact disk" was a phenomenon generally requiring the attention of a surgeon, "servers" were associated mostly with retail dining establishments and ball games employing large fence-like nets separating opposing players, and an occasional conversational outburst of the idiom "hard drive" might not have been totally unexpected amid gatherings of cowboys or professional truckers, but would have been seldom encountered elsewhere.

When the computer was powered up, the monitor didn't turn cyan, or magenta, or any other New Age hue. There was nothing but a dark, blank screen with the word *READY*, in bold white letters, blinking in the upper left-hand corner. In order to get a personal computer to perform any meaningful function, it had to be manually programmed by the user. If the user didn't know anything about computer programming, there was simply little other recourse but to turn off the power and quit (of course there was always the option of trying to synchronize one's heart rate with the blinking *READY* through the application of advanced transcendental meditation techniques).

Dad quickly addressed this deficiency by undertaking aggressive and methodical reckoning of all the amateur programming literature available at the time. This strategy proved to be very successful. Within days he had generated an extensive assortment of mathematically-intensive computer programs that did everything from calculate the translational kinetic energy of satellites in low earth orbit, to figure the daily principal and interest distribution of business loans.

In addition to these stunning practical applications of computer theory, Dad also experimented with a variety of game programs. Of course the computer games he worked on were entirely different than the kind available today. Truly graphical games did exist back then, but typically at no more than a "ping pong" level of sophistication. The majority of games played by amateur programmers of the era were purely numerical in nature.

One popular game that was making its way around the recreational programmer circuit at the time was called *Eject-Eject-Eject*. The game was obtained as written lines of code and then keyed into a computer. Such written programs were widely available from a variety of sources, including magazines and books, or from other programming enthusiasts. Once the user grasped the underlying principles of the program, he or she could then manipulate the code to create their own unique version of the game.

Eject-Eject-Eject and similar games typically generated columns of data on the computer screen but afforded no graphical information. That is, no additional information was provided other than the displayed numerical data. There were no pictures, graphs, or sounds. All flight control was based entirely on mathematically-derived, virtual instrument readings alone. No external reference information was available. Intuition or "feel" was useless.

The displayed data represented key variables in the flight dynamic of a theoretical rocket ship, indicating the state of the flight at any given instant. The listed data included altitude, velocity in three directions (x, y, and z), acceleration (called delta-v, written as DV), pitch, yaw, roll, throttle setting, fuel consumption, fuel and oxygen reserves, and a range of other parameters. These variables were continuously recalculated by the computer, via programmed mathematical formulae based on the Newton's classical laws of motion and gravitation (the same principles used by NASA). Dad's assumptions for engine performance, fuel consumption, and atmospheric resistance were based on published empirical tables.

The challenge of the game was to apply the throttle in a such a way so as to overcome gravity and attain a minimum specified height above the earth, while still reserving sufficient fuel and oxygen to reverse the process in a controlled manner, thereby achieving a soft landing. Optimum flight parameters were maintained by carefully adjusting the power output of the main engine and maneuvering thrusters. Since the state of the flight was constantly changing, continual input by the player was required to keep the flight profile optimized. All power and thruster adjustments were input via the keyboard. A typical screen might look something like this during a flight (see below):

EJECT - EJECT - EJECT
COCKPIT FLIGHT DATA SCREEN

VELOCITY (M/SEC)	ACCELERATION (M/SEC/SEC)	ATTITUDE (DEG)
X = +8230.9	DV(X) = +01.8	PITCH -2.4
Y = +5.4	DV(Y) = +0.2	YAW +0.2
Z = +152.7	DV(Z) = +9.4	ROLL +0.1 /SEC

HEIGHT = 109732 METERS

LIFE SUPPORT	POWER	CONTROL
OXYGEN USE 0.05 %/SEC	MAIN ENGINE 1223.2 NM/SEC	PITCH THRUSTER 0.0 NM/SEC
OXYGEN RESERVE 87.24%	MAIN ENGINE FUEL USE 0.59 %/SEC	YAW THRUSTER 0.0 NM/SEC
CABIN TEMP +26.5 C	MAIN ENGINE FUEL LEFT 64.25 %	LEFT THRUSTER 0.1 NM/SEC
HULL TEMP -214.8 C	APU TIME LEFT 01 H 27 M 36 S	RIGHT THRUSTER 0.0 NM/SEC
HEART RATE 84	MISSION ELAPSED TIME 00 H 12 M 19 S	THRUSTER TIME 80.7 SEC

The goal of *Eject-Eject-Eject* was to start out at an altitude of zero, obtain a height of at least 160,000 meters (about 100 miles), make at least one orbit, and then return such that when achieving a height equal to zero, your heart rate would be greater than zero. Although this appeared at first glance to be a straightforward and simple task, it took many tries to actually achieve such a feat. Anyone who ever did succeed at the game *Eject-Eject-Eject*, would probably be able to fly virtually anything by instruments alone. Numerical games such as these were actually very effective in illustrating the fundamental relationships between power output, fuel consumption, motion, and gravity. Modern flight simulators are based on the same mathematical concepts, except they use more bells and whistles to present the data.

Another game that Dad worked on extensively was called *Unsupervised*. This game mimicked a virtual universe inhabited by pre-teen males existing totally in the absence of adult supervision. It could be described as a computerized version of *Lord of the Flies*. To play the game, the user initially populated the simulated universe with a suite of individuals selected from a menu of predetermined personality types, or *Meanness Levels*. After the population parameters were input, an array of *Hazard Objects* and *Risk Enhancers* were subsequently introduced into the model universe and the program was ran. The computer then calculated a unique resultant solution for each distinct data input ensemble.

UNSUPERVISED 6.0
PROGRAM INPUT SCREEN

MEANNESS LEVEL	INITIIAL POPULATION
Damien	1
juvenile delinquent	24
punk	43
loudmouth trouble maker	52
brat	29
rascal	19
momma's boy	11
chicken	10
sissy	8
girl	3
total population	200

HAZARD OBJECT	QUANTITY	RISK ENHANCER	QUANTITY (KG)
chainsaw	41	gasoline	17,206
semiautomatic shotgun	73	battery acid	2,340
blasting cap	2,560	liquid oxygen	129,350
oxy-acetylene blow torch	65	carbon tetrachloride	1,272
electric sander	139	gun powder	3,560
outboard motor	26	vodka	305
backhoe	15	napalm	20,800
diesel wood chipper	23	VX	420
BB gun	338	smallpox bacillus	19
pick ax	97	CFC	9,000
multi-engine fighter aircraft	4	plutonium 239	6.5

The above input data screen displays are from an actual run of *Unsupervised 6.0*. The object of the game was to formulate an ensemble of inputs that would generate the highest survival (or mortality) rate for a selected behavioral class. The program could be ran in two primary modes: *Pogrom* (as above), or *Custom*.

The Pogrom mode was intended to be an exercise in unlimited pandemonium, anarchy, pillage, and robbery. In Unsupervised 5.0 and earlier versions, this mode had been called *Armageddon*. In this configuration, all of the meanness levels operated as offensive agents against all other groups and the ambient civilian population. Destruction was immediate, encompassing, and brutal.

The Custom mode on the other hand, allowed specific meanness classes to be deployed either against themselves, against other classes individually, or in coordinated teams. For example, in Custom mode the player might field 250 *loudmouth trouble makers* furnished with backhoes and liquid oxygen, against 100 *juvenile delinquents* equipped with outboard motors and napalm. The results of such bouts were often very surprising and always extremely destructive.

My father's most important achievement with respect to the Unsupervised program genre was perhaps his introduction of unconventional algorithms into the code. One of the most successful of these specially-designed subroutines was simply called *the Chicken*.

UNSUPERVISED 6.0
PROGRAM OUTPUT SCREEN

SURVIVOR TYPE	FINAL POPULATION	DEATH RATE(%)
Damien	1	0
juvenile delinquent	4	83.3
punk	2	95.3
loudmouth trouble maker	0	100
brat	1	96.5
rascal	1	94.7
momma's boy	0	100
chicken	8	20
sissy	0	100
girl	0	100

total fatalities	183
total survivors	17
overall mortality (%)	91.5
eyes put out among survivors	29

		CIVILIAN CASUALTIES		
PROPERTY DAMAGE	MONETARY DAMAGE	INJURED	DEAD	MISSING
3 acres veneer walnut trees	$32,000	0	0	0
279 dead cows	$279,000	3	1	0
311 destroyed automobiles	$1,321,437	64	29	1
46 incinerated buildings	$1,675,500	430	113	4
7 damaged bridges	$5,090,300	16	21	27
419 overturned outhouses	$3,134	44	0	1
extinction of 3 rodent species	not quantifiable	0	0	0
1 damaged nuclear reactor	$115,000,000	26,531	45	5
1 oil tanker disaster	$72,341,500	10	4	12
18 derailed trains	$39,500,000	412	310	3
2 damaged hydroelectric dams	$131,880,000	5,954	1,782	202
2 ruptured gas pipelines	$16,435,247	627	324	18
1,349 destroyed mailboxes	$26,800	2	0	0
Totals:	$383,581,918	34,093	2,629	274

What made this virtual entity so interesting was that it was exceedingly difficult to kill. Unlike sissies or girls, chickens had the capacity to survive all but the most determined assaults. In fact, to achieve a 100% chicken mortality rate, the Unsupervised 6.0 model universe had to be tweaked to the maximum. This required a population profile including a minimum ratio of 134 juvenile delinquents per chicken.

Another behavioral algorithm that Dad added to the program code was the virtual entity *Damien*. This level was based on a character in a popular movie series of the period. Damien was designed to be the digital incarnation of the very spawn of hell itself. The player could not introduce more than one Damien into a model universe because any attempt to do so caused the game to automatically default to a 100% mortality rate. Dad referred to this phenomenon as the *Damien Automatic Mortality Normalization,* or the DAMN-Effect. That is, having a single Damien in any universe so drastically increased overall mortality that the application of two or more was both redundant and cruel. This effect could be easily be demonstrated by populating a model universe with one-hundred Sissies and an equal number of Girls, and outfitting both groups with the maximum quotas of hazard objects and risk enhancers. The overall mortality of such an iteration invariably would be zero. In contrast, the subsequent introduction just a single Damien into this same universe, would result in a drastically different outcome: a mortality rate of 99.5 percent.

In fact, this algorithm was so powerful that some users experienced serious application problems. For example, an amateur programmer in Ohio, late one night in a moment of casual lawlessness, deliberately ignored Dad's explicit operating instructions, bypassed the safeties, and ran an Unsupervised 6.0 model populated with ten-thousand Damiens just to see what would happen.

They found the guy three days later drinking gin in a roadhouse south of Memphis. His hair had turned white as snow. After being heavily sedated at a local hospital, he recounted a tale of such dismal horror and disruptive potential that details of the event remain censored by federal authorities even to this day. What is known however, is that on the night of the alleged incident, there was a county-wide blackout, four train derailments, seven computer-controlled equipment failures at local nuclear power facilities, and his house was incinerated, along with a nearby strip mall.

Chapter 21

The Six Kinds of Hitchhikers

For reasons that have never been fully understood, my father was pathologically susceptible to falling asleep while driving a motor vehicle. Among the more prominent outward manifestations of this unfortunate affliction were a robust endowment of surficial disfigurements and generally imperfectly healed fractures, both on his own personal chassis and those of the automobiles he operated. Concomitantly, Dad seemed to be constantly recovering from serious bodily injuries sustained in motor-vehicle mishaps. Presumably, Dad was graced with either an extraordinarily tolerant insurance agent, or the highest inflation-adjusted collision premium of the Modern Era.

For intermittent spans of time cumulatively representing a substantial fraction of my childhood, I recall my father being encumbered with not only a multiplicity of grievous injuries but also with a wide assortment of related medical paraphernalia ostensibly deployed to aid the recovery process. These fixtures included such items as crutches (both singularly and dually), canes (ditto), walkers, leg and arm casts, head bandages, rib trusses, knee gussets, arm slings, neck braces, femur clamps, jaw wires, shin rivets, and traction gantries, or some integrated combination thereof. Also present was a body of associated objects called *scratching jigs*. These were typically produced by unfolding coat hangers and painstakingly re-conforming them into precise geometric shapes so as to be dispatched to specific sites beneath leg and arm casts to combat sporadic outbreaks of severe epidermal itching.

Dad compared the effects of driving to the *Magic Fingers* electronic devices that were once fairly common in motel rooms. The reader may recall putting quarters into a box that caused the bed to mimic the sounds and motions associated with riding in a diesel-powered vehicle cruising down the highway at approximately sixty miles per hour. Like driving, these devices had an hypnotic effect on my father, and would induce deep, REM-sleep in him after only a few minutes.

Alcohol consumption by my father however, was not a factor in the driving-drowsiness phenomenon. Other than an occasional bottle of Merlot, my father seldom drank. The essential factor controlling his alcohol consumption was his dislike of its flavor. This is not surprising. As everyone knows, a lavish slug of 100-proof whisky presented to the unsuspecting or uninitiated, invariably evokes the same series of involuntary physiological reactions that occur upon ingestion of any aggressively toxic liquid, say, like battery acid, rocket fuel, or molten copper. It could be argued that the only thing that prevents our bodies from automatically rejecting any distilled alcoholic beverage is that we will it so. It is a true case of mind over matter. Alcohol is poison after all. It is an aggressive solvent. It can be employed as a disinfectant. It is flammable. It can be used as a fuel, as in motor fuel, like for your Volvo. As a matter of fact, everyone could start running their cars on alcohol tomorrow and nobody would probably notice much of a difference, excepting perhaps a sudden deluge of previously-owned Rolexes on the Middle Eastern pawn shop circuit.

The point is that the compounds we commonly use in our automobiles to make them perform properly come in two distinct classes: toxic and extremely toxic. These include such compounds as sulfuric acid, ethylene glycol, naphtha, benzene, toluene, xylene, methyl ethyl ketone, and petroleum ether, just to name a few. Somewhere down the list are methyl alcohol (wood alcohol) and ethyl alcohol (grain alcohol). The former is a common ingredient in windshield washer fluid, fuel injector cleaner, and a wide variety of other automobile-care products. It will exterminate your run-of-the-mill human being in a dosage of around ten ounces. The latter is the principal active ingredient in those beverages we cherish so dearly, and also comprises ten percent of a popular motor fuel called *Gasohol.* Ten percent alcohol equates to 20-proof in the vernacular of taxable spirits. There is some comfort in this knowledge, in the sense that if one were to ever ingest a harmful quantity of Gasohol, at least there would be a pretty good buzz involved somewhere along the way.

Grain alcohol will render the average person at or near room temperature in doses as little as twelve ounces ingested at once, or in smaller doses taken regularly over an extended duration, say, about four decades. Table 1 below, summarizes the estimated lethal dose for humans per 100 pounds of body weight for some common automotive chemicals.

Table 1
Automotive Chemical Lethality

Compound	LD_{50} Lethal Dosage (oz.)[1]
battery acid	1.8
methyl ethyl ketone	5.0
antifreeze	6.5
diesel fuel	8.7
gasoline	8.7
methyl alcohol	10.5
ethyl alcohol	13.5

[1] based on rat LD_{50} oral dosage extrapolated for 100 lb. human

(LD_{50} = minimum dosage causing mortality in 50% of test organisms)

Grain alcohol fits in neatly among the above referenced chemical classes both in terms of its range of physical properties, types of technological applications, and toxicity. Complicating the situation however, is the fact that our bodies seem to have a profound affinity for the substance. In fact, alcohol is apparently so irresistible to humans that both the retail outlets where it is dispensed and the warehouses where it is stored must be equipped with security systems. The types of the protective measures employed range in sophistication from simple surveillance cameras to steel bars on windows; or from heavily-reinforced concrete bunkers to 14-foot tall electrified, barbed-wire fencing, patrolled by armed guards and attack dogs, depending on the venue. In some regions of the U.S., duly sworn officers of the State armed with pistols and sawed-off shotguns, hand out booze and work the cash registers nine-to-midnight, six days a week. It's like going to a State Police Post to buy your Jagermeister.

From a chemical engineering standpoint, ethyl alcohol has so many useful properties that it would probably be far more widely employed in technological applications were it not such a strictly regulated inebriant. It is perhaps like if opium were useful for a common industrial process, say as a grease for the gears on a cotton picker. It doesn't take some damn Eli Whitney to figure out that before long, the gears on all the cotton pickers would be worn out from lack of lubrication and/or jammed up with the severed fingers of the employees.

Obviously production and commerce would be catastrophically impacted. So traditionally, we have assumed that it is probably good in a societal sense to refrain from exploiting the useful properties of substances that also happen to be intoxicating or addictive. Nevertheless, the fact remains that if we could throw-off this antiquated notion of substance discrimination we might someday actually be able to obtain energy self-sufficiency in this country, and a nice bag of *Panama Red* at a reasonable price.

In light of Dad's driving difficulties, his natural aversion to alcohol is understandable. It is inconceivable that this could have done anything but support his efforts to cope with drowsiness. Conversely however, there unfortunately was another beverage that Dad found equally as repulsive as strong spirits, i.e. coffee. It literally made him gag. He categorically and unequivocally hated all hot brewed liquids as a distinct class of phenomena. He could not understand why any sane human being would want to immerse the delicate tissues of their mouth in a boiling, acidic bean leachate.

Needless to say, either one of the two above referenced naturally occurring traits, (1) a proclivity for driving drowsiness, or (2) an aversion to coffee, would be dangerous enough in our modern technological world. However, when they are both combined in a single unfortunate individual, the peril is compounded to the severest proportions. Dad knew this. So he continually sought new and innovative ways to help him remain alert while operating a motor vehicle.

The Trotting Experiment

One method that my father researched involved trotting along-side the car as it idled down the highway, while holding on to the steering wheel by extending his right arm through the window. To accomplish this he would get the car moving very slowly in first gear and then carefully step out onto the roadway, shut the door, and then steer as described above.

Only a few minutes of this activity was remarkably effective at stimulating his cardiovascular system, thereby defeating the drowsiness. Once he was awake he would open the door, get back into the car and then resume normal highway speed. This method seemed to be the breakthrough he had been searching for. Sure, it was probably against the law, but as far as he was concerned at the time, to do otherwise was to invite certain catastrophe. However, the circumstances eventually became such that what was perhaps the core weakness of this methodology rather awkwardly revealed itself. It happened late one night somewhere in the hills of Kentucky. Evidently, Dad failed to fully anticipate the robustness of the force of gravity associated with a certain segment of the route he was traveling. Apparently, the steepness of the roadway unexpectedly exceeded some critical angle, thereupon impelling the car to an untenable velocity. After that it became a simple exercise in linear reasoning for Dad: either release the steering wheel or start running forty-five miles per hour. He released the steering wheel.

The car continued down the hill another fifty yards and then gracefully pirouetted over a cliff and was torn to bits as it plummeted over three-hundred feet vertically, finally coming to rest on jagged rocks at the base of the mountain, subsequently igniting a considerable forest fire. In his haste to reach the automobile and recover his personal items, Dad neglected to adequately appreciate the scope of the conflagration.

When he suddenly discovered himself engulfed in flames, only then did he modify his angle of approach by a factor effectively equivalent to 180 degrees. He subsequently narrowly escaped untimely cremation as the advancing fireball accelerated up the slope behind him the entire way. But the good side was that his drowsiness was cured for the rest of the trip.

In the considerable legal aftermath, Dad was ultimately compelled to bring to bear the full weight of his formidable forensic skills in order to completely address the manifold concerns of the insurance company regarding the perceived inordinately minor nature of his personal bodily injuries. He subsequently, and no doubt probably quite wisely, elected to discontinue all variations of the "trotting-along-side-the-car maneuver" because of its inherently flawed nature.

This put him back at square one again, that is, driving totally unprotected. It was dynamite just looking for a place to go off. Sometime during this dark period, Dad eventually discovered, via convergent logical analysis, what many other drivers of the period had already determined: that having a passenger in the car to chat with, even a complete stranger, could take the edge off of the drowsiness just enough to literally mean the difference between life and death, or at least having a car that was in one piece and not melted.

So, aside from Dad being a nice fellow, and it being a unique time and place in the universe where hitchhikers and the people who picked them up were commonplace, there was also a very practical reason for providing transportation to the masses. At least that's my theory: passengers helped my father stay awake.

This assessment is supported not only by my own personal first-hand knowledge of the actual events themselves, but also by two significant facts: 1, Dad never had a car wreck while transporting a hitchhiker, and 2, of the estimated 235 reported automobile accidents he was involved in, approximately 219 occurred while he was the lone occupant of the vehicle.

Passenger Diversity

Depending on the time of day, weather conditions, regional demographics, and random chance, there could be a variety of hitchhikers present along any given segment of highway. However, a representative sample of hitchhikers generally comprised six basic categories (see Table 2).

Table 2
Hitchhiker Data Summary

Category	Description	% of Total Riders
1	military personnel	35
2	farm-hands	19
3	stranded motorists	11
4	local nimrods	7
5	interstate nimrods	6
6	kooks	22

Of course ordinary instances of overlap between the above referenced classes did occur, as would be expected in any sample population. It is very likely however, that statisticians conducting an objective study of this group would ultimately conclude that there was a seemingly inexplicable particular skewing of the data toward the last category. That is, it was common to encounter passengers from categories one through five who also overlapped with another category. However, that category was almost always number six.

The range of behavioral propensities exhibited at that time by the cumulative population of hitchhikers in general was what most observers might consider abnormal at the very least. Initially this might seem surprising. After all, in a random sample of sufficient size one would expect a normal range of traits. Apparently inexplicably however, for hitchhikers this was not the case. Fortunately, upon analysis a rational explanation appears emergent from the data. That is, their deportment spanned the full bandwidth of the human experience as one would naturally expect, but there was something more. All of the parameters seemed exaggerated.

After years of reflection I have concluded that most of these phenomena were ultimately reducible to the simple fact that said hitchhikers constituted a select group. Behavioral scientists tell us that it's in select groups where things are happening. Select groups are the result of some agent, combination of agents, or processes in the physical, biological, or cultural environment, acting as a filter. What emerges from the filter possesses properties, characteristics, and/or potentialities distinctly different from that not emerging.

When human behavioral phenomena are reduced to algorithmic or numerical units, which in principle they ultimately can be, then the select group filter may be theoretically modeled as a mechanism that takes certain ensembles of these numbers and squares them, or in some cases undoubtedly compounds them to far greater exponential powers. With hitchhikers, the nice always seemed nicer, the sad sadder, and the ill-mannered coarser.

Although it may appear little more than a petty concern to the modern casual observer, it cannot be overemphasized just how important an issue like good manners often became among a collection of total strangers locked for hours-on-end in a vinyl-lined box made of stamped sheet metal and tempered glass, streaking across the surface of the planet at Mach 0.10.

Ancillary to this was also the issue of some passengers apparently not having been afforded the level of access to modern sanitary facilities as we would have ideally hoped. Taken together, these criteria synergistically coalesced into a gestaltic phenomenon whose indices were inescapably graduated in denominations of abject obnoxiousness.

Being a pre-teen with superfluous time on my hands, I therefore had occasion to construct a clandestine environmental rating protocol called the *Yuck Factor,* or YF for short, that I sometimes employed in my attempts to more perfectly recount these experiences to my contemporaries. It was a simple linear rating index based on the level of atmospheric organic contamination delivered by the subject, taking into account wind direction, relative humidity, dew point, and ambient temperature.

The units ranged from YF-0 through YF-10, with YF-0 being the least offensive, i.e., no detectable contamination, and YF-10 being more or less tantamount to a forty gallon tub of fermented walrus gums, sometime around late July, with a few opossum livers and maybe a rancid halibut or two thrown in depending upon the odds. As one would expect in such a standardized numerical modeling protocol, YF-5 was the break-over point. That is, if the location of the source could not be determined with one's eyes closed, then the index was YF-5 or less. Accordingly, if their location could be accurately pinpointed independently of any acoustic, visual, or tactile clues, they were deemed YF-5 or greater.

Farm-Hands

This group was composed entirely of men in their twenties through sixties who scraped out a living doing farm work, more or less at about the same socioeconomic rung as your modern illegal alien migrant worker, except without the Astrovan. Up through about 1970 there were still a large number of them around. They got to and from work by whatever means they could. Many of them had to hitch a ride at least three or four days a week. This is not intended to imply that there are not non-alien farm-hands in America today. What is implied however, is that for the most part they now own or have access to automobiles, perhaps accounting for a large portion of the near three-order-of-magnitude reduction in the incidence of hitch-hiking observed today.

Farm-hands seemed to be the least conversant of all the rider categories. They were typically mute until spoken to. They spanned a range from about YF-2 to YF-6, with an average of about YF-3. Also, apparently curiously, farm workers almost always had a sack with them. It could be made of paper, cloth, plastic, or even leather. They sometimes had a lunch pail and a water jug as well, but these were optional. The sack however, was omnipresent. The contents of the sacks could sometimes be problematical. Experience had taught Dad, rather bitterly, to assay the ingredients of all sacks or containers prior to allowing their admittance into the vehicle. He was not trying to be difficult or unfriendly, it was only a necessary precaution similar to what today might be called a *security check.*

Farm-hands carried sacks because at least a part of their employment compensation package was in agricultural goods. Their employers usually allowed them take what they wanted from a large garden that they helped tend, or from a personal plot they cultivated on their employer's land. Depending on the time of year, a typical farm-hand on his way home might have fresh corn, potatoes, onions, or a variety of other items in the sack, and usually in quantities sufficient for several meals. And since they took a sack full home virtually every day, there was always plenty available for bartering or gratuities.

Approximately half of the fresh produce served at our home when I was child was obtained from hitchhiking farm workers as either a gesture of appreciation to Dad for giving them a ride, or as a monetary instrument in transactions of unregistered commerce. Nearly all farm-hands were more than willing to share the contents of their sacks simply out of good will and fellowship. The bartering just seemed to make it more interesting and fun. Of course Dad, arguably being among the top, if not the single greatest squirrel hunter of the 20th century, almost always had a sack of his own, full of freshly dispatched squirrels, located somewhere in the vehicle. He would offer these as fungible tender in exchange for the various agricultural commodities.

There was a generally-established conversion rate that seemed to be well accepted by all. Table 3 below, lists the standard trade value of one gray squirrel *(Sciurus carolinensis)* relative to a few items commonly carried in a farm-hand's sack.

Table 3
Farm Commodity Exchange Value
of One Gray Squirrel* (U.S.)
*(unskinned, dead less than 3 hours, c. 1955-70)

½ dozen tomatoes or ears sweet corn
½ dozen eggplants, green peppers, or squash
1 dozen carrots, onions, or potatoes
1 dozen turnips, cucumbers, or beets
1 quart green beans, sweet peas, or Brussels sprouts
1 head lettuce or cabbage
1 cantaloupe, watermelon, or pumpkin
1 quart strawberries, blackberries, or grapes
4 paw paws
½ dozen apples, peaches, or pears
1 quart pecans or walnuts (in the shell)
1 quart sweet milk
1 pint buttermilk
½ dozen eggs
½ pint butter
½ pie or cobbler
½ pint honey, sorghum, or molasses
½ pint home made liquor or wine

Occasionally, Dad would strike a bargain with a farm-hand even though he did not possess any squirrels at the exact time that the deal was made. In other instances he might possess squirrels but the farm-hand would express some displeasure concerning the quality or freshness of the offered animals.

In either of these cases, Dad would abruptly stop the vehicle near the first reasonably-sized patch of woods he saw. Then as the farm-hand waited (often outwardly skeptical), Dad would dash from the automobile and hunt in the woods until the required quota of premium quality squirrels was obtained. This typically required less than ten minutes (and sometimes as little as five). He would even skin and gut the squirrels on site if requested. It took Dad approximately forty seconds to completely skin and gut an average squirrel.

Dad was what can only be described as the Mozart of squirrel skinning. He had mastered its subtleties with the fervor and intricate craft of a seasoned artist. It was a ballet of manual dexterity beyond the reach of most people. That is, it was an expressive symphony of precisely choreographed movements and subtle nuances of articulation arguably lying outside the observational sensibilities of all but the most impassioned practitioners. There truly was no conventional standard by which to measure his talent.

He was a squirrel-skinning statement. His was a revolution of style and form so express and admirable that an audience became instantly entranced by the effortless fusion of movement, the fluid interplay between sheets of viscera, nebular outlays of blood, and fleeting veils of hide. They would watch in rapturous awe as the elements of the base and corporeal were transcended by the superlative essence of graceful motion and the stunning purity of human determination.

Farm-hands would often verbally convey their sincere amazement at my father's mastery of the art of squirrel-skinning. Many of them instantly recognized and freely acknowledged that they were in the presence of a true genius. Although Dad was aware of his stature in this regard, he never let it go to his head. And despite the initial skepticism of the few cynics, once they experienced the full magnitude of Dad's talent, they would usually yield over to him their entire inventory of produce as a nominal gesture of appreciation for allowing them the fortuitous privilege of witnessing such a display.

Farmhand Contraband

There were instances when a farm-hand's sack contained products that Dad considered non-permissible for transactions of squirrel commerce. That is, he assigned no fundamental squirrel-exchange value to said items. These included among other things, radishes, most home-processed meat products, and of course rutabagas.

Radishes upset his stomach, he considered home-made meat dishes to be pathogenically perilous, and he categorically refused to accept rutabagas because of an oath he had made to himself after surviving World War II (see Chapter 5). In addition to the normal items that my father refused to eat or transact on, there was also a special class of materials that he regulated extremely harshly based on their general incompatibility with an overall pleasant driving experience. That is, if the constituents of a container were obnoxious, offensive, hazardous, or questionable in any way, my father would first invite the prospective rider to place the object(s) into the trunk of the car, or if we were driving a pickup, into the bed of the truck.

If said hitchhiker refused to comply with these minimal safety requirements, he was cordially denied admission to the vehicle. Most riders were more than happy to abide by the rules and generally were sympathetic to my father's reasoning when he requested their cooperation.

Of course there were always a few malcontents who expressed their displeasure at Dad's policy. Some even vehemently argued with him, maintaining that they were "entitled" to a ride without condition whatsoever. Dad honestly did try to be nice to such people, but it was sometimes very difficult for him to remain a gentleman under such circumstances. There always seemed to be a few hitchhikers who outwardly maintained that anyone who owned and operated an automobile did so at the expense of, and/or "upon the backs of the poor."

They somehow believed that all car owners obtained their vehicles either by aristocratic inheritance or by stealing them from the government. In their minds, a car was tantamount to State Property, that is, they owned it just as much as my father did. So therefore, Dad was obligated to give them a ride anywhere they wished. They did not seem to grasp or recognize the concept that cars are bought and paid for like all other property. Dad attempted to explain that this was America, not the Soviet Union. This only seemed to make them madder. Table 4 below, lists some of the most common controlled cargo and the remedial action that Dad mandated.

Table 4
Farm-Hand Special Cargoes

Item(s)	Events	Remedial Action
home-made cheese or whey	38	bed of truck only
tripe, chitlins, snouts, tongues, glands, or slop	92	bed of truck only
hog, cow, or goat heads	21	bed of truck only
live pigs or calves	41	bed of truck only
rabbits, weasels, minks, beavers, or muskrats	39	bed of truck or trunk of car
chickens, ducks, coots, pigeons, crows, or turkeys	55	of bed of truck or trunk of car
cardinals, blue jays, robins, hawks, or mockingbirds	24	bed of truck or trunk of car
groundhogs, opossums, raccoons, or armadillos	42	bed of truck or trunk of car
live snakes or lizards	25	keep walking
live frogs or toads, or newts	47	bed of truck only
live crayfish or mussels, tadpoles, salamanders	76	bed of truck or trunk of car
rats (dead or alive)	47	keep walking
skunks (dead or alive)	29	keep walking
turtles, carp, shad, eels, gar, mullet, or skipjack	54	bed of truck or trunk of car
live bees, hornets, or wasps	37	keep walking
crickets, grasshoppers, grubs, or earthworms	28	bed of truck or trunk of car
live horseflies	1	keep walking
live leaches	12	keep walking
manure (any quantity)	52	keep walking

I was sleeping soundly on the back seat when a farmhand carrying a seventy-five pound bag of live horseflies got into our automobile somewhere near Mt. Unpleasant, Kentucky. Via the richly detailed accounts of my father I have been able to reconstruct, more or less, the gist of the initial conversation that occurred. Dad opened the dialog with a direct question:

"What's in the bag?"

"Horseflies."

"Horseflies?"

"Yep, horseflies."

"Dead or alive?"

"They're alive alright. They're the big black sumbitches too. Species *Tabanus* I think. The bastards are meaner than hell...got a bite on 'em like a rat. They're about three inches long. They're the .357 magnums of the bloodsucking insect world! There's about 235,000 of the rascals in this sack here!"

"What in the world are you going to do with 235,000 horseflies?"

"I give them to my boys to play with."

Dad peered over his shoulder to check on me as I lay sleeping in the back seat, angelic-like no doubt. I suppose he was desperately trying not to visualize me being engaged in the exploitation of multiple-kilogram quantities of disease-ridden vermin for some kind of disgusting, perverted amusement.

"What do your boys do with so many horseflies?"

"Well, they mostly make little planes out of them and then have air races."

"How do they make planes out of horseflies?"

"Easy, they just pull the legs off and then glue the flies belly-down onto the wings of paper airplanes. Works great! You ought to see it. But if they use enough horseflies they can get just about anything to fly. I helped them glue about 300 of the bastards to a license plate one time."

"A license plate! So what happened?" Dad queried.

"We let it go and the damn thing took off and flew around the back yard a couple of times and then it went clean out of sight! I got a phone call about a week later from an old fellow over in Clay County. He said he found my license plate in his wife's Nash. I said 'Oh hell!' And then I told him: *maybe you should take her to see a doctor!* He mumbled something and then hung up on me."

"That's interesting. What's some other things you've done?"

"Well, the boys like to take a live rat and glue maybe fifty horseflies onto its body. They hold the rat in a little harness until the glue dries, otherwise the rat would just pull the horseflies right off and kill them faster than they could ever glue them on."

"Anyway, when the glue is dry they go out in a field and turn the rat loose. The sumbitch tries to take off running but he just goes straight up like a rocket. After the rat gets up so high though he eventually levels out. Some rats start pulling the horseflies off about this time and it's usually on one side or the other so that it gets the power distribution out of balance."

"When that happens, it causes the rat to fly in circles. He eventually looses altitude and crashes into something. But I've seen them hover around for an hour or so before they slam into the side of a barn or hit a power line. And sometimes the rats just fly away - we don't know where they go."

"How often does that happen?"

"Oh, they do that all the time."

"They just fly away?"

"Oh yes. Some of them take off like a bird, go right out of sight, almost always heading south or southwest. It's the damnedest thing you ever saw! When we get a fresh sack of flies like this one here, the boys will outfit a couple hundred rats and release them all at once. It's quite a show for a while as they buzz around above the farm sporting with each other. Every once in a while they try to land on something alive. The cattle have learned to head for the pond if the rats get to flying too low. Believe it or not, the cats hide under the barn. The boys like to use pick-ax handles to swat the rats out of the air."

There was a pause as my father contemplated the overall ramifications of these mutant hell-spawn being out there somewhere. He envisioned the horrible fear and confusion of some poor average Joe minding his own business, sitting out in his back yard, enjoying a nice glass of lemonade perhaps, when one of these pestilent, bloodsucking, insect-rodent abominations comes seemingly from out of nowhere and lands on his neck. Then he entertained the image of a tranquil sky suddenly darkened by swarming legions of the aberrant vermin. In his mind's eye he watched them descend on a major urban area and shuddered at the ensuing bedlam. It arguably matched scenes out of *Revelations*. Dad sensed his imagination teetering on the brink of an uncontrolled spiral into paranoia. He had to get a grip.

"So how many boys do you have?" Dad asked.

"Just four these days."

"You used to have more boys?"

"Yes sir, I had five boys up until last summer."

"What do you mean?"

"Little Johnny died."

"I'm very sorry to hear that. What happened?"

"He had *encephalitis* and *tularemia*."

"Aren't those diseases associated with *horseflies*?"

"Well, some people say they are. But it was never proven that the flies did it. The vet over in Hockertown still says it was just all the uncooked rabbit meat he ate that actually killed him."

Dad nodded affirmatively as though he understood completely, as if this were a common everyday topic, and a routine occurrence. That is, for a kid to contract encephalitis and tularemia - a kid who has daily exposure to hundreds of thousands of bloodsucking flies and presumably hundreds of quite probably neurotic and/or homicidally pissed-off rats, and then kicks the bucket, and for the family veterinarian to be the final medical authority.

"Uh huh...oh yes, tularemia, raw rabbit meat, oh yes...veterinarian... uh huh..."

But my father did this frequently. What it meant was that his brain was crunching the permutations. He was cogitating his options for freeing this guy from the interior of our car before the horde of winged .357 magnums freed themselves from the interior of the sack. It seemed like a good time for a security check.

"Is that sack tied-off properly?" Dad queried.

"Oh sure, see here...watch this..."

I don't know if anyone on this earth can precisely articulate what freakish events transpired in the immediately subsequent seconds. I can tell you that I only remember being awakened by a terrible commotion. I cannot describe the complete scene. But I do know that by the time I achieved the first glimmerings of consciousness, the car had skidded sideways down the center of the highway for approximately three-hundred feet.

We had clipped a mailbox and ran over a cat as well. The automobile finally came to rest across the road in a beet field, pointed in the opposite direction. The instant the car stopped everybody bailed out, including the narrator, who didn't know what he was bailing out of, into, or why it was necessary. But somehow I did know that it was necessary. It was pure gut instinct that guided me in those first few seconds of quasi-awareness. Even though I didn't have a clue as to what was happening, my body somehow executed the proper steps, in the correct order, to facilitate my survival. Outwardly this took the appearance of my arms flailing and swatting wildly while my legs transported me generally away from the vehicle, establishing an appreciable distance between themselves and the source of the ungodly, excruciating, four-dimensional buzzing.

Within a few more seconds, Dad had spotted me and was quickly moving toward me. Our guest rider then let out a gleeful "Yee haw!" Meanwhile, a dark, droning, pestilent mass lingered around the car.

"Hot dang! That's the second time this week!"

Dad did not appreciate the humor in the guy's confession. He quickly surveyed my chassis for incidental damage generally attributable to bloodsuckers and then that of the car for the same. He found none to speak of. Luckily for our guest this was the case.

"Whew, that was close partner! Good thing nothing got tore up." the fly-man enthusiastically exclaimed.

Dad glared at the farmhand with a countenance of absolute disgust.

"What about that mailbox?" Dad asked.

"Oh, no thanks, you go ahead, I already got one. But I will take that dead cat if you don't mind."

It took Dad threatening the guy with a rigorous "head skinning," to get him to completely clear all of the horseflies from our car, including about a thousand dead and wounded ones covering virtually the entire interior of the automobile. Needless to say, this was the last time that Dad ever allowed sacks of horseflies, or any harmful insects, into the vehicle. And from this point on he got a whole lot more serious about security checks.

Stranded Motorists

This group was composed almost entirely of women. They could be almost any age, but typically were under thirty. Of the few men who did qualify as stranded motorists, most were either elderly gentlemen, preachers, or insurance salesmen. Stranded motorists typically exhibited environmental ratings of YF-0 through about YF-6, and averaged about YF-2. Almost invariably the women would be adorned with hair-curlers, dressed in bathrobes, or arrayed in some other configuration of ill-preparedness, making them slightly vulnerable and often a little testy. Good-looking gals usually ended up with what amounted to a pit crew to assist them, often in as little as a few seconds after stalling. Everyone else had to wait for my father to come along.

Dad helped all stranded motorists. It was just something that a man did. No questions, no philosophizing, he just made a sincere effort to get their car started for them. If he could not get it running he would give them a ride to the nearest service station. It was that simple. The most common automotive problem was a flat tire. The second most frequent problem was *out of gas,* and the third most recurrent problem was a tie between a *broken fan belt* and a *blown radiator hose* which were also more serious. However, Dad assisted motorists with virtually every conceivable mechanical problem at one time or another. It did not matter who these people were.

For example, I was once with him when he helped a man from Alabama. His car had a broken fan belt. It was on a Sunday in late July. The weather was sweltering. No one seemed willing to stop and assist him. When Dad saw a car with its hood raised, he just pulled over automatically. The stranded man was nervous and a little apprehensive. He told Dad that a State Trooper had ignored his efforts to flag him down over an hour ago and that some other men had driven by repeatedly, shouting rude epithets. This news incensed Dad. He did what he could to reassure the man. He told him not to worry and that he personally would see to it that his car was repaired. The man then got a look on his face of complete calmness. I could tell that he trusted my father. It was one of those special moments in life that are too rare. Since it was on a Sunday, and no service stations in our town were open, he drove the stranded man to a truck stop at least forty miles away to find a replacement part, then came back and helped him repair the vehicle. It took nearly all day to do this. But Dad got him back on the road. About a month later he received a nice Thank You card in the mail. The card was signed: *Rev. King.*

Many of the stranded motorists Dad assisted were from the lower echelons of the socioeconomic landscape. Some were outright destitute. When these people ran out of gas, Dad would usually buy them some, no questions asked. My father's humanity was even more expressed when people were suffering. I remember once when we stopped at a terrible traffic accident. There were at least four cars involved in the wreck. Dad and I were the first people on the scene. There was a crying woman standing in the middle of the road. She was shaking uncontrollably and blood was streaming down her face. Dad made me stay in our car while he went and aided the victims. He helped the woman sit down and tried to console her. He then took her hand and gently showed her how to place it over a cut on her forehead. He told her to keep pressure on the cut and that the bleeding would stop. In the process she informed him that her husband was trapped beneath their Lincoln. Dad then quickly extricated a well-dressed man who was trapped beneath the overturned car.

The man had a serious compound fracture in his left arm and was bleeding profusely. Dad picked this man up and carried him to a shady spot on the opposite side of the road. He then removed the man's necktie and wrapped it around the injured arm. The woman stopped crying at this point and offered to assist him. Dad instructed her on how to loosen the tourniquet every two minutes. She stayed with her husband and performed this duty while Dad left them to go help the others. He went to each car in turn and checked the condition of every passenger. He methodically applied first aid to those who needed it and gave moral support to all. By the time the ambulances arrived, Dad was covered in blood. As they were putting the well dressed man into the ambulance, his wife informed the emergency personnel about Dad's heroics. The paramedics told my father that his actions had clearly lessened the suffering of the injured, and quite probably kept the well dressed man from bleeding to death. Dad accepted their thanks, shook hands with all present, then got back into his car and drove away.

Most people freely expressed appreciation for Dad's gallantry and kindness. Many offered him money. He categorically refused to accept anything from them other than their honest gratitude. He made many friends in this way. Sometimes however, for unknown reasons, motorists were unappreciative of Dad's humanitarian gestures.

An episode I recall in particular occurred when we were headed south somewhere on U.S. 41 and Dad suddenly had to swerve to miss an entire car engine laying in the middle of the road. I recall him commenting something to the effect of: "Either a junk dealer has lost part of his cargo or we are getting ready to meet somebody with one hell of a case of car trouble."

Sure enough, as we rounded the next curve we observed a woman decked-out in hair-curlers, wearing only a bathrobe and house slippers, standing beside a brand new Cadillac. She was holding a gas can in one hand and zealously flagging us down with the other.

"I think I'm out of gas." she said as we slowed to a stop next to her.

Dad had a pretty hard time communicating to her that being out of gas was not the problem.

"*But it's a Cadillac!*" she kept insisting. Even after Dad raised the hood of the car and confirmed that the engine was gone, she was not convinced.

"What makes you such an expert anyway?" she said in a very obnoxious tone.

"Well, it doesn't take an expert to know that a Cadillac motor is blocking traffic over there, and that right here is a Cadillac car without an engine. You must agree, it is logically compelling at the very least."

"Oh yeah, how do I know that it wasn't you that put that engine in the middle of the road?"

"What?" Dad said as he closed the hood on the Cadillac.

"And keep your damn hands off my car!" she protested rudely.

"Lady, please calm down. I'll give you a ride to the closest service station."

"Don't tell me to calm down! I'm not riding with you anywhere you sonofabitch, especially in a stupid truck!"

"Okay then, do you want me to go call a wrecker for you?"

"Listen, all I want you to do, is go fill this can with gasoline and bring it back to me as fast as possible! If you can't do that then get the hell out of here or I'll call the sheriff on your ass. And I mean right now mister!"

By now Dad had endured all that was healthy. The time had come to move on. But he could not resist one little jab:

"Ma'am, with all due respect, the only good that a can of gas will do this car now is to pour it on it and burn it where it sits. That would at least make it easier for the salvage company to load onto the scrap trailer when they come to haul it off."

"That does it! I am going to tell the sheriff everything you said. They'll lock you up so long your stupid-looking little brat won't recognize you, assuming that he can now!"

I was just a kid, but I knew I had just been dealt an insult of the most heinous and loathsome order. So did my father. But he remained a gentleman.

"Lady, obviously you are very upset about your car. While you cool off a little I'm going to drive up there and move that engine out of the road before somebody has a wreck."

"Listen you obnoxious bastard, if you so much as touch that engine I'll sue you for every dime you have! Junior won't get any new shoes until he's fifty!"

"Okay, fine, if you don't need my help, I'll be moving on, have a nice day."

We got back into our truck and drove away. I remember Dad telling me that sometimes it is difficult to keep our hope for humanity alive when we encounter people like "Cadillac Woman." He wanted me to understand that people like her constitute a minority and it was always better to have hope than not to. He told me to always remember this one simple axiom:

"Hating humanity is really just hating yourself."

He also told me that it went against every instinct he had to not turn around and move the engine out of the highway.

A few days later a county sheriff came to our house and served Dad with a summons and informed him that he was being sued for $300,000 by the driver of the Cadillac. Evidently, a few minutes after we left Cadillac Woman that day, an elderly couple were injured when they struck the motor in the road with their car. Not surprisingly, Cadillac Woman sued claiming that it was my father's fault. She alleged among other things, that Dad damaged her car, and that he refused to move the engine out of the road after placing it there against her wishes. Prior to the trial, her attorney repeatedly offered Dad the chance to settle out of court for $15,000 cash, and threatened to accuse him of attempted assault if he refused. Dad elected to fight it.

As promised, her attorney zealously tried to make Dad look like some kind of a predatory pervert in the opening examination. There was a problem however. The judge categorically refused to accept the validity of the accusations. It turned out that the judge sitting on the bench that day was none other than the well dressed man whose life Dad had saved a few months before. The judge dismissed the suit after only ten minutes of testimony. He also harshly admonished the opposing attorney for sensationalism, demagoguery, and outright deceit. Dad was absolutely elated. It was a great victory.

But it still cost him $125 in attorney fees, plus another heavy tax on his hope for humanity. Contrary to what one might expect however, after this episode he actually redoubled his efforts to assist stranded motorists. I believe he did this to make up for allowing one person's bitterness to affect his hope for all of humanity. As far as I know, he never let that happen again for the rest of his life.

My father was hope. He tried to be everyone's hope. He even came from a town called Hope (*New Hope* to be precise). He brought hope with him when he walked into a room. In the darkest times, when all around was lost, he was light, certainty, and hope. Wherever he was, hope was there too. They were inseparable. When he was there, we were going to win.

What this ultimately means of course is that there is hope for humanity. There has to be. There are many, many reasons to think so, but only two matter, and they are irrefutable: 1, Dad was always right, and if he had hope, then there must be something to it; and 2, there are other people in the world like Dad. It is part of the natural human condition, genetically ordained to be such. And as long as these people exist, humanity will exist. Just a few of them are all we need. Luckily, we have billions.

Local Nimrods

This group was comprised of neighborhood men, usually down a little on their luck, hitching to or from work. About half were drunks headed either to or from the bootlegger's. Environmentally rated YF-2 through about YF-7. They could be practically anyone who had lost their driver's license or vehicle for one reason or another, or were unable to afford an automobile. Some belonged to a special class who never learned to operate a motor vehicle at all. This was a common occurrence during the time period in question. These people were arguably the last remnants of the original population segment who had refused to make the transition from the foot-based to the automobile-based transport paradigm. Each passing year their numbers became fewer until around 1970, they more or less became extinct as a class.

Local nimrods also included a peculiar subgroup who were apparently intoxicated farmers. I have yet to formulate a comprehensive rational explanation for this phenomenon, but nevertheless it was real. Drunken farmers were particularly pompous, loud, and obnoxious. I recall a case where such a farmer wrecked his tractor in a ditch and subsequently repeatedly attempted to persuade Dad into pulling it out with our brand new car we had literally just picked up at the dealer. Dad graciously declined several times on the grounds that such an endeavor would undoubtedly result in damage to both vehicles. And since we were on our way home to get my mom and take her out for her birthday dinner, he really did not want to risk hurting the car.

After a nauseatingly lengthy debate, the farmer reluctantly got into our car and we all drove away. But within a few minutes he started complaining about the tractor again. Dad tried to reason with him but it had little effect. The guy apparently was either too drunk to realize it or too distracted to grasp what Dad was saying. He subsequently berated Dad harshly, calling him a wide variety of unflattering terms. Dad struggled desperately, far beyond the standards of routine civil discourse, and endured this verbal abuse. We eventually located a service station and tried to leave the guy there but he refused to get out of our car on the grounds that he did not like the way he had been "railroaded" into riding to a service station when all he wanted was somebody to pull his tractor out of a stupid ditch. He went on to state that the only way he would vacate our car was if we went back and pulled the tractor out of the ditch.

Dad debated with him for about another sixty seconds and finally got out of the car went around to the passenger side door and literally attempted to forcibly extract the farmer from the vehicle. But the farmer turned sideways, leaned back in the seat, put one arm over the back of the seat and one arm under the front of the seat, thus securing himself very effectively, and then kicked extremely vigorously whenever Dad tried to remove him. Complicating the situation was the fact that the farmer was also wearing an enormous pair of extremely heavy duty cowboy boots with razor sharp spurs which when thusly deployed, constituted a formidable defensive capability. It was a really bad scene. Several onlookers began to gather and stare. The only way for my father to effectively counter such a defense was to respond with like force, that is, get a run at it and dive through the door feet-first, and try to "kick it out with him," so to speak. Not a pleasant thought obviously. But Dad knew he had little choice because the guy had already slowed us down so much that we were running late for Mom's birthday dinner.

So, reluctantly but determinedly, he prepared to make his move by planting his feet firmly on the pavement and leaning slightly forward as though lining up for a hundred-yard dash. But then he paused for a second and noticed all of the spectators starting to gather. Dad hated "scenes" in general, and as far as being an agent in one, it was not an option. So he unhesitantly stood-down from his offensive posture and simply glared at the farmer in disgust, apparently trying to formulate an alternative plan.

A seeming deadlock had developed. Dad could not extract the guy without getting down to some serious scene-making. And even if Dad did elect to proceed with a first strike, the jackboot technology commanded by the farmer again highlighted the fearsome disadvantage that would have to be overcome in an unlimited stomp-a-thon. Obviously, the prospects of such an engagement were not merely distasteful, but too bitter to contemplate. Just when it seemed that all was lost, luckily, my natural kid-associated pyrotechnics expertise actually turned out to be useful. That's when I told Dad about the sack of smoke bombs in my coat pocket. Dad smiled, and the rest is history. It literally required all twelve of my Mt. Vesuvius Death Smokers to flush out the obstinate farmer, but it finally worked 100% completely. The down side was however, that the guy ended up soiling himself and the interior of our car in the process. Dad considered it a lousy break, but an acceptable cost overall for being able to unequivocally bring closure to the affair without having to resort to a kick-to-the-death.

When we got home that night Dad had a really hard time explaining to my mom not only why we were over an hour late but also why the interior of our brand new car smelled like a whisky barrel full of burned shit. And as usual, not only did he totally vanquish her fury with his boundless charisma, but he also must have deployed his formidable powers of persuasion to mitigate any lingering doubts she might have harbored, because before the night was over, she cooked us a nice steak dinner and painstakingly disinfected the interior of the car with concentrated chlorine bleach.

Interstate Nimrods

Mostly would-be artisans, disgruntled Peace Corps members, college students, Marxists, beatniks, free-thinkers, pilgrims, etc. Smelliest of the six categories. Rated from about YF-4 through YF-10. Averaged about YF-7. Large overlap with Category 6. Some of the most animated conversations occurred while members of this class were in the automobile.

Although most of these individuals considered themselves substantially beyond the common and base bearing of regular men, frankly, much to their displeasure, and ultimate denial, many of them were wholly unprepared for the intensity of my father's tactical forensic maneuvers.

Dad was never defeated in an argument. But he chose his battles carefully. He would go on the offensive only when his opponent's position was verifiably erroneous, or if he felt they were overdue for an encounter with reality. Which interestingly, was almost always.

We picked up some would-be, do-gooder anarchist east of Paducah one time. As soon as he got into the car it was clear that he had a major chip on his shoulder about something.

"So what's your beef with the world?" Dad abruptly asked him.

"It's rather simple actually. The current problem is that there is too much cheap food. A globally-enforced ban on all forms of mechanized agriculture would expedite the transition to a balanced, ecologically sustainable society."

"What?"

"There are too many people for the planet to support. The world needs to be depopulated to less than two percent of current levels. If we just banned chemical fertilizers, pesticides, and mechanized agriculture, the human population would re-adjust to a sustainable level. There's no reason for us to be so arrogant to think that we shouldn't have *die-backs* every so often."

"Die-backs?"

"Yes, without a major dieback within the next twenty years, all natural resources will be exhausted and wildlife will become extinct. It is our moral duty to save the world from this."

"So to save everybody we must kill them?"

"That's more or less the essence of it."

There was a pause as the full meaning of the guy's statement crystallized in Dad's brain. Finally, Dad responded with a question.

"Why do you hate everybody?"

"I don't know what you mean."

"I think you do. Don't you want to have a wife and a kid someday and be a productive citizen of the greatest country the world has ever seen? Whose side are you on son?" Dad asked.

"I wouldn't subject a child to existence in this country! Nor would I ask our Mother Earth to support another human being. And your idea of the American Dream to me is a nightmare!"

"But your kid might have some fun. You wouldn't want to rob a child's chance at happiness, would you?"

"Any child who has fun or who is happy, does so at the expense of Mother Earth! Happy children are the most damning evidence of all that environmental ruin is being perpetrated by their parents, or that their government is oppressing someone."

"So let me understand correctly, you want to create a society where everybody is on the brink of starvation all of the time, nobody is happy, and kids can't have fun?"

"Okay, yes!"

"Then North Korea is place for you." Dad quipped.

"We are fighting for the earth pal! We are firemen! Nothing is going to please me more than the day when I can sit back under a giant redwood tree, drink a glass of herbal tea, and gloat over all you sonofabitches that I helped depopulate!"

"How would you like to depopulate this car?" Dad finally asked the guy.

"I'd like that pretty damned good! Stop right now. I've had about as much of you as I can stand. Let me step back out into nature again and breathe the fresh air! Let me bond with the Earth and her creatures as only the truly enlightened can."

"You want out here?"

"Listen mister, unless you want to spend the rest of your life in prison for kidnapping, you better stop this smoke wagon right now!"

Dad pulled the car over. The guy got out. But before he closed the door he looked in and asked:

"Could you spare five dollars?"

"What?"

"Do you have five bucks you could give me?"

"What for?"

"I haven't eaten today."

"Well, you should be happy about that!" Dad replied as he pressed the accelerator.

It was about an hour before sunset as we drove away. The passenger door was still open as the guy just stood there in stunned silence, watching us leave. Before closing the door, Dad used a newspaper to flush out most of the approximately ten-thousand mosquitoes and horseflies that had entered in the few seconds the car had been stopped.

As we looked back the guy was suddenly becoming aware of his surroundings. But he was too occupied with swatting to think about us. It was about this time that we were startled by the loud thud of a mutant horsefly-rat striking our windshield. And then another, and another. It quickly became obvious that we had serendipitously discovered the location of all the missing mutant horsefly-rat-vermin previously outfitted by the strange farm hand and his few remaining boys. There were hundreds of these flying devil-seed saturating the air. As they pelted our automobile with a continually increasing frequency, our drive the exit this rude theater suddenly took on a grave sense of urgency.

It just so happens that the place the Eco-Nazi made Dad let him out at was about 17 miles down a dead-end logging road, in the middle of a maze of such roads extending through hundreds of square miles in the sparsest populated, swampiest, most snake-infested, mosquito-ridden, horsefly-glutted, coyote-crawling, leach-saturated, chigger-breeding-grounded, God-forsaken patch of wilderness in the state of Kentucky. There were also very reliable reports that the area contained herds of rabid wild pigs, ill-tempered bobcats, and giant carnivorous snapping turtles that weighed over 350 pounds each. We knew in our hearts that the Eco-Nazi was about to receive a complimentary crash reality course in the routine operations of Mother Nature's hostile side. This seemed fitting since he apparently had up until then thought that it was only Nature that needs the protection.

My father was never able to comprehend the Eco-Nazi mindset. His early life had been one of constant struggle. He had come up through an era of real poverty and adversity. It was a time and place where widespread suffering and hunger really existed in America. He had endured great injury, illness, and pain. He was caught up in the rigging and trampled by a team of horses when he was twelve, putting him in a coma for two weeks. He fought infestations of parasites of some kind or another for his entire childhood. He fought other men when he had to. And when his nation called him, he fought the forces of real tyranny.

He knew what it was like to be covered in filth and vermin and to not have the means to do anything about it. He knew what it was like to not have adequate food, clothing, money, or freedom of movement. He knew what it was like to be gravely ill and wounded. He had suffered rheumatic fever, pneumonia, fractured bones, a ruptured spleen, crushed hands, puncture wounds, third-degree burns, snake bites, perforated ear drums, concussions, severe lacerations, dislocated joints, broken vertebrae, cracked elbows, and knocked-out teeth, all before his 25th birthday.

None of these afflictions were the result of recreational activities. He never broke a leg skiing or white-water rafting. Everything that ever happened to my father occurred during the rigors of toil, combat, or of life itself. But he was never bitter about any of it. Nor did he ever feel sorry for himself. He just viewed it as nothing more than the cost of pursuing happiness.

He got shot-up in a brutal war and saw hundreds of his comrades murdered and mutilated defeating tyranny of a most despicable kind. He saw America not as something that oppresses people but as something that allows them opportunities to rise up out of oppression and hopelessness, to defeat poverty, and to be happy. That is why he could not understand why anyone would promulgate a philosophy that promises to make us poorer, hungrier, and sadder. Since it made no sense, he could only conclude that such people were insane, or that they were crying for attention at any cost. That is, he saw them as people whose desire to be different was so exaggerated that they let their power of reason be overwhelmed by their own vanity. He saw no fundamental difference between the ambitions and methods of the Eco-Nazis and the those of Hitler, Stalin, or Mao.

That is, they were all groups whose expressed objective was to restrict the freedom of human beings based on a political interpretation. Anyone disagreeing with their interpretation of course suffered the ultimate restriction of freedom: forced termination of life, liberty, and the pursuit of happiness. Until the day he died, my father would have suffered through all his trials and tribulations again, all of the pain, all of the errors, everything, for just one more day of life. Why? Simple, because each day is another opportunity to be happy.

Kooks

This class included everything from the mildly schizophrenic to the czar of the Josef Stalin Fan Club; from the pleasantly argumentative to the radically misanthropic. YF-2 through about YF-10. There were representatives of each of the seven deadly sins, sloth for example. Then there were the theme-kooks. These included snake handlers, witches, incubi, Freudians, Jungians, flat-earthers, anarchists, theosophists, and the occasional nefarious Yugo apologist still in denial. Collectively perhaps they could have been described as new-math iterations of the human equation.

They typically gave the outward impression of being sweet, harmless, misunderstood, charismatic, and personable individuals, full of love and hope for the human condition. Translation: they were a pack of raving, paranoid lunatics. But, for the most part they were harmless. However, there also was a dark subset of these individuals who seemed to be the personifications of every vile and contemptible face of human perversion and depravity. Some of them constituted a clear and present danger to say the least, mostly because of their unpredictability. A few were extremely scary. The majority were simply pathetic. I recall a big mean-looking fellow Dad picked up once. This guy just stared out the window and kept whispering to himself: *"City of the Damned...highway of the wounded dog...City of the Damned...highway of the wounded dog..."*

Since we picked him up about ninety miles from the nearest paved road, we never really figured out exactly what city, or highway he was so displeased with. It didn't take Dad long however, to dial-in on the fact that this guy's cotton picker had wandered a row or two over into the cocklebur patch. Dad asked the guy straight out what the hell he was talking about:

"Hey buddy, what the hell are you talking about?" Dad said.

"City of the Damned, Highway of the Wounded Dog!" the guy replied.

"Yes, I think we understand that much already. What city? Where? Do you mean U.S. 41?"

"Follow the wounded dog to the City of the Damned. There you will see."

"See what – the wounded dog? What is the wounded dog? Where is the City of the Damned?"

"The wounded dog has a broken heart. The City of the Damned is where he is. Go there and you will see. Do not go there and you will not see."

Dad paused and looked toward me. It was not a comfortable look. I could tell that he was more than a little bit worried. He perceived this passenger as potential trouble and was obviously deeply concerned about my safety. Dad decided to humor the guy until he could engineer a plan to get him out of the automobile.

"Is that where you want to go, to this so called, City of the Damned?"

"I seek the City of the Damned, true, yet never can I escape it. The wounded dog seeks me."

"The wounded dog seeks you here?"

"Even now my son."

"Right here, this very moment?"

"Yes."

"Where?"

"Directly behind this chariot of bloody iron and fire - on the heel of everlasting sin and damnation!"

"I thought the wounded dog was in the City of the Damned." Dad observed.

"He is."

"Then this is the City of the Damned?"

"Yes, my son."

There was a pause as Dad and I looked out the windows at the strikingly beautiful but otherwise unremarkable rural landscape whizzing past us at seventy miles per hour. There were a couple of windmills scattered hither and yon. There were a few cows in a field, some ducks on a pond, even a tractor parked in a barn, but little else except the rolling immensities of verdant maize and pasturage arrayed as far as the eye could see. There certainly was no city, nor did we observe any dogs of any kind, wounded or otherwise. We then looked at each other in puzzlement.

"But we're out in the country!" Dad said.

The guy laughed as if we were complete idiots, morons, and hayseeds freshly escaped from *the Home*. He finally replied:

"That does not matter. It surrounds us, it fills this car."

"Then the whole world is the City of the Damned?" Dad asked.

"Yes. You learn quickly my son!"

Dad hit the brakes and pulled the car over.

"Get out!"

"What for my son?"

"This is as far as I can take you."

"But this is not the place that I seek."

"Too bad Einstein, now get the hell out of my car – and don't step on the wounded dog!"

"You are the wounded dog!" the guy yelled as we drove away.

Military Personnel

My father gave rides to soldiers anytime he was able because he enjoyed talking with them about military topics and he sincerely felt it was his patriotic duty. To me at least, military personnel seemed to be more courteous and appreciative than some of the other passengers that Dad had occasion to assist (however, a really detestable passenger did guarantee alertness for many miles). Dad provided transport to enlistees of virtually every branch of the service. However, U.S. Army personnel constituted the vast majority of his riders because we lived near Fort Campbell – headquarters of the 101st Airborne Screaming Eagles.

My father probably hauled more Screaming Eagles than just about anybody short of the Army itself. Sometimes the soldiers would be traveling in groups of up to a half-dozen, especially around the holidays. There were occasions when the car would have so many Screaming Eagles inside they'd have to hang their wings out the windows. If we were in Dad's truck, a couple would get into the cab and the rest would ride in the back. There were many times that he took them directly to Fort Campbell, especially in the winter. Some offered him money for his kindness but he would never accept it.

If we were not in a major hurry, Dad would always pull over at the nearest restaurant and buy dinner for everybody, especially around Christmas. He always made a point to pick up people around that time of year and treat them to a lavish dinner at a nice restaurant. They didn't always have to be a soldiers either, just somebody who looked like they needed that special little glimmer of hope that only comes when a stranger offers kindness. He may have done this because of what happened to him during the war, when his convoy was overran by German tanks and he subsequently didn't get to eat for twelve days and almost froze to death. So my father empathized profoundly with anyone hitching in the winter, and especially soldiers.

I considered being with my father in a car full of active duty U.S. paratroopers as the coolest thing in the world. I seldom spoke, being perfectly content to only listen. The dialog was quite entertaining at times. These spirited conversations would typically commence immediately after they got into the vehicle and would not terminate until we delivered them either at, or at least appreciably nearer to their destination.

The range of subject matter invariably consisted of two related, but very distinct categories: 1, military technology, and 2, military history. They discussed detailed specifications and performance information about a broad range of military hardware (if the Commies had hidden a microphone in Dad's car it would have been disastrous for the Free World). They articulated precise, minute-by-minute accountings of actual combat action from the squad level up through theater-scale, in both the WWII and Vietnam operational theaters.

Paratroopers of the 101st Division are an enthusiastic group, as copiously blessed with élan as any military organization in the history of the world. It is a tradition that even weathered the Vietnam era. This was perhaps most obvious whenever my father would articulate a few anecdotes concerning his combat tour with the 423rd Infantry Regiment of the U.S. Army 106th Division in WWII, because there were never any audience attentiveness problems. They savored every detail and asked germane questions throughout. And when Dad recounted details of his survival amid the rolling Juggernaut of Nazi tanks and how members of the 101st had rescued him, many of them would reach out to shake his hand and then sincerely thank him. But he would always say it was he who should be thanking them, not the other way around.

When my father was laid to rest in on February 26, 2000, his military flag-folding ceremony was conducted by active duty soldiers of the U.S. Army 101st Airborne Division. They traveled all the way from Fort Campbell on short notice, without hesitation, to perform this honored service. It wasn't planned that way. It just happened. It would perhaps be better left unexplained. What can be said is that nobody there that day appreciated the significance of it, nobody at all. *Nobody except my father and a few Screaming Eagles.*

Chapter 22

Song of the Clay

Halo of nothing, numb emptiness: how can this zero be somewhere?

I remember a dream. It seems like a long time ago. There was an island, a blue island with white clouds, all alone in a dark sea. Then I awoke in that roar around me. There was an explosion of colors and commotion, *my time*. Sunlight spilled through trees. Now it's the cold, black static of Brownian motion again.

In the refuge of sleep, I have slipped through. Doors here lead to unknown things. There are mysteries in here, but no magic keys. Who ran these rooms for so long? Which door did he take? Where are the colors, the sounds, and connections? Who will speak for me now?

I have my limits, yet there are *the infinities*. The Greatest Thing is: *that something knows*. There is a thought in here so substantive and so true that when it is stumbled upon, a universe explodes from nothing. It is the Original Thought. It was the last thought of another universe. That is where I will go. The clay presses against me now, *but there will be other adventures*.

THE END

Acknowledgements

The author wishes to express sincere appreciation to the following individuals for their assistance in the preparation of this book: Idris I. Ahiezer, Pamela Day, Sam Elder, Eric Fry, Kiah Furher, R.G. Higginbotham, Ken Merten, Andrew B. Nelson, Dan Nelson, Mike Osha, Keith Pearson, Michael Phipps, Keith Souders, Rick Vance, William R. Wills, and Donald R. Wilson.